Making Healthy Families

With notes from the Web

Volume 1

Gayle Peterson, MSSW, PhD

SHADOW AND LIGHT PUBLICATIONS
Berkeley, California

Other Books by Gayle Peterson

An Easier Childbirth: A Mother's Guide for Birthing Normally
Birthing Normally: A Personal Growth Approach to Childbirth
Body Centered Hypnosis for Pregnancy, Bonding and Childbirth (audiotape)
Body Centered Hypnosis for Childbirth: A Training Videotape

Web Resources by Gayle Peterson

www.AskDrGayle.com
www.parentsplace.com/expert/family
www.cheerios.com

Published by
Shadow and Light Publications
1749 Vine Street
Berkeley, CA 94703

Cover Design: © 2000 by Stuart Gold

Page layout and design: Ernest Grafe

ISBN Number 0-9625231-5-1

Library of Congress Catalog Number 99-97006

Peterson, Gayle H.
Making Healthy Families
1. Psychology. 2. Marriage and Family. 3. Parenting

To my husband, my children,
my grandchild, and all the families
I have worked with throughout the years
who have taught me so much
about the meaning of family

CONTENTS

PART II: BECOMING PARENTS

PART III: CRISIS AND TRANSFORMATION
ON THE FAMILY LIFE CYCLE

ACKNOWLEDGMENTS

I would like to express my gratitude to Greg Bogart for editing this book with skill and love; and to my colleagues, Bruce Linton, Fortunee Kayra-Stuart, and Barbara Lewis for their expert feedback and advice on clinical cases that furthered my understanding of healthy family relationships. I also want to thank Jackie Needleman and David Cohen for giving me a voice on their wonderful website for parents. And to my children, Sorrel and Yarrow Madrona, and my grandson, Nicholas Madrona Duchesne, for their daily teachings throughout the years of motherhood. And finally, my deepest love and appreciation to my spouse and life partner, Stuart Gold, for his ever-present enthusiasm and support throughout this book project.

PREFACE

www.parentsplace.com

The questions and answers that bring this book to life appear on the author's family therapist column on parentsplace on the world wide web. The founders of this site, Jackie Needleman and David Cohen, launched this grassroots resource network for parents from their home in Berkeley, California in 1995. New parents themselves, Jackie and David understood the needs of parents and pioneered making quality parenting resources available. Their website brings families together with others going through similar struggles in parenting and supplies current and valuable information for assisting parents at critical junctures of the family life cycle.

The author has been writing for *www.parentsplace.com* since its launching in Berkeley and continues to answer questions on her column for ivillage.com, which now coordinates the parentsplace channel from New York.

Overview

What makes a family healthy and what *predictably and scientifically* contributes to success in family relationships? *Making Healthy Families* describes leading edge research on what contributes to the making and sustenance of healthy, functional families. This book is organized in the framework of the stages of family life, from "Becoming a Couple" to "Becoming Parents" and "Raising Adolescents." It educates parents about the predictable life stress of each transition, and offers guidelines and hands-on exercises for achieving optimal adjustment. But it does not stop there!

A chapter on "Trouble-shooting" offers couples an opportunity to plot their own predictable stress points on their family journey. Knowledge and workbook exercises allow parents to predict which stages will be more difficult for them to traverse, thereby allowing them to better master their own unique life struggles. The chapter on "Divorce" offers advice to parents through trying times, bringing forth the best research available for helping both children and parents through this transitional family crisis in the best way possible. The "Making Healthy Stepfamilies" chapter provides wisdom about the realistic stages of stepfamily development that can make remarriage rewarding, and helps readers avoid the pitfalls so many fall into, which cause over half of second marriages to fail. Also, those in mid-life transitions and personal crisis will find the information on what contributes to healthy families and healthy passages illuminating.

The cutting-edge research on what makes families work—from structure and communication to family style and characteristics of healthy family systems—is presented in an accessible format with questions from parents that have been answered on the "Ask Dr. Gayle" family therapist column on *www.parentsplace.com*

INTRODUCTION

The birth of a baby is the birth of a new family. Families exist to nurture us, not only when we are vulnerable and as helpless as a newborn—but later, as we face the challenges of adulthood. We need to be able to depend on our intimate relationships for emotional support. Healthy families serve as a nest for our human growth and development.

Our families impact the very quality of life, including who we are and who we will become. We can learn much from the past forty years of research on family structures, styles, rules and communication, which can help us create a healthy family system capable of adjusting to the ever changing needs of its members.

Traveling Through Time on the Family Life Cycle

Sociologists have attempted to research and describe the continuous process of growth that a family experiences as it travels through the family life cycle.[1] Newborn babes are raised to adulthood, only to join with new adults to establish their own families. The ever-changing flow of life through the generations has predictable growth pains. Most professionals agree that knowledge of the life cycle stages helps parents and spouses traverse difficult and trying periods. Critical points on life's timeline can prove overwhelming in the moment when perspective is lost. Knowledge of the normal challenges and transitional flow of these stages can be a life-saver!

Often, the stages on the family life cycle that are troublesome can be predicted because they are the same stages that our parents had difficulty coping with in some way. We may find ourselves at a loss as parents to provide our children with what they need because we do not have childhood role models who were successful with a particular stage of the family life cycle. For example, if you left home early as a teenager (before high school graduation) you may have difficulty sustaining your

---

1. E. M. Duvall, *Marriage and Family Development*, 5th edition (Philadelphia: Lippincott, 1977).

teenagers through the "launching" stage of leaving home. Becoming aware of the psychological tasks of successive stages enables us to provide opportunities for our children that we may have missed in our own development. Without such an overview, it is likely that we will pass on unresolved emotional pain in some form to our own children. By increasing awareness of what is needed at various stages, we are more likely to learn from others, thereby changing what is passed on to future generations. Armed with knowledge, we can develop new and healthier patterns for growth.

For our purposes, this book series will focus on the contemporary middle class family in the United States. Description of the family life cycle will unfold as family researchers describe it today in our culture and time. Extreme wealth and extreme poverty do alter these stages, as do cultural variations. Other naturally occurring facets of the family life cycle include divorce, single parenting, remarriage and stepparenting. These transitions pose variations of stages on the cycle, and will be addressed in this volume.

You will be better able to deal with sensitive parenting issues once you are aware of the larger perspective of the family life cycle stages. "Trouble-shooting" (in part three) will elucidate where you and your partner may experience difficulty in the family life cycle, based on unresolved traumatic stages in your own individual childhood histories.

Now, let's take a look at the basic stages of the family life cycle. Case vignettes and questions from parents facing struggles in marriage and parenting highlight healthy family processes and will help you clarify your own family journey.

Part I

Becoming a Couple

ONE

Creating Your Garden

Living on our own, we establish intimacy with others outside of our families. We endeavor to become independent, both emotionally and economically. By doing so, we achieve a healthy separation that allows us to think for ourselves, rather than feel compelled to make choices that may have been right for our parents, but are invalid for us. If things go well, we enjoy an ongoing connection and warmth with our families, while engaged in substantiating our independence. This period is the stage of the *unattached adult* in the family life cycle.

Still, it is not unusual to marry precipitously, for a variety of reasons, even skipping this stage altogether. Early marriage may leave us with a less developed sense of our individual identity and needs. When marriage occurs without enough clear establishment of a separate sense of self, the new couple system can become secondary to the needs of the previous generation, causing difficulty in the *coupling* stage. Preoccupation with fulfilling the needs or fantasies of our parents, can interfere with establishing a healthy alignment with our new spouse. Bill and Mary had this problem.

Bill and Mary got married while attending college. However, the year of their marriage, Bill's parents divorced after having stayed together "for the kids." Bill's role in the family had always been to make dad feel better when he felt sad or angry with his wife (Bill's mother). When the divorce took place, Bill was unable to focus on his marriage, instead spending every weekend with his father. He

1

still felt it was his job to keep his parents together. He ignored his wife's pleading to stay home with her on weekends.

Finally, Bill's job took them to another part of the country, which prohibited him from actively trying to play the role of marital mediator for his parents. However, he and Mary never resolved the damage done to the marriage as a result of his overriding loyalty to his parents' troubled marriage. Bill and Mary did not discuss the alienation that had occurred at that time, as neither was clear about what their commitment to one another should look like. Mary felt somewhat guilty that she was asking for Bill's attention at such a difficult time for his parents.

Symptoms of unresolved family loyalty showed itself in the fact that they spent every Christmas with his father. Even though they had two children of their own, it was not until the children were teenagers that they spent the holidays in their own home. They had developed few traditions of their own, and by the time their eldest was fourteen, Bill became more argumentative with his wife and verbally abusive to his children, resulting in Mary seeking help from a family counselor regarding the viability of their marriage.

Bill and Mary's case illustrates how getting stuck in resolving problems of the last generation can prevent couples from successfully launching their own families. Bill was preoccupied with saving his parents, leaving him little time or energy to establish his marital bond with Mary. Mary did not see her role as his wife as a legitimate avenue for meeting her own needs for intimacy and forming family. She retreated into her own world, dealing with him peripherally for years, until his verbal abuse of the children became overbearing.

The psychological task of the stage of *coupling* is to establish appropriate boundaries for the new family system. Regardless of whether marriage occurs precipitously, or not, misplaced loyalties can be problematic to the health of the new couple's relationship. The couple's bond must strengthen and become a primary basis for decision making. Though newly married couples may enjoy help and suggestions from in-laws and others, they must develop their own capacity to resolve differences and find successful solutions. If they fail to develop a cohesive bond to deal with life's problems together, they become vulnerable to erosion of intimacy and mutual respect as the years wear on.

A healthy realignment of the new couple and extended family system occurs when family and friends accept the primary bond of the couple and include the new spouse in their social circle. Loyalty and commitment to the other in the couple system becomes the first priority. Ideally, couple bonding is respectful of the primary intimacy between partners, but inclusive of others as a supportive network. An "inner circle" is created that consists of the newly formed couple system.

Establishing effective boundaries, making decisions with your spouse, and establishing appropriate authority with your own parents are all necessary ingredients to secure your relationship in this stage. The following question and answer illustrates the dilemma that many couples face in realigning their marriage.

Establishing boundaries

Dear Dr. Gayle,

I have been married for three years and have the most amazing wife and six- month-old daughter. The problem comes in when we are around my parents. I came from a very close knit family and when I'm around my parents, I can't seem to break the parent-child relationship. Any time there is friction between my wife and parents, my inclination is to say nothing and hope it works itself out. My wife ends up feeling left out.

I keep trying to avoid making anyone mad, but I'm making my wife very angry because she feels secondary to my parents. My parents live out of town, but we see them about four times a year for about a week each time. My parents will be visiting again in about three months and I am extremely nervous. Any suggestions?

Bob

Dear Bob,

Your insight and your acknowledgment of your wife's experience are both remarkably clear! You are already aware that your contribution to your problem is to remain silent and in a child's role, instead of an adult role at your wife's side. So what is stopping you from taking action to align yourself with your wife and set boundaries that are appropriate with your parents?

Your loyalty must rest with your wife, but this does not mean you do not love your "folks." Talk with your spouse about her feelings and needs in the conflicts that arise with her in-laws. Empathize with her, but do not stop there! Identify what behaviors you both agree must change.

What changes do you need in order to feel respected by your parents in your new role as a husband and head of family? What does she need to feel comfortable in her roles as wife and daughter-in-law? Do not shy away from taking the lead to talk with your parents about specific behaviors which need to stop. Let them know that while you do not require that they love your wife as you do, you expect them to respect your boundaries around these issues as a couple and to "live and let live."

You may begin this process by phone. If you do, be sure to speak with each of your parents separately. This way you will feel less intimidated, and have a fair chance at having an adult-to-adult conversation. You might decide to address it by letter first and let them know you are calling and want to establish separate adult relationships with each of them, now that you are establishing a family of your own.

Focus on your desire to develop an adult friendship. Let them know you want to change the nature of your relationship with them from child to adult. Keep this focus the foundation of your discussion. Address the issues you discuss with your wife. Be specific about the behaviors you want changed, but keep this part short. By setting the framework for a discussion about your needs for a change in how you relate to them, you are more likely to create the necessary shift that is at the root of this transition.

Whatever your reason for avoiding conflict, this pattern could spell trouble for the future of your marriage. Conflict-avoidance can lead to unresolved feelings that result in a fractured relationship. You will need to strengthen your communication skills not only to address your parents, but to maintain a healthy and vibrant marriage.

It is not always possible or necessary for in-laws to "love and cherish" your spouse. It is important that family members tolerate differences without intrusion and judgment that curtail family interaction. Holiday visits, celebration dinners and grandparenting roles are all a part of family life. Establish goals that include your parents but do not insist on "instant love." Blending families, including in-laws, can require time and patience from everyone involved.

If your parents feel (and raised you to believe) that to have differences is disloyal, you may be suffering under the belief that differences cannot be accepted in a family. To take your place as an adult with them may include expressing your own views of family, including tolerance for differences!

Sometimes it is hard to grow up because we idealize our parents. Still, it may be your turn to teach your parents something new about family. Do not forget that we are all, forever, growing up!

Resolving prior stages of the family life cycle

The stages of the family life cycle are successive and depend on resolution of the preceding stage. In the above example, and for Bill and Mary, it is clear that when the second stage of the family life cycle (coupling) is compromised the couple will be divided. Alienation is likely to corrupt ongoing intimacy.

Sometimes couples can continue for a very long time in this arrested state of development, but deterioration of the marital bond shows itself in the long run. Mary coped by taking care of the children as they arrived on the scene, and Bill coped by devoting himself to his job as a traveling salesman, which took him away from the family on frequent and prolonged intervals. They continued their marriage with specialized roles in the family that did not require much couples communication and a minimal amount of joint decision making. They stayed out of each other's way.

Sometimes the goals of a married couple can be held up by loyalty and commitment to aging parents. Finding a balance, without putting your own life's goals out of reach is necessary for the health of any marriage. The following question and answer illustrates this dilemma.

Children or caring for my parents?

Dear Dr. Gayle,

My husband and I have been married for one year, and we have been together for seven. I am thirty and he is thirty-four. I am an only child. My father is eighty-four and my mother seventy. We have no other extended family living near us and now that my parents are getting old the burden of responsibility for caring for them is mine exclusively.

My father is very frail, and my mother, being much younger, looks after him. She is a very bitter person, and is getting worse all the time. On one hand she does not want anything to happen to my dad, but on the other she resents that he is old and can't do very much anymore. I try to do what I can for them, take them shopping, take them out for the day or a weekend, to try to make their life a little better. They have no friends either, so they are house-bound and isolated.

My responsibility to my parents, and my parents themselves (particularly my mother) is causing problems for me in my marriage. My mother is a very difficult person, very negative and easily angered. She does not care for my husband, and she lets him know it. He does not want to be around them much, and I can understand that, but he also feels I should not be so involved in their lives, or worry about them so much. I realize my own health is suffering because of my worrying, but I don't know what else to do. I am the only person who can help look after them.

We would like to have a baby in another year, but by that time my parents will be even worse off, and I don't know if I can take care of them and a baby too. My husband and I have had numerous fights about this. I feel he can't understand what it is like for me, since he came from a broken home and was raised by a stepfather he hated. How can I make everyone happy, least of all me?

Dawn

Dear Dawn,

It is not your job to make everyone happy. Your responsibility is to your own life and marriage first. This does not mean that you turn your back on your parents. It does mean that you set limits to what you can do to help them, and consider possibilities of elder homecare or a retirement residence for assisted living.

Your husband may be at a loss to influence you in this direction because you discount his views. Because he experienced divorce in his childhood does not mean that his feelings and observations do not have merit. Nor does your having a biologically "intact" family experience in childhood mean that your family patterns are a picture of health. Often, children from divorce benefit from the mistakes their parents made because the negative patterns of interaction were obvious. Adults from intact families may not have clarified toxic patterns of interaction because their parents remained married. There is a difference between staying married and staying in a bad marriage!

Certainly your husband's experience may give him greater opportunity to know what doesn't work. And your parents' interactions do appear to have a somewhat toxic effect on you. Consider that what he is saying to you may be in the best interests of the marriage. Perhaps he is the voice for the emotional health of your own marriage because you are not! You are too embroiled in your parents' marriage and life problems to focus on your own family's development.

Examine the guilt and overresponsibility you are feeling towards your parents. You cannot change their marriage, their current isolation or their growing frailty. It may be that your parents' situation is caused and exacerbated by their difficult relationship with one another. Their growing dependency compounds their marital stress.

Encourage their independence in realistic ways. This will be better for their mental health as well as your own. Separate your feelings about their relationship to one another from their growing frailty. Do what you can to help them with external services and environmental changes that can ameliorate the negativity between them, but let go of hearing about any distress your father has caused your mother. It is unhealthy for you to be an emotional dumping ground for their marriage.

Research government resources for ways to help your parents with daily living that will decrease your responsibility and open up your time with your husband and child. Or ask your husband to help you with this! County agencies usually have offices that specialize in aging that can help identify possibilities for assisted living. This could help relieve your mother's stress and increase her freedom. There are some very lovely retirement residences that include cleaning, cooking, social activities, transportation, and outings that your mother might enjoy. She needs to make some friends!

It is not in your mother's or your best interest to continue to use you as her only social outlet. You cannot be her best friend. And she is nonsupportive of your marriage to boot! This undermines your relationship with your husband, putting yourself in the middle.

Take yourself out of the middle. Be aware that though this may be a familiar position for you, it is harmful for you to be used to buffer the stress between your parents. The down side of being an only child is that you have no other siblings to unite with to see your parents more objectively. "Only" children can sometimes be easily swept into a dysfunctional negotiating role in the parents' marriage. But it is not your job to make them happy together. Their marriage may be miserable, but you have a right to succeed where they have failed! It is not too late to change course and put your own life and family in focus.

Maintaining boundaries that support the growth of the new couples system is the first order of business. Once boundaries are intact, we are free to focus on other elements of our family's development.

Fortifying Your Couple's Bond: Creating Your Family "Style"

When two people come together to create a family, they each bring their own unconscious version of how family members relate to one another. As children, we spend years growing up in our own families, observing and imprinting upon the ways that our families, as a particular group of people interact to solve problems, to express feelings, to make decisions and raise their young. How our parents raised us resulted in a unique family culture. We are conditioned to imprint these same influences (both positively and negatively), onto the next generation.

When a child is born, old family styles of relating are awakened. The couple's relationship undergoes tremendous stress. Marital partners who have basked in positive feelings in their partnership can find themselves falling into negative automatic behaviors. Where they once spoke proudly of their open and direct communication, their equal and respectful relationship to one another, they may nevertheless find themselves falling back on old familiar, though unpleasant methods of interacting (blaming, withdrawing) reminiscent of what their parents did when dealing with conflict.

Family Style

Family researchers, such as Robert Beavers, have defined *family style* as "the degree of centripetal and centrifugal forces in a family."[2] "Centripetal" is analogous to petals on a flower, tightly formed and organized around a center. It is meant to describe a quality of interactions that draws people closer together. "Centrifugal" refers to the quality of centrifugal velocity, which forces us to drift at an increasing rate, away from one another.

Healthy family styles blend characteristics of both of these polarities at differing points on the life cycle. Young families with small children are naturally centripetal. Parents must be accountable to each other for coordinating childcare and their young children require close proximity to

---

2. R. Beavers, "The Beavers System Model." In F. Walsh (Ed.), *Normal Family Processes*, 2nd edition (New York: Guilford Press, 1993).

them. But families with adolescents grow towards some incorporation of centrifugal forces, as greater independence is not only necessary but desirable for healthy growth. Let's take a closer look at what is meant by these two polarities, how to recognize their extreme or "dysfunctional" forms, and where our own childhood experience placed us on this continuum.

Freedom and connection: Finding a healthy balance

In the extreme, rigidly centripetal families create a culture in which they bind together against the outside world. Outsiders are distrusted. Only the family is perceived as safe. Family members can express positive feelings towards one another, but repress negative or ambivalent feelings, resulting in warmth that can often feel false or superficial because the underlying conflict is never truly expressed or resolved. Leave-taking may be difficult in such a family and it is not uncommon to have an adult child return home or never leave home, and for somatization of feelings (headaches, aches and pains, fatigue) or scapegoating of one member to manifest as a release valve for the repressed negative feelings in the family. Positive feelings of love are acceptable, but anger is not tolerated. Members may feel that to be loved they must give up a large part of themselves. Dependency is encouraged, individualism punished.

In the extreme, a rigidly centrifugal system trusts outsiders more than their own family members. Dependency is perceived as weakness and so expressions of love and caring are repressed, while anger and even hostility are accepted modes of relating. There is a tendency for children to leave home prematurely, before they reach adulthood. Independence is encouraged and precipitous, while dependency needs are sought elsewhere, outside of the family.

In the most positive light, centripetal forces encourage *warmth and connection* in a family and centrifugal forces emphasize *freedom*. In truth, we need both to achieve a healthy connection and the ability to relate honestly and intimately. Let's explore your own childhood family " culture" and its impact on your current family relationships.

Exercise: What are your family "blueprints"?

Gaining an objective perspective of your family-of-origin allows you to keep what you value, but improve on what did not work well. Take thirty minutes to explore the past with your partner. If you are a single parent, answer these questions for yourself, or if you wish do this exercise with a friend or relative with whom you feel safe. Keep in mind that you may have experienced these areas differently than your siblings, or differently at one time in your childhood, than another. Use the age of twelve as a reference point in time for answering these questions about your experience of your family-of-origin (unless otherwise stated, or you have a strong preference to use another point in time).

1. What was the quality of your parents' relationship? Was love expressed in words? Was anger expressed verbally in your family and between your parents? Was the expression of anger "safe" in your family and in your parents' relationship, or emotionally "threatening"? Was the expression of love openly shared or repressed?

This dimension refers to the relationship between love and anger. It is desirable to be able to express anger without attacking character (or violating safety), while simultaneously being able to stay in touch with your love for that person. This balance creates a range of expression in the family that encourages connection over disconnection. Anger can be expressed safely, without denying love.

Rate from 0-10, with 0 representing that in the family atmosphere only positive (loving) feelings were comfortable being expressed and 10 being only negative (angry) feelings were commonly expressed. 5 would represent an equal ability *to express anger without denying love*.

| 0 | 1 | 2 | 3 | 4 | 5 | 6 | 7 | 8 | 9 | 10 |

2. How did your parents resolve conflict with one another? How was conflict resolved in your family in general?

Rate from 0-10, with 0 representing that conflict was never overtly expressed, and so left unresolved and 10 representing that conflict was repeatedly expressed in anger and disrespect, but without mutual resolution.

It is desirable for family atmosphere to allow for passionate discussion without discounting or denigration. This increases the possibility for successful negotiation. 5 would represent an atmosphere in which differences could be expressed and explored without attacking character, and mutually acceptable solutions would be found.

| 0 | 1 | 2 | 3 | 4 | 5 | 6 | 7 | 8 | 9 | 10 |

3. Was communication clear and direct? Or was it ambiguous, nonverbal, coercive?

Rate from 0-10, with 0 representing pressure to mind-read people's needs (saying "yes" when they really mean "no") to 10 representing repeated and consistent misinterpretations/accusations of others' behavior. ("If you loved me you would have . . . . ").

A family atmosphere in which a full range of emotions is acceptable allows members to release tensions and frustrations without damaging relationships. Feelings do not necessarily require action, and so understanding between people is more likely. Discussions can develop and be sustained, which encourages connection over disconnection. 5 would represent non-blaming clarification of feelings and differing points of view, *and safety in the family system for anything to be discussed*. There would be room for feelings to be expressed and explored. *Feelings are not seen as actions*.

0   1   2   3   4   5   6   7   8   9   10

4. What was your family's relationship to the outside community as you grew up? What was your relationship to your parents and to the outside community as you grew up? Where did you go for help as a youngster, a teenager?

Rate from 0-10, with 0 representing complete dependence on family to answer all needs to 10 representing complete dependence on others outside the family for help, guidance and nurturing. Families benefit from outside support, which promotes feelings of connection inside the family. 5 would represent *a balance of both, changing appropriately with age*.

0   1   2   3   4   5   6   7   8   9   10

5. Did your parents support your growing independence from the family as a child, an adolescent, a young adult?

Rate from 0-10, with 0 representing much difficulty and feeling pressure not to develop your own interests and ideas in adolescence, to 10 representing being "on your own" as a teenager with little guidance. Reflect also on how you did leave home. Were you adequately supported to develop your own independence?

A family atmosphere of emotional commitment to fulfill the changing needs and to act in the best interests of children promotes connection between family members over a lifetime. 5 would represent *feeling supported to develop your own interests as an adolescent and to leave home as a young adult, but with emotional support from your family as you established your place in the world.*

0	1	2	3	4	5	6	7	8	9	10

Where does your childhood experience put you on the spectrum? (0 is extremely centripetal, 10 extremely centrifugal) Mostly, you will find a mixture of these two styles. You may also find that your family culture tended towards one end, and your partner's towards the other. By learning this, you can consciously choose to adopt new guidelines that solicit your strengths, and correct for your weaknesses.

Learn from each other! Identify what you consider strengths and weaknesses from both of your family cultures. Perhaps your partner's family was good at encouraging individuality but short on emotional connection, and your family was quite warm but family relationships were at times emotionally suffocating. Or you may discover one area such as avoiding, rather than resolving, conflict that left you lacking in the ability to negotiate with your spouse, while your partner's skills in that area are more developed. Consider ways to increase the strengths and desirable qualities while decreasing tendencies towards the extremes in family style. Pay attention to what your family's balance is, and what you want it to be, at any given point in time.

Our parents are our first role models. Our job as parents is to sort through our past, taking what we want to continue in our own families, and letting go of that which we do not want to repeat.

After discussing and exploring your own family blueprints, do the following worksheet to further develop your vision for your present family relationships. Be conscious of childhood patterns and how they may be influencing your present family processes.

Worksheet

Assess the capacity of your present family atmosphere in promoting connection (over disconnection) in these five dimensions of health:

1. Are verbal expressions of love and appreciation daily occurrences between spouses, between adults and children in your family? Are expressions of anger or disappointment acknowledged without withdrawing love and appreciation from the family member with whom you are angry or disappointed?

Reflect on the last forty-eight hours. Did you give any verbal appreciations or expressions of love to your family members? Did they give any to you? List them here. _____

_____

_____

_____

_____

_____

In the next twenty-four hours, consciously give at least three verbal appreciations to your spouse and children. List them here with the effects you feel doing so had on family relationships. _____

_____

_____

_____

_____

_____

In the last week did you withdraw emotional support from your spouse or a child because you were angry? Did you break a commitment to a family member due to disappointment? Write down your experience of expressing and receiving anger in the family, and discuss the event and whether anger is expressed safely in the family or in a way that threatens emotional connection between members. _____

_____

_____

_____

_____

_____

Write down how you want to handle future angry or disappointing incidents in the family. For example: if you withdraw emotionally (not talking, avoiding sex) when angry with your spouse, consider making a commitment to express your feelings without retreating from the relationship. If you withdraw your commitment to taking your teenager to his baseball practice because he swore at you, consider a consequence that does not interfere with your commitment to drive him to practice (such as no television, or other "privilege" that evening). In other words, examine your actions to determine whether they are retaliatory in nature or clear and effective communications of your own needs and limits.

Being able to express anger without attacking character or threatening a relationship, coupled with the ability to express caring openly, creates a range of expression in the family that encourages connection over disconnection.

Write down your family's strengths and weaknesses in this area, and any ideas for improving this dimension of your family atmosphere _____

_____

_____

_____

_____

_____

_____

2. A family atmosphere that allows for expression without discounting or denigration of others' points of view promotes healthy negotiation.

How is conflict negotiated between you and your spouse? Yourself and your children? Reflect on the last time you experienced conflict in the family. Did you find a mutually acceptable solution to the problem? Was it overly painful to reach a compromise? Do things not get done because successful negotiation does not occur in a timely manner? Write down your assessment of your family's strengths and weaknesses in problem solving and allowing for differing views to be expressed in the family.

_____

_____

_____

_____

_____

_____

Write down any ways you feel you would like to see your family improve in this dimension and discuss it with your spouse. (For example, you may identify the need for more "teamwork" in the family towards achieving goals and finishing projects). _____

_____

_____

_____

_____

_____

_____

_____

_____

_____

3. A family atmosphere in which a full range of emotions is acceptable allows members to release tensions and frustrations without damaging relationships. Feelings do not necessarily require action, and so understanding between people is more likely. Discussions can develop and be sustained, which encourages connection over disconnection.

Do you feel that your spouse is direct and clear with you about his/her feelings or are you often "in the dark" about your spouse's experience? Do you say what you mean or find yourself "beating around the bush" to avoid hurting others in the family? Discuss with your spouse or reflect on your own clarity of communication over the next twenty-four hours.

Room for ambivalence is a healthy aspect of adapting to change and disappointment on the family journey. Is this an area in which you want to envision change in your family atmosphere? (For example: You can communicate your desire to express an unpopular feeling and communicate that it is simply a feeling you need to "get off your chest" and not an assessment of the viability of the marriage!) Are there any areas you feel are "taboo" to discuss in the family, including any feelings you harbor that you feel cannot be shared? Does the family atmosphere allow for feelings to be expressed without jumping to conclusions?

Write down your assessment of your family's strengths and weaknesses in this dimension and any ideas for increasing the range of expression you would like to envision. For example, some families simply do not make the time to listen to their spouse's or child's feelings. Repeated incidents can pile up in which family members ignore feelings to get tasks done. Introducing a mechanism like calling a family meeting or having a daily time to check in with a child or spouse about his/her day may allow a greater range of feelings to surface. _____

_____

_____

_____

_____

_____

_____

4. Families benefit from outside support that promotes feelings of connection inside the family.

Do you have a "best friend" to talk with about personal issues? Do you feel that your family life (and marriage) is supported by friends or community involvement? Or do you feel your spouse is your only friend and confident? Do your children enjoy friends and community activities? Write down who the people are or what activities you turn to when you are feeling down or distressed about something in your life, and your observations about who other family members get support from, outside of the family. _____

_____

_____

_____

_____

_____

Write down ideas for increasing outside support if necessary—for example: developing personal friendships, joining a parents' support or activities group, enrolling your child in a play group, exploring church involvement or coaching your child's soccer team. _____

_____

_____

_____

_____

_____

_____

5. A family atmosphere of emotional commitment to fulfill the changing needs and to act in the best interests of their children promotes connection between family members over a lifetime.

Reflect on whether your parents supported your need for support and growing independence throughout your childhood. Periods of development in which you felt unsupported will naturally be charged times for you in your child's development. It is helpful to observe the feelings that arise about your own development, so that it is not projected onto your child, either by repeating patterns or overcompensating for them.

Write down any periods in your childhood that were particularly painful for you and share them with your partner. (For example: If your parents divorced at age three or you lost a parent at age fourteen, these will be particularly charged periods of time as your children pass through these ages.)_____

_____

_____

_____

_____

How well do you think you are supporting your children's growing independence? Write down the ways you currently encourage your children to make their own decisions at their current ages. Write down any ways you wish to consider supporting them to develop their ability to make decisions and pursue their own interests in the next year? The next two years?_____

_____

_____

_____

_____

_____

Observe the five areas just discussed with an eye towards flexibility and balance. Taking the time and effort to consider and reflect upon your family's style is by itself a healthy start. By talking about the blueprints of our family of origins, we are able to more clearly decide the atmosphere or style we want to adopt for our own families.

Recognizing our unique strengths and weaknesses also makes it possible to feel connection and intimacy as a couple. To develop ourselves as individuals and yet be able to depend upon our partners as *loving* critics develops a sense of trust and pleasure. We often choose our partners for the very qualities we subliminally recognize as undeveloped or missing in ourselves. Too often, we as partners do not take responsibility to develop the qualities we were attracted to in our loved one, and end up polarizing instead of learning from or appreciating the balance of the other. These patterns of non-appreciation are learned and can be unlearned. Remember that as parents, we are now the leaders of our families, and it is our turn to set the style for growth and development.

Summary

Below is a list of the five areas of health research shows contributes to healthy family relationships. Use these as a guide towards developing your family's unique and healthy style. (Consider tearing this list of five dimensions of family health out to put on your refrigerator or somewhere else that will help remind you of your desires regarding family interactions.)

Five Dimensions of Marital and Family Health

1. The ability to express anger without denying love

Children as well as adults need to be accepted for the full range of human expression to feel loved. Conditional love involves an emotional disconnection when anger arises. An inclusive love accepts anger without emotional disconnection. Practice saying to your children, "I do love you and I am very angry about your actions." Parents find that by saying this out loud to young children, they can actually feel the difference of their emotional love *and* anger simultaneously in their physical bodies. Both they and their child are reassured, and anger can be expressed without the emotional withdrawal that so often accompanied our own childhood experiences. Once you have mastered this response with your children, try it with your spouse when the opportunity arises! Can members of your family express anger without emotional withdrawal or lashing out?

2. The ability to accept differences in opinions and feelings

Psychological safety is created in an atmosphere that does not discount or denigrate an individual for his or her opinion, but does allow for the passionate expression of differences. This sets the stage for effective conflict resolution, too. Problems can be solved and compromises reached when empathy develops out of safe and full expression of differences. Is there room for different viewpoints and opinions in your family?

3. The ability for clear and direct communication that allows feelings to be expressed separately from action

It is safe to have feelings when these feelings are acceptable to have and not "acted out" on a family member. Families that develop an atmosphere that tolerates ambivalent feelings accepts the realities of the human experience. For example, a mother may feel disappointed that she cannot attend a social gathering of her colleagues due to family responsibilities. Her feelings of disappointment can be expressed (and met with empathy) as she chooses to forgo her event. By making room for "unpopular" feelings, resentment and guilt are more likely to be replaced by appreciation and a fair sense of give and take in the future. Is there room for feelings in your family?

4. The ability for family members to depend on the larger community

Families do not exist in isolation. Resources outside of the family must be incorporated into family life for children and adults to feel a part of a larger "whole" and to acquire needed resources for development. A family atmosphere that is supported by outside forces, such as a father's group for a new father, or a mother's group for the mom allows for affiliations and outlets for life's frustrations that may otherwise result in internalized pressure in the family.

Friendships, hobbies, and activities that help us release tension give us more of a buffer in our daily lives with those who are most intimate to us. Though we develop family spirit and togetherness, it must be balanced with a support network that extends beyond the family. How healthy is your community network? Do you have close friendships (other than your spouse, for example) that you can talk to when you feel down or pressured? Men are particularly vulnerable to ignoring the need to develop male friendships and may overburden their marriage with *all* of their emotional needs. If you are a single parent, who do you turn to for discussion of your own ups and downs and troubles that naturally arise in relationship with your children?

5. The ability to gradually hand over age-appropriate decision making to growing children and support independence

In a healthy family system, support to eventually separate from the family is not viewed as a betrayal, but a natural resolution to a child's growth. Connection allows for a child's growing development away from the family, and healthy family connection continues when there is a slow and evolving change towards adult friendship, which gradually replaces parental-child interactions. Families sometimes get stuck in negative parental-child relationship patterns when parental responsibility is abrogated too early, or a child's growing independent decision making is discouraged. Finding a healthy balance is the key to maintaining healthy connections to your children over a lifetime! How did your parents do? Did they maintain a vibrant relationship with you through your adult years? How do you envision your relationship with your children as adults?

TWO

How Does Your Garden Grow?

Characteristics of Healthy Families

A healthy family is neither necessarily average,
nor merely lacking in negative characteristics.
Rather it has described positive features.[3]

What are the hallmarks of families that seem to flourish in an atmosphere of warmth and ease, even under stressful life events? Why does crisis pull some families together, while driving others apart?

Too often we study what goes wrong, but this does not always give us a picture of how things go "right." Sometimes our attempt to study health is limited by our unconscious or conscious biases. Paying attention to positive elements in human relationship results in more than the sum of its parts. By studying the characteristics of what contributes to health and well being in family systems, you may find yourself thinking differently about your own family experience.

In 1976 a group of family researchers collaborated in the Timberlawn study of healthy families.[4] Their work produced the first published report of a detailed examination of well-functioning families. Robert Beavers, MD continued to develop research on healthy family systems and what

---

3. N. Epstein, D. Bishop, C. Ryan, I. Miller, & G. Keitner, "The McMaster Model View of Healthy Family Functioning." In F. Walsh (Ed.), *Normal Family Processes*, 2nd edition (New York: Guilford Press, 1993), p.139.
4. R. Beavers & R. Hampson, "Measuring Family Competence: The Beavers Systems Model." In F. Walsh (Ed.), *Normal Family Processes*, 2nd edition (New York: Guilford Press, 1993).

makes them tick. The following description of the characteristics of healthy families is the culmination of thirty years of research. Additional studies have corroborated these findings, underscoring the importance of encouraging processes in families that promote connection over disconnection, and acceptances of differences. The characteristics listed below describe what goes on in families that promote healthy relationships. It is not all inclusive, nor does it express one way to be as a family. These are simply observations from a variety of family cultures that have been identified as having positive impact on growth and adaptation.

All families, no matter what their unique culture, do basically the same thing. They nurture the growth and development of their members. Each family is like a garden. The characteristics below are some of the nutrients you may wish to consider in tilling the soil.

Seven Characteristics of Healthy Families

1. Orientation: Creating a safe atmosphere for learning from our "mistakes"

Mistakes are accepted as an opportunity for learning. Family members are assumed to be inherently "good." When mistakes are made, attention is focused on understanding the "bad" behavior. Responsibility, rather than blame is encouraged. Natural consequences may be given, but punishment for the sake of humiliation is avoided.

For example, a ten-year-old girl steals lipstick from a department store. One parent's response was to cut her daughter's bangs abnormally short and call her a "thief." Her mother felt that by doing this, she would be shamed away from the behavior. The child continued to steal, but learned how not to get caught. Ignoring the behavior does not make the family "safe" either. Instead, being able to make a mistake and depend on parents to understand their behavior as well as to guide and set limits, lets children know there is help when they go astray.

Children who hear that their parents believe in them, recognize that a mistake was made, and seek to get to the bottom of feel safe to bring up problems with when they do arise. "I know you are not a thief. Why in the world are you stealing? Tell me how this happened." When parents' orientation is to confront negative behavior, without shaming, children learn to trust their guidance. The family atmosphere is a safe place for children to bring their problems when they are in trouble.

2. Clear boundaries

In healthy families, responsibilities of adults are separate from the responsibilities of children. Parents are in charge of the decision making although they do receive input from children about their feelings and viewpoints. Clear boundaries keeps children from feeling overly responsible for "adult" problems, allowing them to feel secure enough to grow- up gradually.

3. The relationship between power and intimacy in the couple's relationship

Spouses are able to relate intimately when they feel they have equal power. This is because when we get frightened, two options are available to us: to relate through loving and caring to get our needs met, or to control others or a situation. Family relationships are strengthened when members relate to one another in order to solve problems, rather than seek to control one another. Unilateral decision making by one spouse dampens affection, trust and love. Equal power in decision making is necessary, or intimacy suffers.

Classic examples of this can be seen in the housewives of the 1950s in this country, when men assumed deference in decision making because they brought home the paycheck. Because dad made the money, oftentimes mom's feelings, her needs, her schedule, were ignored unless it fit into dad's needs and work schedule. Mom's emotional caretaking of family members was unpaid work and therefore of secondary importance. She became a second-class citizen in many families, and everyone suffered because of the loss of intimacy inherent in such an arrangement.

This does not mean that one or the other partner cannot specialize in homemaking and the other in working outside the home for money. But it does mean that both partners' viewpoints receive equal attention, making joint decisions promotes intimacy because those decisions are made in consideration of others. Intimacy erodes when money is not shared as an equal resource. The following question and answer illustrates the relationship between equity in decision making about financial resources and the health and intimacy of the relationship.

Marriage and money: Communication and control

Dr. Gayle,

My husband and I have been living together for four years, but we are still arguing about a lot of things, especially money. Both of

*us are working full time. My husband is earning twice my salary.
He pays all our bills and his bills, and I pay my bills (personal) and
the rest of my salary goes to our savings account.*

*Lately, he is demanding for me to pay half of our bills. Helping
my husband with the expenses is no problem, I think that is what
marriage is about. But my husband also refuses to tell me where his
money goes.*

Linda

Dear Linda,

Decision making is one dimension of marriage. It appears that
you have allowed your husband to make decisions in the past when
it comes to money. But you seem to be uncomfortable doing so.
Decisions cannot be made unilaterally in a marriage without detrimental impact on your relationship.

Have a discussion with your husband about the nature of partnership. According to law in most states (such as California), all income
in a marriage is shared jointly. This means that you are entitled to
fifty percent of your husband's income, as he is to yours. And if
divorce takes place in a community property state, everything you
have is divided in half. But you do not want to have to divorce your
husband to feel entitled to your fair share!

Require that all financial knowledge, including what each of you
makes and where it goes, is known and accessible to both of you.
Information as well as decision making needs to be shared in order
for equality to exist between partners.

Reflect on whether you have been reticent or unwilling to accept
responsibility for financial information or decision making. Did you
want your husband to "take care of things" so you did not have to
worry about finances? If so, you may have initially contributed to his
"taking over" in the present. Women are often acculturated to not
take charge of money or financial decisions. Perhaps your father took
care of finances in your family and it seemed natural to abdicate this
area to your husband. But in your current situation, it is clear that
you are being relegated to a child's role in this area of the marriage,
and you are neither happy nor comfortable with the result.

Establish a partnership in this area. Be honest with yourself if you
have in any way acted like a child in relationship to finances. If you
have contributed by taking the role of a child, acknowledge that and

be willing to accept responsibility educating yourself about finances. Claim both responsibility and your half of the decision making power in the relationship. This does not mean a power struggle with your husband, but creating equality in decision making about how money is handled. If a power struggle escalates from your attempts to establish equity in decision making in your marriage, seek counseling to resolve the conflict. Unrelenting overt or covert power struggles that defy resolution can lead to divorce.

Intimacy wilts under inequity, but flourishes when partners respect and enjoy equality in decision making. Let your husband know the way that you feel when overpowered by him in this area has the cost of damaging the affection you have for him. This is not a retaliation on your part, but merely a natural consequence. Very often we cannot see the forest for the trees. "Getting your way" at any cost means just that. Though your husband may feel in control when he makes unilateral decisions about finances, he is paying the price in deadening the affection in the marriage.

Ask your husband to consider the cost of his behavior to your marriage. Is the need to control greater than the desire for a loving and affectionate relationship?

4. The ability to speak honestly

In healthy families, love is not withdrawn if people think differently. Ambivalence and uncertainty are also acceptable to express. Freedom of expression (without denigration or discounting others) supports individuality without threatening belonging. This contributes to an atmosphere in which lively discussions can develop and people can enjoy one another.

5. Humor is your ally!

One aspect of mental health is the ability to laugh at ourselves good-naturedly. This is not the same as laughing at, or making fun of someone at his or her expense. Instead, it is a shared experience of humor that lightens up the potential to take ourselves too seriously, and to not be able to see the forest for the trees. Humor often allows us to regain an overview or larger perspective that has been temporarily lost in the stress of everyday living. Many medical researchers have even linked it to physical health and recovery.

Humor plays an important role in family bonding and maintaining a healthy perspective in life. It can help free us from the natural ruts we often find ourselves in when we feel the overwhelming need to be right when arguing with our partner, or child. Use it to recover from overly alienated or polarized positions or when you feel backed into a corner, or find yourself saying something that really isn't you!

6. Teamwork: The ability to organize and negotiate in a timely fashion

Family life is full of tiny, small and larger tasks to coordinate. The list can be endless, but reasonable organization must be maintained and decisions about coordinating activities in the family must be reached in a manner that feels fair. Many of these decisions must also be made in a time frame that allows for discussion, but does not bog things down. Quite a tall order!

In concert with the other characteristics of healthy families, parents can take charge without being overly controlling in a situation. Because there is a spirit of camaraderie, trust is built up over the years and organization flows more smoothly. Develop teamwork. Remember that when responsibilities are clearly delegated in a family, negotiating does not have to be repeated on a daily basis.

Does having a toddler mean that the house has to be a mess?

Dr. Gayle,

Clutter seems to be a constant battle in our house. We live in a small home, which makes it worse. My wife and I have an eighteen-month-old boy, whom we both love dearly, and we have decided to have another child.

I work four twelve hour days, and have three days off. My wife stays home. When I go back to work, after the second or third day, the house looks bad. Laundry piled up, diaper pail full, towels on the floor, toys and clutter everywhere.

This puts me in a rotten mood as soon as I get home. I understand that raising a child is a lot of work, our boy is in need of almost constant attention. This has been going on since he was born. I feel that having another child with no concession from either one of us will compound the problem and surely end our marriage. Am I wrong in feeling that at least the clutter can be controlled?

I do a lot to help out. I don't want to live like a slob, but don't want

to be thought of as a controlling dictator either. When there are dia-
pers piled up on top of the pail lid tree high and his bedroom stinks,
she moves the toy box into the living room and his toys are scattered
everywhere. She puts the laundry in drawers in the living room to get
it out of sight until she can sort it. The thing is when I need some-
thing, then the hunt is on and it takes forever to find anything.

When I am home, I do the dishes, water the plants, take out the trash
that piles up, maintain the vehicles. Am I wrong in thinking she needs to
be more active? Is she right in thinking that's the way it is with kids?

Douglas

Dear Douglas,

Organization is one dimension of family health. Without enough of it, families suffer the consequences of a chaotic environment. It is true that a wide range of styles or methods for organization abound. However, it appears that your wife is simply withdrawing from the challenge of creating order, not arguing over different methods for achieving it. Do not accept motherhood as an excuse for chaos. Instead, invite your wife to be a team player. Ask for her help to create the organization that is an inevitable requirement of family life.

It is true that having a child requires greater organizational effort in a family. It is often the case that lowering expectations for tidiness is an appropriate measure to reduce stress while maintaining an overall sense of orderliness. However, in your family it appears that there is no systematized approach to organize the many tasks at hand. No wonder your wife feels overwhelmed! You are right to consider that adding another child to your family without incorporating a method for handling increased responsibilities may cause you to progress from chaos to anarchy.

It is possible that you and your wife specialize in different qualities. She may be more spontaneous, while you are more goal direct-ed. Whatever your unique differences, it is your job as parents to come up with methods to organize your life in ways that simplify your stress rather than exacerbate it. Ask your wife to consider the possibility that order can become her friend rather than her enemy!

We often learn our organizational skills from our parents. It is possible that your wife grew up in a family that functioned poorly in terms of organization, or was rigidly structured to the point that she developed a rebellion against all organizing. Regardless, she chose you as a husband. Clearly you represent a different perspective, and one she may very much need to incorporate. Marriage is a partnership. There is always room to learn from each other.

Share your feelings with your wife. Let her know that she has many qualities you admire and that you appreciate the loving care she provides as a mother and wife. Express your experience of overwhelm about the level of disarray in your family environment and the fact that you are not comfortable with adding the responsibility of another child until the two of you are able to create a shared vision for your family environment. This is not a threat, it is simply a reality of the conflict between you over organization in the family.

You are a family member and a co-leader of the family. Your distress matters. Ask your wife if she will meet you halfway in considering a change. No doubt, disorderliness also slows her down and it may make organization more difficult for your children as their lives become more complex with school activities, homework, and more. Take a long range view. Ask your wife how her family organized family responsibilities. Reflect on how your family handled organization and identify what kind of benefits a modicum of order brings each of you.

Establish a shared vision for organization in your family and keep in mind that both of you matter! You must achieve a satisfactory middle ground or you are not truly resolving the problem. Once you have agreed to a vision for achieving order, brainstorm ways and methods that will simplify. For example, put toys away at a certain time in the evening or twice daily. Or, maintain certain areas as "clean zones" and others as "toy zones." Establish follow-through procedures in the family. For example, put dirty diapers in the diaper pail immediately after a diaper change. These are merely good "work habits," as many parents will attest.

All systems require organization to perform tasks and function smoothly. Running a family is no exception! From government to girls' scout groups, order creates the space for creativity and meaningful interactions between people. Smooth functioning requires that you institute systematic methods to complete tasks in a timely manner.

Creating order will assure the space and time to relax, have fun, and generally enjoy your family relationships. Ask for your wife's help to envision and implement a balance of order in your lives that is family-friendly!

7. Family value system: Feeling a part of a larger "whole"

What makes life worthwhile? Coping with the inevitability of death at the end of the life cycle requires some kind of transcendence beyond logic. "Family spirit" and values may play an essential role in preparing our children to cope with life's ups and downs, as well as its inevitable losses.

Values are guidelines that exist to help children learn how to best live the lives they are given. Values are learned through our actions and verbal expression. Family processes provide children initial guidelines for how they are expected to treat others on their life's journey. Children learn that lying and stealing are okay in order to meet their needs, or not. Guidelines for negotiating their own needs and desires in the world may include treating others respectfully, or disrespectfully.

Healthy family relationships teach children not only to develop trust and to be trustworthy, *but that they are a part of something larger than themselves!* In the passage through life, we hope that our "spirit" lives in our family's future generations because of the way we have lived our lives, and what we have meant to each other. Something as simple as taking your family on a vacation that brings them close to nature can acquaint children with their part in a bigger picture.

In addition to a basic positive view of humanity and of life in general, healthy families also deal with the inevitable losses that occur in the family life cycle. To do so, families employ varying philosophies, religious or otherwise, about the nature of life. Healthy families include some larger concept of life that encompasses the fact that we all die.

Therefore we must inevitably be able to find some meaning in something that is a larger whole. The individual must be able to find significance in the contribution to something greater than the self. The capacity for symbolism must therefore be a part of the family's emotional wealth, since we cannot answer the basic question of "why" that our children ask us with anything but intuition, faith or philosophical speculations.

Whether in society, family, grandchildren, god, politics, or social change, an individual must be able to find meaning that in some way transcends the ultimate loss of individual life. Along the way, there are usually a number of naturally occurring deaths in the family that help prepare us, as we are faced with carrying that family member in some other form than the physical. The following question and answer illustrates this process.

What to tell three-year-old about dying grandfather

Dear Dr. Gayle,

My father-in-law is dying of a liver disease. What do I tell my three-year-old? He and his grandfather are very close, and this disease took a dramatic turn very quickly. He went from seeing a happy vibrant man, to seeing a little old man lying in a hospital bed, with tubes in him, talking nonsense. We aren't religious, so there haven't been any stories about heaven to fall back on. I haven't had anyone close to me die before, so I am absolutely ignorant of anything to say.

Tina

Dear Tina,

Your son is fortunate to have known his grandfather and enjoyed him while he was still a vibrant figure in his life. It is positive that your son is seeing his grandfather change, however dramatically, for it will prepare him for his death. Your son's experience of his grandpa's transition from vibrancy to complete absence (without any in-between transition) would have created an even greater change to assimilate.

Naturally, it is important to monitor your son's reaction to seeing his grandfather's process of dying. Support him by talking about what is happening. If he does not want to see grandpa in the hospital, do not force him, but do encourage a brief visit, if he is interested. Even a visit to the hospital gives him some place and time to process the fact that grandpa will no longer be with him in his daily life. Funerals, too, provide a ritual for sharing and easing the pain of loss. Including children in memorial rituals in an appropriate way allows them to share their grief instead of becoming confused by it.

Many books can be useful to help children process the concept of death by putting it into the context of nature and the natural beginnings and endings of all living things, including fish, dogs and grandparents. One such resource is *Lifetimes*[5] by Bryan Mellonie and Robert Ingpen. Reading material aimed at this age will give your child and yourself a reference point to talk about grandfather's dying. Answer his questions as best you can, and do not be afraid to tell him if you do not know the answer. Seek to be emotionally reassuring to him, but truthful.

---

5. B. Mellomie & R. Ingpen, *Lifetimes* (New York: Bantam Books, 1983).

Even though you do not follow a particular religious path, it does not mean you do not have your own brand of spirituality. You will find yourself developing a philosophy for handling loss in the family. If this has not happened for you previously, then you, too, will be experiencing this process for the first time. You may find that other, less intense losses, such as the death of a pet, may come to mind to help you share a context of loss with your son. Whatever experiences you and your husband bring to this event should serve to guide you towards helping your son retain the value of his relationship with his grandfather throughout his lifetime.

Remembering the good times with his grandfather may continue throughout the weeks, months and year ahead. And his special relationship with his grandfather will likely become a positive memory that will guide his behavior towards his own grandchildren, surfacing at the appropriate moments in his development. Your job is to support the natural process as it unfolds. And within this process, you will develop a familial context for death and loss. Some families make collages of the person who died, to honor his memory. Memorial services that include retelling the family's best stories about the deceased is another common ritual.

Part of the task of parenthood is to integrate that which is unknown. All families struggle with the process of explaining death, for it is after all a natural part of the family life cycle. Your father-in-law's death will stimulate your family's handling of the spiritual in a way that is unique and universal at the same time. Your son will no doubt benefit from your obvious sensitivity to the need to address rather than attempt to sidestep this very important transition in the family.

Judith Viorst, in her book *Necessary Losses,*[6] elegantly describes the process of growing up as a series of continual losses necessary for growth throughout the life cycle. Leaving childhood is necessary for becoming an adult. Letting go of our children as they leave home is necessary for their development as adults and for our growth as parents. We all move on in life. Our connectedness remains but our relationships and how we depend on one another change. The following question and answer illustrates the midlife challenges that can present themselves when children leave home and we are left to face our lives and marriages.

---

6. J. Viorst, *Necesary Losses* (New York: Simon and Schuster, 1986).

Without a life after children are grown

Dear Dr. Gayle,

Things change in a marriage after raising children. I think it was once called the twenty year fracture! My husband and I made the mistake of giving our entire beings to our children. I was a stay-at-home mom and now find myself without a life. Literally, I don't know how to get the joy back I once had. I don't feel good about myself at all. I know what I should do, but I can't seem to get myself going. My husband has his career and I feel left behind. I'm stuck and it affects my marriage in a big way. I still have a high school junior at home, but he needs his independence and I need a life of my own. What to do?

Shar

Dear Shar,

Your feeling of "being without a life" now that your children are leaving home is not simply due to being a stay-at-home mom. I have had a career throughout raising my children and when both of my children left for college, I felt a huge hole in my life. In the two years following their departure I felt lost and somewhat aimless even though I loved my work!

You have spent twenty years in a primary nurturing role in the family. Because you have done such a terrific job, your children are striking out on their own. You recognize this and support it, but it does leave a void in your life to fill.

Being in touch with your children's needs on a daily basis, loving them and caring for them is a vitally important part of life as a mother, whether you work outside the home or not. The nurturing you give also nourishes and rewards you in the circle of that love. Living together is an intimate connection we take for granted. Grieving their daily presence is natural and inevitable if you have connected deeply. Other feelings of joy, relief and pleasure related to this change may also occur. However the overall adjustment is one of loss for the daily intimacy and structure in your life that having children at home provides.

Family life gives us a way to organize our lives. And healthy family relationships require that you derive meaning from being involved in your children's lives. This is what gives them the sustenance to become independent. You cannot protect yourself from this loss. If you've done your job well, you will hurt! But the good news is that your life will also change and evolve. You are entering a life transition and it feels like one, with all the ambiguity and uncertainty that is a part of a major life change. Transitions by nature are "liminal" periods. That is, they are times when we are without form, "on the threshold," "betwixt and between."

Murray Stein in his book, *In Midlife* [7] describes liminal periods to be periods as times when we feel unformed, like the elements of life before life itself is created. Liminal periods are essential to the birth of new forms. It is a place of the "naked soul." Despair and a sense of emptiness are common reactions while traveling through transitions of any kind. But it is also a place of struggle towards the birth of a new identity.

You are in the family life cycle stage of "launching children." Talk with your husband about mourning this change in the structure of life you have shared together for so long. He is bound to have feelings about children being gone from the home as well. Share your grieving even though it will be different for each of you.

One of the tasks of this period is the renegotiation of the couple's relationship. Emotional support from your husband is important now. Spend time together. Take walks or do things you may not have been able to do because of the demands of raising children. Weekends away are important. Getting reacquainted with one another without the interaction of the children between you will help to establish a new kind of relationship. Start courting each other again. And don't be surprised if you feel shy or awkward at first.

Using the support of husband and friends can be the springboard to explore new interests and activities or rekindle old interests left behind in the process of raising a family. The fact that you know what to do, but just can't seem to get yourself to do it is an indication that you are mourning. Allow yourself a period of mourning as a part of this transition. When you acknowledge your grief as appropriate and a natural part of life change, you will be less likely to blame yourself for past choices. You are not hurting because you were a stay-at-home mom. You are grieving because you love and have cared for your children well and now need to let go.

Turn all of the loving care you have given to others on yourself now.

7. M. Stein, *In Midlife* (Dallas, TX: Spring Publications, 1990).

This may be an excellent time to engage in some personal therapy or marital therapy to get support in exploring your options. A woman's support group may also serve you during this transition. It usually takes about two years to reestablish structure in your life, so be patient. You will not always feel this way and each day, week, and month will lighten your sorrow and consolidate your new sense of self, including rewarding adult relationships with your grown children.

An Exercise in Reflection on Family Experience

The following worksheet provides opportunity to reflect on your current family relationships. Take time now to explore these characteristics with respect to your own childhood family background and to your current family. Use the worksheet to help you sort through the past and create your future. Discuss the following questions with your partner, a trusted friend, or you may decide to journal your answers on your own.

Family beliefs

Ask yourself: What were the basic attitudes, beliefs or philosophy that influenced me in my childhood family? Did family members believe in the basic "goodness" of one another? Were limits set neutrally, without emotional rejection? Or was emotional rejection and judgment part or all of the response to mistakes or misbehavior? Was this a family in which members strived for perfection but accepted the inevitability of mistakes? Could members show fear and uncertainty with expectation for reassurance and understanding? Write your observations of your family-of-origin's orientation towards mistakes and the belief in "goodness" of its members. _____

_____

_____

_____

_____

_____

_____

Describe your present family's orientation, reflecting on these basic questions related to family relationships and the overall atmosphere of warmth and caring. Write your observations of your family's strengths and weaknesses in this area and ideas for improvement if necessary. ____

_____

_____

_____

_____

_____

_____

_____

Remember that if your family atmosphere is not where you want it to be, you can change it! You are not stuck in the past. Although it is natural to recreate a family atmosphere similar to the one you grew up in, once you are able to objectively identify elements you would like to change, your observations lead you to different outcomes. And change takes time. Each incident or event you turn around builds on itself to create the future. Patience and compassion are your best allies to evaluate your present family orientation.

Boundaries

Ask yourself: Were the roles of parents and children clear in my childhood family? Did I learn to take responsibility as a child, and gradually make my own decisions? Was there too little guidance, or too much? Did I enjoy an identity with my family, yet connect with outside members of the community and extended family for greater resources? advice? information? Write down your observations about boundaries between you and your parents in childhood. _____

_____

_____

_____

_____

_____

_____

How do I see my present family with respect to clarity of roles and expectations? Are responsibilities in the family clearly defined, or fuzzy? Is there an extended network of support, or is our family more isolated than I would like? Write down your observations of your family's strengths and weaknesses in this and any ideas for change. (This may overlap with the first exercise to some extent. Anything already addressed need not be repeated.) _____

_____

_____

_____

_____

_____

Consider ways to create greater clarity regarding responsibilities, if you feel it is needed in your family, or to take some action towards developing a connection with community resources or to make time for developing friendships and a social network, if needed. Your experience of your family is a "work in progress." You have every right to develop and influence the course of your family's direction!

Power and intimacy

Ask yourself: How were decisions made in my childhood family? Were people's feelings considered? Did any one person's feelings or needs dominate over others? If so, why? Was any attempt made towards fairness in considering members' needs when they conflicted? Were children's feelings heard and taken into account by parents in their decision making in the family? Write down your recollection of how and whether family members treated each other with respect. _____

_____

_____

_____

_____

_____

What are the answers to the above questions for my present family? Do all members have the same opinion as I do? Do any members feel that their feelings do not matter when it comes to important decisions? Does your partner feel considered and respected with regard to feelings in conflict situations? Gather information from your spouse and other members of your family about their experience. Evaluate the "spirit" of the family's dynamics from various perspectives. Is it what you want it to be? What is positive about your family's spirit? Is anything missing that you want to develop in your family's atmosphere? (For example: greater respect or consideration.) _____

_____
_____
_____
_____
_____
_____
_____

Honesty and freedom of expression

Ask yourself: Did I experience pressure to lie or hide my true feelings or opinions in my childhood family? Were members open to differences in the family, or extremely threatened by feelings or ideas that conflicted with their own? In my present family is honesty of feelings and opinions prevalent? Are individuality and expression of a range of feelings and opinions acceptable? (This may overlap with the first exercise, but is meant to explore your childhood from another angle that may jog your memory and clarify family patterns.) Write down your experience of being able to express your views in your childhood family.

_____
_____
_____
_____
_____
_____

Gather information from your spouse and other family members about their experience. Becoming aware of each family member's experiences is the first step. Awareness itself opens the door to change in small, but subtle ways. For example, one mother observed that her daughter rarely ever complained, though her brothers often expressed what went wrong at school. She began to check in with her daughter about what things were difficult for her, as well as what was going well. This opened up a whole dimension of closeness and sharing that had been dormant between mother and daughter. Write down your present family's strengths and weaknesses in the area of self-expression and any ideas for increasing the range of expression, if you feel there is a need for one or more family members to feel more comfortable expressing themselves.

_____

_____

_____

_____

_____

_____

Warmth and humor

Ask yourself: Can I remember good times, fun times, and times of mirth and laughter that bonded you as a family in childhood? How often or how rare were these occurrences? Write down the good times you remember with your family in childhood. Whether they were abundant or few and far between, they are important resources to recover.

_____

_____

_____

_____

_____

_____

Do you laugh together as a family? Do family members seek each other out to talk and check in with one another at some point in the day or week? Are there family rituals, like dinnertime, weekend trips or other activities that family members look forward to sharing together? Write down the family rituals you have, or want to have in your family and the ways you use humor, or want to begin to utilize more humor, if you feel it is missing. _____

_____

_____

_____

_____

_____

Humor and warmth make relationships rewarding. Simple, playful banter while cooking can create an atmosphere in which people want to relate, rather than isolate—even teenagers! Evaluate this kind of connection in your family relationships. If you feel you are lacking something here, introduce a little humor, for fun's sake.

Organization and negotiating skill

Ask yourself: Were family tasks done with ease or with difficulty in my childhood? Was there a reasonable amount of order in the household, or did weekends get bogged down in repeated attempts to organize basic family tasks? Could I count on things being done regularly and did I have regular family chores myself or were things more haphazardly maintained? If organizational structure was maintained was it flexible enough for updating from time to time as needs of family members changed, or was it overly controlled and rigid, allowing for little or no adjustment over time? Were problems resolved, or did conflict drag on, with repeated struggles over the same issues? Write down your impressions of the level of successful organization in the family and the spirit in which it was carried out.

_____

_____

_____

_____

_____

_____

In my present family is there reasonable order that is sustained over long periods of time with appropriate flexibility, or are there repeated arguments over basic chores and lack of clarity regarding how they will get done? When conflict arises, is it resolved without excessive emotional pain and tension? Reflect on this aspect of your family experience, and gather information from your spouse about his/her experience of family life together. Write down your strengths and weaknesses in the area of organization and the spirit in which it happens, and any ideas for change, if needed._____

_____

_____

_____

_____

_____

_____

Consider and evaluate whether you have transferred any ineffective patterns of organization from childhood onto your own family, and decide what kind of organization you want to have in your current family. It is possible that to succeed in this area, you may need to consider revising your priorities (maybe the kitchen floor will not be spotless while my children are young!). Or you may find that your inability to reach timely and effective compromise with your spouse creates an undercurrent of tension in your household, affecting the overall family atmosphere in a negative way. If so, put this problem between you on the table for discussion and, if necessary, seek help and resources to detoxify this aspect of your relationship. The ability to problem-solve is an essential element of healthy family relationships.

Values

Ask yourself: What philosophy or values did my childhood family hold regarding life? What did my parents tell me about the nature of life, the meaning of family? How was disappointment or failure handled in my family? How did my family handle the subject or experience of death? Did I experience myself as a part of a larger whole in the context of my family's past and its previous generations? Write down your impressions about how well you felt your parents helped to connect you to your family's history or introduced you to a larger meaning in understanding life.

_____

_____

_____

_____

_____

_____

_____

_____

What kind of values do I want to pass on to my children? How do I address the meaning of life? How do I handle disappointments? The subject of death? Do I feel a part of a "larger whole" in context of my family? My community? Past generations? What do we do as a family that gives us an experience of "we"—such as family picnics, outings, nature hikes, camping, daily family dinners? Write down what values you want to pass onto your children and how you help them to connect with their family's history and heritage. _____

_____

_____

_____

_____

_____

_____

_____

Discuss these questions with your partner. Evaluate your own and other family members' experience of the family and the larger community. Remember, it is never too late to begin having family dinners if you have not, or to instigate Friday night as "family pizza night," or to make a family trip to visit a "forgotten" relative, if you want. This is your family. You can try new and different things than those you were raised with, as well as embracing family rituals you found enriching in your childhood.

This sorting through process allows you to develop your own family vision! Make a list of strengths and weaknesses and any changes you want to implement in any of the above areas in your present family life. Review this list and update your impressions six months from now, and one year from now.

Family structure: Who is in charge?

In order to create the families we want to have, we must be clear on our leadership. Although boundaries have been discussed, it is necessary to delve deeper into the marital partnership that makes up the foundation of family life. What does being "in charge" really look like?

Clear generational boundaries are necessary for a healthy, functioning family. There should be no question as to who is parent and who is child. This is true whether your child is fourteen or two, though naturally responsibilities change as your child grows.

In healthy families, parents do not feel as though they must disclaim their adult power, and children do not feel called upon to assume premature adult responsibility. On an emotional level, this means that a child doesn't feel compelled to fill the needs that parents must provide for one another. If this happens, the emotionally "parentified" child is at risk for becoming the "problem" that parents polarize (or unite) around. With muddy boundaries, the child can become overburdened by adult problems. When this happens, generational boundaries collapse, often leading to unhealthy alliances, such as mom and child against dad or other painful strategies in a failing attempt to resolve conflict.

Parents sometimes unwittingly develop unhealthy family structures by putting their child in the middle of an argument; for example, "The baby is crying and she needs *you* to come home." Rather than, "I really need you."

You can learn to nurture clear generational boundaries in your own family. Doing so supports intimacy in the parental relationship, as parents must be more direct in communicating their needs to one another. This ensures your relationship will grow! Clear boundaries also allow a special bond to develop between siblings. Painful undermining of a secure family structure can take place when cross-generational alliances override the bond between generations. This occurs when the parental bond is weak, and children are used as emotional replacements for the opposite sexed parent. A daughter may feel that she is daddy's favorite, while mommy likes her brother best. Sisters and brothers share a similar position in the family and benefit from healthy peer relationships. When generational boundaries are intact in the family, a child's place is secure.

Solidifying the couple's bond: What you can do!

The first step in building a healthy family structure is to strengthen your couple's relationship from the beginning. Your relationship is the garden in which your child grows. Your relationship also determines the emotional atmosphere of the family. Nurturing this important generational bond is essential to a strong family foundation.

Take time daily to express your needs and share feelings with one another

Schedule quality time to enjoy each other. Make this a priority from the start. Even if it is only once a month, it is a statement that you need each other. In fact, attention to one another is necessary for children to feel loved. Even young babies benefit from parents taking a night out for themselves to nurture each other.

Couples commonly come for counseling when their first child is between one and two years of age. Often, they have neglected their couple relationship through the plentiful changes of this period. When they finally turn their attention away from parental duties, they have been lonely for each other for a long time. Their need for meaningful contact is expressed through accusations of neglect and failure. As time goes by, lack of intimacy between partners becomes a family pattern that takes its toll. The following question and answer presents this common pitfall in early family development.

Balancing kids and marriage

Dr. Gayle,

I am a mother of three and I have been married for six years. My husband and I always had a wonderful relationship, but things seem to be going downhill. We never have time to be together. I feel like I am always answering my husband with, "I can't, I'm feeding the kids" or "I am doing something with the kids." I can tell he is as frustrated as I am. I love my children dearly but I am at my wit's end. What do you recommend?

Janet

Dear Janet,

Mothering three children means that you and your husband are outnumbered! Yet, it is in the best interests of your children that mom and dad take some quality time for their relationship. Since you have identified the problem, why not start there? Securing time together on a daily basis now may save you the expense of later marital counseling or an unrealistic, last-ditch push for a weekend away to save your marriage.

Two things must happen to get your marriage back on track. First, organize! The larger the family the more important it is to develop productive routines so that you do not waste energy reinventing the wheel each day. Divide duties between yourself and your husband so that lunches get made, teeth get brushed, and homework is supervised. Initially, effective scheduling takes effort, but planning will pay off in time saved and lower frustration levels.

Secondly, you must carve out time for your couple's relationship on a daily and weekly basis. You are each other's nourishment. Your energy is derived in part from the heart and soul of your marriage. In other words, the love, attention and appreciation you give one another is what helps you through the day.

Your children by about age four can learn to respect twenty to thirty minutes of "parent time" each evening after dinner. And while children are younger, you and your husband can create this time after their bedtime. Children's bedtime needs to occur in a timely fashion that also allows for this quiet sharing and "down time" together. Use it to catch up on your day and consider a family business meeting once a week to brainstorm planning strategies for the family schedule as things are constantly changing. Soccer schedules, kids' play dates, and school activities can be devastating to family organization and morale if you play it by ear in a larger clan such as yours.

The secret of enjoying larger families (though it is beneficial for smaller ones as well) is to delegate. As your children reach appropriate ages, it is possible to obtain their help in a cooperative fashion, which both increases their sense of worth and helps you out.

Develop a strategy for handling daily chores in a routine manner with children pitching in to help. Washing dishes, putting toys away at a specific time of day, and encouraging children to play on their own for twenty minutes while you and dad have "talking time" can become their "jobs" in the family. Age-appropriate duties encourage children to become responsible adults, and some form of "helping" can start as early as two years of age. Middle aged children (eight to eleven years) can become increasingly helpful, and adolescents may blossom into helping out by cooking one dinner per week, shopping for the weekly staples at the grocery store, and other time consuming family tasks. Delegation can make running a family smoother and more enjoyable.

The key here is consistency and establishing a routine. Children do flourish in a stable, structured environment, which is also balanced with family fun and predictable activities that serve to bond families together. If kids are rewarded with enjoyable family time together, chores can represent a sense of belonging. Self-confidence develops for the child when routine duties are balanced with predictable family outings, whether it be Friday night pizza at the local family bistro or Sunday afternoon walks to the park. Create ways to balance spontaneity with consistency and order.

Now, back to you and your husband! Talk with your partner about realigning your relationship. Make a regular weekly (or bimonthly, if necessary) date. Take Saturday afternoon or evening time to remember what it is like to be alone together. Maintaining a boundary around your time alone together with your husband models intimacy for your children. Your marriage is the foundation on which their lives are built. Like watering a garden, spending quality time together assures your children's sense of security and continued growth.

Balance your schedule so that you can enjoy family and couple's relating. For example, you could create a weekly schedule that alternates couple's time one week with a family outing the next week. Once predictable times for enjoying family relationships are established in this manner, you can always look forward to the next time you have carved out together. In this way, the relationship serves as a buffer to the many stresses of daily living.

The early years of raising children are particularly time intensive and physically demanding. The time you create to be together as a couple may feel like an oasis in a desert in the early years, but with consistent reinforcement you will find yourself in more lush surroundings as your family matures.

Now is the time to make order out of chaos. Family researchers contend that it is the processes and quality of family relationships that determines health or dysfunction. Establishing routines that nurture and activities that bond now will bode well for your family's future!

Parenthood reactivates your own childhood

Your own childhood is reactivated when you become a parent. This makes you particularly vulnerable during the first year of your child's life, as you are making this important family transition. Old wounds are reopened, but this time you are the parent! And your partner feels more like the opponent than your teammate. You may feel you are losing each other at the very time you need one another the most. This brings us to a second very important approach you can take towards building a healthy family structure from the very beginning.

Adopt a team approach

Make decisions together. Remember that the two of you share the same responsibility. For example, no matter which one of you is carrying out the responsibility physically, both should be sharing in the discussion and decision making about how a child is disciplined or whether a job change is right for the family at this time. The following question

and answer illustrates the problems that occurs when couples are undermining each other instead of working out their differences together.

Husband is undermining my parenting

Dear Dr. Gayle,

*I have a ten-year-old daughter and my problem is not my daugh-
ter but my husband. When I ask my daughter to read a book or to
practice piano, most of the times my husband takes my daughter's
side. It's always too early to do it or I am asking her to read too
many pages. I am playing the bad guy, while my husband is playing
the good guy. I don't believe that my requests are unreasonable and
even if they are, I don't think that my husband should question my
request in front of my daughter.*

*When my husband is around, I am completely ineffective as a
parent which worries me a lot given that my daughter is entering
adolescence and why should she listen to me when even my husband is criticizing what I say? What kind of relationship can I have
with her when I am perceived as the bad guy? My husband is an
educated person, and we both adore our daughter. How can I make
him understand that his behavior is damaging our daughter?*

Ruth

Dear Ruth,

You are right to be concerned. Your husband's criticism of your
parenting in your daughter's presence undermines both your effectiveness as a parental team and your relationship with your daughter.

Negotiate appropriate guidelines with your husband concerning
parenting. Require that negotiations between parents take place separately from your child. Invite him to disagree with you in private,
where the two of you have an opportunity to hear each others' feelings and opinions about what is in your daughter's best interest.
Once you have had time to discuss differences, you may find that
you are not as far apart as you thought on what is best for your
child. Then you will be able to give your daughter clear direction
that does not involve her in your marital conflict!

Your husband's constant challenge to your parenting that results
in his being the "good guy" is not only damaging to your daughter,
but to the marriage. Remind your husband that he is married to you,
not your daughter. Your relationship is the foundation for your

daughter's development, including her eminent separation from the two of you as she grows older. The stronger your bond is, the easier it will be for her to develop her independence without guilt. Involving her in discussion of who is "right" and who is "wrong" can not only confuse her with respect to what the rules are in the home, but more importantly it can complicate her relationship to both of you.

If this pattern of triangulation in your parental conflict continues, your daughter may resort to manipulation in order to get what she wants, but the emotional result will be that she has daddy on her side against mommy. This cripples the affection she can feel for mom and puts her in a psychologically compromised relationship with dad—that is, she experiences closeness to dad at the expense of her mother's feelings of hurt/dismissal. Neither of these positions is in her best interest, as she is at risk for loss of an appropriate relationship to either parent.

Be honest with yourself. Are you willing to give your husband's opinions full consideration? Have you in any way contributed to his not seeking you out for discussion by blocking any of his perceptions when he has tried to discuss his views with you?

Assure your husband that he has legitimacy as a parent and that you are willing to hear his way of looking at a situation. It is his job, as it is yours, to help you identify your own "blind spots." For example, if he feels your "timing" is off in your directions to your daughter, ask him for constructive alternatives and suggestions. But refuse to accept further discussion or discounting in front of your daughter. It is through discussion that the two of you have the opportunity to grow closer and feel your importance to your spouse. This sense of importance to one another in your primary bond as parents contributes to affection in the marriage. And an atmosphere of affection and respect in turn promotes problem-solving!

You may also benefit from exploring the roles that each of your sets of parents played in your respective childhoods. How was conflict handled between your parents? Were there "good" guys and "bad" guys in your family histories? Were spouses committed to respecting one another's opinions and feelings or did they triangulate children or others in order to get their way? Did fathers and mothers work together as a parenting team or give conflicting messages to their offspring?

Get your marriage back on track by establishing a parenting team. Remember that your child will not only benefit from your solidity as a couple, but your marriage relationship will be more likely to endure through the time when your daughter has flown the nest and you are left facing each other!

Team sharing

Feeling supported instead of alone throughout your day is a result of sharing feelings as well as responsibilities with your partner. This kind of team sharing and support strengthens your "couple bond," making you less likely to turn to your child for emotional needs that should be met in your relationship with your partner. In this way, clear boundaries between generations are off to a healthy start.

The quality of your relationship is like a plant—it requires watering on a regular basis, or it will whither. Taking the time and attention to nurture your relationship in the ways discussed will help lay the groundwork for a healthy family system in the years and challenges ahead. Think of it as an investment in your family's future!

As we travel through the life cycle we continue to grow and learn. The older we get, the less we find we know. Helping each other through this process of living the best way we can is what family is all about.

THREE

Pregnancy and Childbirth
Opportunities for Empowerment

Even when the couple's bond is weak, or depleted by loyalties to their families-of-origin, pregnancy and preparation for childbirth can bring a couple together. Although no family researcher has included the period of pregnancy and childbirth as a separate stage on the family life cycle, it is of singular significance due to the incredible potential of this period for growth and change, and deserves to be defined as such.

Preparing for the labor and planning the circumstances surrounding the birth can provide opportunity for realigning the couple system. It is during this period that couples reflect on their own parenting styles, and talk at length about how they want to raise their own child. Active involvement in the childbirth can empower a previously burdened couple to focus on their own beliefs and family experience. Even when there has been trouble due to split family loyalties from the beginning, a second baby can help a couple to establish a strong bond and new efforts at communication. Such was the case of Tom and Sarah, expecting their second child.

Sarah was six months pregnant, suffering extreme nausea with her second child. She had hoped for support from her mother and her in-laws, moving temporarily to be geographically close to them for help. Her five-year-old son traveled with her, while her husband stayed behind to work at his job, in a city 5,000 miles away where they had been living together as a family. Because of extreme nausea, Sarah's obstetrician recommended no airplane travel, once her situation had stabilized with medication. Return home to her husband was impossible until after the birth.

Through this period of time, Sarah became disillusioned with the support she had thought she would receive from relatives, and sought counseling. She became aware of how she and her husband had remained loyal to their family-of-origins emotionally, rather than depending on one another for their main nurturance. Communicating by phone daily with her husband established a deeper connection and they were able to talk together about their disillusionment with his parents and her mother. They discovered for the first time how each felt about the fact that they had not developed a strong couple's bond, which included her depending on him in this situation.

By the time they were reunited, prior to the birth, Tom and Sarah were able to recognize their need to form a strong couple's bond, and began to realign their boundaries with both of their families more appropriately. This new communication strengthened their own sense of family and commitment to the needs of each other. They not only established new guidelines for interaction with relatives that created less disappointment, but freed up energies that had previously been spent accommodating others to attend to the primary needs of their own family.

Devaluation of the feminine

The experience of pregnancy and childbirth is uniquely female. Not all women give or want to give birth. However women who do give birth whatever the circumstances, are faced with the reality of one of nature's most powerful events. The fact that women can express extremely *negative* or incredibly *positive* experiences of childbirth is evidence of the generic power of the experience itself. This most basic fact, that childbirth is a powerful force to be respected, has been lost in the overall devaluation of the feminine in our society.

Women often feel alone with the responsibility of motherhood, even when they have supportive partners. Mothers are criticized quickly when things go awry in childrearing, while their positive contributions go unsung. In fact, many aspects of female development remain invisible to our culture at large. Childbirth is no exception. *The message of our soci-*

ety is that the experience of childbirth is unimportant. The following question and answer illustrates the feelings women may have about childbirth and the impact the experience has on a woman's psyche. It also emphasizes the importance of the role realistic preparation for labor plays in psychological outcome.

Having nightmares about my baby's birth

Dear Dr. Gayle,

I am twenty-seven years old and have been happily married for nine years. We have two great kids, a son who is eight, and our daughter is three months old. My son was born by cesarean and my daughter was a vaginal birth. The delivery of my daughter was very difficult (over fifteen hours) and painful. It has been over three months now and I still am having nightmares about the day she was born. I go through the entire labor in my dreams. Even while I'm awake I have daydreams and can hear the sounds in the delivery room. They used a vacuum suction and I was not prepared for the pain of childbirth. I still remember how out of control I felt. Is this normal? Am I nuts? If I could just get over her birth, I would feel a lot better. Am I going crazy?

Dawn

Dear Dawn,

You are not crazy. Labor and childbirth is an impactful experience that needs to be integrated due to its enormity. Because the experience is devalued, attention to women's needs to prepare adequately and to process the birth following delivery is greatly neglected in our society.

It is true that labor is painful and preparing to cope with it actively is important in order to feel some sense of mastery of the physical experience. But even without realistic preparation, and after the fact, talking about the experience can help you to better integrate it.

Let's take a look at how much went well in your birth. You were able to deliver vaginally in fifteen hours. Given that she was your first baby to come down your vagina, this was excellent time. The average total time for a first baby is generally about twenty-four hours. Though you needed help to push her down, she came through the birth passageway even though you were quite distressed with the pain. Perhaps you were shocked by the sensation of labor and did not expect such intensity. It is natural to feel afraid when you are faced with sudden, unexpected pain.

But let's go back to visualize a different experience. A positive visualization can help you to heal the post-traumatic stress that you are experiencing. Imagine that you had the help of a doula (labor coach) and your husband, who was able to help you breathe and even yell your way through contractions. Supported with the sense that you would make it through, and resting in between contractions would have helped you feel less traumatized by the process. In fact, women who are supported through the birth and realistically prepared for actively coping with pain, often feel a sense of empowerment afterwards. It is not too late to create a visualization (perhaps with a friend's or even a professional counselor's help) of doing just that. My book, *An Easier Childbirth*,[8] also offers exercises for healing a past traumatic childbirth.

Childbirth is a powerful force that is nothing short of an ordinary miracle. It is an experience of many dimensions. It can be very positive or very negative, but it is rarely neutral. Women deserve support to integrate the magnitude of this experience, which is so denied and misunderstood by society and many in the medical profession.

You are right to pay attention to your feelings about the birth. Address your experience through visualization and/or counseling so that you may integrate the depth of this experience instead of feeling overwhelmed by it. The experience of labor is a part of you that needs assimilation in order to resolve your sense of trauma. And like any event of great magnitude, learning about ourselves with respect to it can yield insight.

With support, you may find that you uncover a deep appreciation for yourself and a new realization of the strengths within yourself that brought forth your daughter's life!

Empowerment and choice in childbirth

When given the opportunity for talking about the emotional aspects of their pregnancy, birth, and motherhood, most women will tend to make choices for childbirth that suit their needs. Their sense of empowerment lies in their exploration of themselves. After all, they are giving birth to a new identity of motherhood! When women are assisted in

---

8.   G. Peterson, *An Easier Childbirth* (Berkeley, CA: Shadow and Light Publications, 1993).

learning about themselves and the physical process they are undergoing, they come to realize that even a choice of medication in labor does not entirely shield them from experiencing pain in the process, contrary to widespread belief. It is common for women to conclude that a natural or close to natural delivery is their most positive choice. *But what is key is the process of personal growth, not the type of childbirth planned or had.*

What Contributes To Self Esteem In Birthing Women?

Research does show that childbirth experience has an effect on women's self-esteem after birth and can impact her emotional availability to her baby immediately afterwards.[9] Giving birth will tend to be integrative or disintegrative, depending on the support, preparation and acceptance of her feelings before, during and after the birth. Her sense of maintaining psychological wholeness throughout the labor, whatever the method or kind of birth, is key to a positive sense of self. Giving birth is an experience of great magnitude. It naturally follows that the more intact a woman feels emotionally, the easier it is for her body to adapt to the intensity of the labor, as heightened amounts of fear can give messages in some women for the brain to shut off labor. Self-esteem *is* a part of health.

In my clinical experience and research, the main factors that contribute to women's positive self-esteem in childbirth are:

1. that she feels herself to be an active participant in the process, including decision making.

2. that she perceives her feelings throughout the process are acceptable and that her caregivers support her free expression and release of these feelings before, during, and after childbirth.

3. that she has been realistically prepared for coping with pain in labor, with active coping techniques, rather than mere relaxation.

---

9. For more research on women's experience of birth, see the references in G. Peterson, *An Easier Childbirth* (Berkeley, CA: Shadow and Light, 1993), and G. Peterson, *Birthing Normally* (Berkeley, CA: Shadow and Light, 1984). Also see P. Simkin, "Just Another Day in a Woman's Life: The Nature and Consistency of Women's Long Term Memories of Their First Birth Experiences." In *Birth*,19:2, (1990); and P. Simkin, "Childbearing in Social Context." In *Women And Health*, 15:3 (1989).

4. that she is not perceived by others or herself to be *in control* of the process, the baby or the outcome of labor; she is only responsible for doing her best to cope with the power of contractions in whatever form she is experiencing them. It is understood that in the case of desire or need for surgical or other intervention or medication, planned or unplanned prior to birth, she is entitled to *respect* and supportive assistance in responding to her physical *and* emotional needs.

5. that she is given ample opportunity to express her feelings about motherhood, including her experience of her own childhood family relationships.

6. that she is given ample opportunity to explore her feelings and circumstances surrounding her own birth, her mother's childbirths, and any previous pregnancy and childbirth experiences of her own.

7. that she and her partner explore the childhood role models of their respective parents relationships for intimacy, conflict resolution, and expectations for caretaking, with an eye towards developing their own plans and values for their relationship as partners and as parents.

Women and their families need support through this life transition. When women are given an opportunity to integrate the process of giving birth and becoming a mother, childbirth flows more smoothly as does postpartum adjustment. Whether a woman gives birth vaginally, naturally, with medication, or by cesarean, it is an event any one of us can help her accept and integrate.

Pregnancy loss

Miscarriage or stillbirth are experiences filled with lost dreams and promise. It can break a relationship apart, or make it stronger. Much depends on whether the couple can accept differences in the grief experience, yet find ways to come together to face the future. The following question and answer illustrates the effect of pregnancy loss on marriage and the different paths recovery can take.

Differences in grieving over miscarriage

Dear Dr. Gayle,

I recently had a miscarriage after an unplanned pregnancy. My husband and I were a little upset when we discovered I was pregnant and then at almost twelve weeks we lost the baby. I was devastated, but I almost feel as if my husband was relieved, though he never said so. I have wanted a baby so much since then that I almost can't think of anything else. My husband cannot understand it. I really love him, but this is driving me CRAZY. How can I accept his feelings?

April

Dear April,

Both you and your husband shared initial upset and ambivalence when you believed you were to become parents unexpectedly. The visceral experience of pregnancy no doubt helped you attach to this reality in a deeper and more immediate way than might have been the case for your husband. You may have been working on the bonding necessary to welcome your child, while he was working through the anxiety you both shared. It is natural that you would be expressing the grief about this sudden change in events, while he would be experiencing the relief.

Your husband's "relief" in no way obliterates loss, however. It is possible to experience both sadness for the loss of the pregnancy and relief that your preparation for parenthood is now extended. Do not expect him to grieve in exactly the same way you do, but do not mourn in isolation. Plan a ritual together for saying good-bye to this potential child. Take a walk to a special place in nature, plant flowers, or throw a stone out to sea. Create a ceremony to help you release your sadness and crystallize the feelings that this pregnancy has brought forth for each one of you.

Talk together about what this journey has put you through, and the feelings that have arisen. Create a safe atmosphere for differences so that your sharing is productive. Honest expression of feelings and the ability to accept similar as well as different emotions about this experience can provide opportunity for greater closeness instead of distance.

It is not unusual for a miscarriage to blossom into a commitment to parenthood. In your case, pregnancy has clarified your desire and readiness for motherhood. Share this transformation with your husband. Perhaps he has experienced something similar. Your next pregnancy may well be a planned one. Perhaps you will find that this pregnancy had its own purpose that has been fulfilled after all.

Pregnancy loss creates an opening for not only bonding, but appreciating your partner's differences in processing life experience. Like any life event, it can bring you closer or drive you apart. Find a way to connect through your grief. Like any family process, the meaning you create through your sharing will make the difference on your life's journey together.

Part II

Becoming Parents

FOUR

Tilling Your Garden

The psychological adjustment necessary to successfully navigate the period in family life of raising young children is quite momentous and generally underestimated in its magnitude. The psychological tasks of this period include maintaining a relationship with your spouse while integrating the new roles and responsibilities of parenthood. Not an easy job! Making room for the children is important, and saving time for one another is necessary. After all, your marital relationship is the garden in which your children grow. They will bask in the genuine glow of affection you show to each other. Or they will experience the wake of unresolved tensions that you create together.

In the beginning of new parenthood, there are two difficult situations that commonly complicate this stage of adjustment. If a marriage is weak to begin with, the couple may turn to the children to fill the void. The relationship grows cold with children experiencing the load of emotional involvement that should be placed elsewhere. The other pitfall is a marriage in which the spouses enjoy such a tight relationship with each other that there is no room for the children. Couples who are overly involved in each other, perhaps taking primarily separate vacations from the children, or being unavailable due to heavy career and work demands, can leave precious little time for children's needs. The unwillingness to spend time on child-focused activities is a symptom of a couple system that has not adjusted well to making room for the children they have spawned.

A balanced couple system accommodates the young child's needs, limiting adult centered activities, both in work and socially to make room for these new family members! These new members are welcomed, despite the confinement they bring. Family traditions are established. The meaning of life has changed. Together parents celebrate and commiserate in their new lifestyle as parents of young children. Parents bond with other new parents, and a whole new social support network develops to embrace the needs of the growing family. Gradually, couples develop boundaries around their own time together and strike a healthy balance between couple's activities and child-focused ones.

Major stress in this stage of raising young children is establishing family responsibilities and roles, especially with respect to the division of the workload by the parents. Gender roles and expectations in the family weigh heavily, and children benefit from a family that values nurturance over work in the early years of development. Respect and value for the work of nurturing as well as the importance of economics and work outside the family will be an issue the parents must resolve together. The satisfaction each spouse feels about how work in the family is shared will foreshadow the success or failure of their marriage.

Traditional family roles, in which mothers do all the nurturing and fathers withdraw into outside work activities, leave mothers overly responsible for the emotional health of all members. Many family researchers recommend sharing the role of nurturing, as it leads to healthier and happier families. Researchers have found that traditional roles contribute to dysfunction due to the alienation of the father in the emotional life of the family and the over-functioning of the mother in an impossible attempt to make everyone happy. The following question and answer illustrates this dilemma, which can often result in misunderstandings.

Cultural influences on motherhood, and creating a parenting "team"

Dear Dr. Gayle,

It seems in our marriage that my wife and I are reversed from the stereotypical styles. She tends to be more brash, while I am more laid-back and sensitive. She is more concerned with how much has been accomplished in a day, while I strive most of all to keep life a positive and joyful experience, especially for our children.

As a stay-at-home mother of three (eight years, four years, and one year), she seems frustrated eighty percent of the time, ending up speaking in a "scolding" tone to the kids a lot. I see this reflected in a whining response from the kids, compounded by her making threats without carrying through on warnings. Of course, this leads to some discipline challenges, which further irritate my wife, to the point where she's "had it" by the time I come home from work most days.

Whenever I try to talk about discipline, or trying to use a more cheerful tone with the children, she becomes defensive, with the remark, "easy for you to say, you don't have to put up with it all day long." I've tried to get her to do things with women in our church, but she was raised to not be selfish (to take time for herself).

Any clues on how I can help my wife relieve some stress?

Barry

Dear Barry,

Your wife has a point, as do you. Her focus on getting things done and your contribution to sustaining joy in the family suggest that your marriage holds promise for great collaboration! Perhaps you could create more teamwork, which would allow her to reflect on her own contributions to "martyrdom" and you to experience more of the front-line parenting.

Let your wife know that you love and respect her, and that you want to take her complaint seriously. Consider relieving your wife of her responsibilities for a weekend. Let her know that you appreciate her and want to reward her by giving her time to be "selfish" and giving yourself an opportunity to experience at least a part of what she herself does for the family. Mothering, unlike your job outside the family, is unpaid work with little recognition. This cultural reality sets a different tone for women than for men in our culture.

For example, if you are pushing a baby stroller down the street you will likely get a lot of smiles. If you are paying for groceries with a crying baby, you may find women and men offering you help. While if your wife was in an identical situation, others would be less likely to smile adoringly or suggest help. Reactions could range from silence to irritation and criticism if she is unable to quiet her young.

It may be true that your wife is overly sensitive to your criticism. Still, you may be falling short in comprehending the cultural differences that are experienced by men and women when performing the same parental duties. Women are expected to nurture, while men are appreciated if they are sensitive and caring to their children. This difference in gender expectation can be experienced as an overall lack of appreciation by your wife, which can contribute to her defensiveness. Acknowledge the cultural loading for women that accompanies motherhood. Let your wife know that you are working hard to appreciate her experience and that your intentions are not to merely criticize but to offer your loving support and input as a parent. It is also possible that the two of you may be reversed in nature from the roles you have agreed to play. As you suggest, perhaps you would enjoy caring for children twenty-four hours a day more than your wife does. However, you have agreed to organize your responsibilities along gender lines for now. Communicating your feelings about the worlds you live in can create a bridge for empathy. Mutual understanding can pave the road for accepting rather than rejecting feedback from one another.

In any healthy marriage partners give and receive and are willing to consider one another's viewpoints. Invite positive suggestions from your wife rather than dismissal of your concerns. She does have an obligation to the marriage to be willing to listen and consider what you have offer.

Your feelings as a father are also important and need healthy dialogue if you are to experience inclusion rather than exclusion from the intimate workings of the family. Too often, fathers are relegated to the periphery of the emotional connections in the family due to specialized roles. You are right to insist on input into the intimate family atmosphere. It is your avenue for emotional involvement instead of remoteness as a father figure. Your wife chose a man capable of this relatedness. No doubt part of her reason for marrying you was because your heart is in the right place! Now it is her job to incorporate your involvement as a committed parent. Ask her to value rather than block your active participation as a parenting partner.

Be certain that you are also nourishing your spousal relationship. Take your wife out to dinner. Suggest a leisurely walk away from parenting responsibilities to create an open discussion about what kind of family you want to have together. Explore your different family backgrounds. How did each of your parents handle decision making together? How was work and play balanced in your respective families? Did parents offer their help to one another, or did they each run their own sphere of the family with little input from the other? Were there any "martyrs" in the family? If so, identify the role guilt played and the effects of running a family this way. What kind of role models do you want to be to your own children? What do you want to teach them about women's and men's roles in the family?

And what does it mean to be "selfish"? Is there ever a time in which selfishness can be healthy?

This is your family and you have the right to create new and healthier improvements in the last generation. Yet, old patterns die hard. Be patient, understanding, but firm in your desire to create a shared vision of family.

Tell your wife that you want to help her reduce, not increase her stress. Strengthening your emotional connection is the best stress-buffer any marriage can have. Invite her to become a part of the change necessary to beat, rather than become victim to, the daily stress that is a natural part of family life in our society.

Nurturing the couple's bond

In the midst of all this change, it is still important to remember that your primary and intimate bond is with each other. When the time is right take weekends away to be together, and nights out to nurture the intimacy that you alone share. As lovers and as friends, it is important for the couple to protect the primacy of their bond, which is the foundation of their growing family. It is this relationship that will teach their children how to love their husband or wife when they grow up to marry and have children of their own! The following question and answer elucidates the stresses on marriage when a baby is born, and offers suggestions to keep your relationship viable when you become parents.

Redefining relationships after baby arrives

Dr. Gayle,

My husband and I always have had our disagreements, but we were able to forgive each other and make up when we had a fight. Since our baby was born, four months ago, we can't say a word to each other without an argument. I feel very sad because of his lack of support and understanding. As a result, I am becoming very attached to the baby and moving farther apart from him. He doesn't want to go and talk with a therapist. We are thinking about separating.

Angela

Dear Angela,

Becoming parents together is one of the greatest transitions of marriage. Increased demands for nurturing a newborn can only cement family relationships when a couple can channel their energy to meet the new challenges. Unfortunately, if couples are not able to negotiate the changes required by this stage, their relationship can deteriorate quite rapidly.

The birth of a baby is also the birth of a new definition of family. You must redefine your relationship to include the very meaningful roles of mother and father to your newborn. You are clearly attached to your baby, but is your husband bonding to his child? Has he spent any time caring for her without your presence? Does he feel that he influences the growth and development of his daughter? Does he feel empowered in his role as a new father, or alienated?

Two crucial developments could serve to save your marriage. First, build a communication bridge between you. Take long walks with the baby, perhaps while she naps in a stroller. Or, after she goes to sleep at night, begin getting reacquainted with one another. Start by sharing feelings about the changes in your life that have evolved since the baby arrived. Be sure to make room for negative feelings that either of you may have, but are afraid to express.

For example, your husband may be feeling resentful toward his daughter because of the amount of attention you give her. This is a common reaction for fathers, especially if their own childhood experience was somewhat painful or neglectful. Just witnessing, or experiencing, the love between mother and daughter can bring up primal feelings about our past relationships with our own parents. If your husband feels on the outside of this circle of love, he could be experiencing profound alienation.

You, too, may find yourself completely immersed in the mothering experience. If your own parents did not maintain a connection to one another in your childhood, you could be neglecting your own marriage as well. These are common pitfalls of this stage of family development.

But this is no reason to run away from the problem! It will only get better by facing it, and forming an alliance to move beyond such pain—toward a new definition of family.

Secondly, invite your husband to increase his participation in the direct physical care of your daughter. Encourage him toward finding the emotional meaning in parenting that you have developed. Joining a support group for new dads can help him find his place in the family. Invite your husband to be a partner in creating the family you want to be, rather than aborting it in midstream.

Adjusting to the stresses of new parenthood

The first year of life is a significant one in family adjustment and deserves special attention. Maturation is necessary as parents learn and develop a new balance in their relationship. Like riding a bicycle, some of what needs to be learned will involve falling down, however if communication predominates over "acting out" behaviors, a new sense of self will be restored. How the couple or single parent adjusts to the stresses of new parenthood can determine the family's foundation for the years ahead. A new balance in meeting one's own and our partner's needs has to be achieved.

Identity as a mother

With the birth of a new baby comes the birth of a new identity of motherhood. It is the psychological task of pregnancy to begin formulating a sense of what it means to be a mother. It is necessary for the new mother to sort through her childhood experience of her own mother, incorporating the things she finds to be positive and determining in what ways she chooses to parent differently than her mother did. It does not mean you do not love and cherish your mother. But it is your job to discriminate your own parenting values and raise your child accordingly. The following question and answer is an example of the pain that can come up for women as they sort through their own mother-daughter relationship when it is fraught with conflict.

Toxic relationship with mother

Dear Dr. Gayle,

I am thirty-three years old and have experienced many years of verbal and physical abuse from my mother. I have received counseling and have asked her to also seek help for her anger and depression.

I am now happily married and expecting my first child. I recently made a decision to cut my mother out of my life, and my life has been so much better. I feel free for once, and close to happy. Even though I do feel at peace with my decision, I have a sense of numbness where my mother is concerned. I would really like some input from you, and some guidance.

Monica

Dear Monica,

You are not your mother's "keeper" or her "scapegoat," yet you have been placed in this role since childhood. No wonder you have "had" it!

The psychological task of becoming a mother has no doubt caused you to want to protect yourself and your child from your mother's toxicity. In fact, it is possible that you needed to "cut her out" in order to lighten your load, and make space for pregnancy.

Your need to cut her out of your life at this time reflects the decision to choose to live your own life instead of hers. But sadly, it also reveals the poisonous nature of your relationship with her. She must have hurt you very deeply to cause you to cut off from her at a time when women often need, and rely on, their mothers. However cutting off from her is not a decision that needs to be set in stone.

Protect yourself by taking distance from your mother. Explain to all concerned that you need some space to sort through your own feelings. But do not label your actions as "cutting her out." This is not what you are doing, but what she would accuse you of doing to her. Do not fall into this trap! You have a right to take some time and space to yourself now. When you are ready, you may want to relate, if only at a distance with a different set of behaviors and expectations for this relationship. If you decide to do so, it will be in your time, and when you feel you would benefit—coming from a place of strength and power to master this situation.

It is natural for pregnancy to bring up tremendous amounts of feelings, and it is possible that you need the "peace" you describe by simply not being responsible for her in any way. Your commitment to your child requires this shift in allegiance, and you are right to take it. But you may find that talking with a counselor now about these feelings will make it less likely that cutting off from your mother will set the stage for a postpartum depression.

The aim of this therapy should be focused on your needs, feelings and desires and how to achieve them in your current family. Develop your own vision of motherhood, and eventually you may desire to focus your attention on strategies for effectively changing your relationship with your mother and re-establishing contact.

Do not commit yourself to an endless moratorium on this relationship. Consider that you are taking a break. Feel your own power through establishing your family. Though you are in no way responsible for destroying family relationships, your own reactivity may come back to haunt you later.

Take care of yourself. But do not back yourself into anyone's corner. Stay open to a change in your feelings as you establish a clear sense of your own power and boundaries around the "poisonous" elements of your maternal relationship. Seek and depend on the support and care of your friends and family who understand. Your job is to focus on your own family now. Upcoming motherhood requires your undivided attention, as there are many things you will have to sort out regarding the kind of family you and your husband want to have and the kind of mother and father you each want to be to this child.

Your numbness will eventually thaw, and you will grieve the lost childhood in the future as you may have done in the past. This grief does not need to envelop you or your joy and happiness at this time. But it will need expression. Some of this may come in acknowledgment of the way you mother your own child differently.

A relationship like the one you have experienced in your family with your mother is a life's work. But it does not have to be a constant focus. Use it as a reservoir for learning and growing. Some of the most abundant blossoms result from sowing the greatest amount of manure!

Remember, too, that your father's responsibility to you was to balance your mother's toxicity. Perhaps he also failed to protect you from scapegoating in the family.

Identity as a father

Recently, fathers are recognizing the need for developing and sustaining a nurturing relationship with their children, rather than taking an emotionally peripheral or merely disciplinarian role. Men *and* women contribute economically in over eighty percent of American families, shaping us towards more interchangeable roles. Men have to move into the role of nurturance or women will continue to experience an overload of responsibility in the family for both economic and emotional caretaking.

However, sorting through the fathering relationship can be particularly painful for many contemporary fathers, as they often feel the lack of a nurturing bond with their own father. Having little emotional closeness with their own fathers (part of the cultural legacy of the 1950s), the next generation of fathers who desire to embrace the role of nurturer must develop it, from scratch. It may feel as though he is a "weak" male in the beginning, but the rewards of intimacy make it worthwhile. Forging an identity based on participation and everyday care earns him closeness in place of the emotional distance he may have witnessed in his father.

But when expectations are unrealistic and communication breaks down, the most loving relationships can falter. The following question and answer illustrates the struggle of one family to integrate the father into the family, after the birth of a child, and in the midst of numerous changes and competing time commitments.

My husband says I don't give him enough attention

Dr. Gayle,

My husband and I are currently going through an informal separation. This was his idea. Ever since our son (two and a half years old) was born he says that I don't pay him enough attention like I used to when I was pregnant. I have tried to explain to him that our child should come first and he agrees but he still feels that he should be first and foremost in my mind. I love him with all that I have. This "separation" is merely a mental separation and not a physical one. Our sex life is definitely better because of it, and I have been trying to compromise by giving ample enough attention to both my husband and son. I don't want to lose him.

What do you think I could do to improve the relationship with my husband while not jeopardizing the amount of attention that I give my son? I am currently working full-time and going to school for my degree as well.

Jennifer

Dear Jennifer,

Although it is fair for him to want the quality of your relationship to be the same, his expectations for the amount of attention he receives from you may be unrealistic following the birth of a child. It is not fair for him to have his cake and eat it too! If he wants a separation, why is he enjoying a sexual relationship with you? Perhaps he wants the life of a bachelor back, but this is not possible.

Working on the relationship within the context of living together is far different from working on it when separated. It is the very intimacy of living together that is being avoided. Such an arrangement contributes to the fantasy that your husband can return to single life and still enjoy the benefits of being a member of the family and a father. Yet he is distancing himself from his son and from you.

Having sex in this situation seems to reward him for leaving and separating himself out from the family. This may be a temporary shortcut to hot sex, (spiced with the threat of abandonment?) but it is not an answer to the problem of forging a vital couple's relationship in the context of a family unit.

Relationships are healing vessels for past wounds of childhood. Your husband seems to have a found a very loving and responsive mate in you. And such healing may be a part of what he needs in a relationship. It is not the case that you are between him and your son. You and he must put your son first, for this is the responsibility of both you and your husband. But it is also critical to your marriage that there is consistent quality time that can be counted on in the couple's relationship. Making consistent weekly dates with one another could be part of the change that needs to occur.

Your husband's withdrawal from you in this situation could prove to be damaging to your marriage. It is important to work things out, however this means spending time talking through these changes that have come about since you became parents. Your child's well-being rests on the strength of your couple's bond. He benefits from what you give to one another, not just what he gets from each of you directly. It is important to process the things that were given up by becoming parents. Grieve the life you left behind, but accept the responsibilities of what you have entered into together. Perhaps your husband is looking for an escape from mourning life before children. Instead he is attempting to return to being single.

Perhaps your partner should join a father's group where he can share his feelings with other men going through the same life phase. Or he could go into individual counseling to explore why your loving attention is not enough, and what the reasons are for his continued jealousy of his son. It is not the feelings of jealousy that are the problem, as this is a common response in new fathers. But it is the fact of his withdrawal from the family, based upon these feelings that could communicate a destructive message to his son. Is he developing a relationship to his son that is separate from your mother-son relationship? What is he doing to feel a part of the family, other than through your love and attention? It is not your job to dole out nurturance. And you need nurturing, too. What is your partner doing to nurture the relationship with you, and with his son separately? For therein lies the connection he longs for. Sex is a transient and empty substitute for enduring intimacy. It is common for men who have experienced difficulty attaching to their own mothers as infants to seek connection through sex. However sexual connection alone never satiates the deep need for intimacy and contact that is an important part of finding your place in a family.

Your commitment and devotion to him should give him cause to consider looking inside for some of the answer to his own need to feel included in your love. And if the two of you are both working full time and parenting, it is true that your attention to one another is curtailed. Going to school in addition to working could also leave little time for each other or parenting. Is there anyway to balance time and commitments that give more time to relationship and connecting, both as a family and as a couple, and less time working or going to school? Could you both continue to pursue work and educational goals, but at a slower pace that would allow for more family and couple time together?

Perhaps your marriage is simply the casualty of too much to do with too little time to do it. If this is the case, discussion and prioritizing might be in order, rather than separation. Ask your husband to talk with you about prioritizing. Request his help and his positive suggestions for solutions. What is the emotional meaning of his moving out? Is he angry at you, but not asking for changes surrounding time and commitments on your part? Ask him to tell you what his vision would be of a loving relationship with you. And ask him to give you positive and realistic suggestions for how things could change, and what he is willing to do to help it to happen.

In short, develop a shared vision of what you both want together. But pay attention to the difference between balancing parenting, work, school and marriage and unrealistic expectations for couple's relating after a baby arrives. There are changes that must be accommodated to when a child is born, and this does include reduced attention to the couple and increased attention to a child. But tease out whether, with the work and school commitments, this means less time together versus no time together!

Couple's identity and new family formation

We have already seen how marriage is the coming together of two different family cultures. Family backgrounds differ and conflicting patterns and expectations are inevitable obstacles to work through. The couple must come up with their own new family form. Realignment of relationships to include new parenting and grandparenting roles, as well as adjustment in the marital relationship cries out for new order at the time of the birth of a child.

In addition to the development of parental identities, the couple bond is also stressed by the necessary forging of new family boundaries. Partners must sort through alliances with their childhood families, making sure that these alliances are secondary to, and supportive of, the decisions they make together as a couple. New families need both appropriate boundaries and, ideally, appropriate support from the extended family network. Pitfalls can arise when husbands or wives have difficulty setting limits with intrusive or judgmental in-laws, due to feelings of disloyalty. Everything from differentiating their own parenting style, the values by which they raise their child, to what holiday traditions they will build into their own family structure can cause stress. This stress is healthy fuel for alignment of the new family identity that must emerge.

A new family culture must be forged between husband and wife. The couple's task is to develop a shared sense of child-rearing values. This can be difficult if in-laws are critical instead of supportive when the couple's actions reflect a difference in values or parenting styles from that of the extended family. It is important during this period of adjustment that the couple's bond is strengthened and not divided by the extended family network. Maturation involves differentiating yourself from your family-of-origin, and taking your place in alignment to your spouse in working through these family concerns. The following question and answer illustrates the need to maintain the couple's boundaries in the creation of your own family unit.

My mother-in-law is running our lives

Dear Dr. Gayle,

My problem concerns my mother-in-law. She and I got along great until I married my husband and gave birth to our daughter seven months ago. I feel that since the baby was born, she has been trying to take over my life ! (Did I mention my husband is the only child?)

My mother-in-law is very possessive and demanding and from the time I have became pregnant has acted as if the baby was

*hers (she calls the baby "hers," and fantasizes about doing
"mommy-daughter" stuff with my baby). I think my mother-in-
law is trying to live vicariously through my family. I am feeling
very rejected, hurt and smothered. This has created so many
problems in my marriage that my husband and I almost separated because of it, even though my husband agrees his mom's
behavior is very inappropriate.*

*We tried talking to her about the problem once, but she freaked
out and denied everything. My mother-in-law used to be an alco-
holic (my father-in-law still is), so they have the "don't talk about
problems" attitude. I find it very hard to visit them (which my
mother-in-law is demanding more and more frequently) and I find
myself getting desperate to move far away. I am ashamed to admit
I have even considered leaving my husband and daughter just to
get away from this woman. I feel so trapped and I don't know
what to do. Help!*

Michelle

Dear Michelle,

Your husband must align his loyalties with you if your marriage is
to succeed. The good news is that he knows his mother's behavior is
inappropriate. Now it is time for him to do something about it!

Each day your husband does not set limits with your mother-in-
law strains your marriage. This is the stage of development in the
family life cycle in which it is essential that the two of you create a
boundary around your nuclear family. You are a new mother and it
is important that your authority be recognized in the extended family. But it is your husband's job to talk with his parents about this
boundary in the beginning.

He must show his mother that he supports you in your parental
authority and require that you be accepted as his wife and the mother of his child. Not saying anything for fear of his mother's reaction
only worsens the situation and reinforces her fantasy that this is
"her" child and you are a "third wheel." Let your husband know that
you do not expect him to love his mother any less, but that you are
now the center of his life and need his support.

Do not despair! You *are* the wife and mother in this family.
Instead of feeling trapped, find your voice as a mother. You and your
husband set the guidelines in the family. Explain to your mother-in-

law that you appreciate her as a grandmother and ask her how she would like herself referred to, in this role. Would she like your daughter to call her grandma, nana, or some other appropriate endearment? Let her know that you do not want there to be any confusion about who is mom and who is grandmother for your child. Clarify your expectation for her to speak accordingly to your child. "My grandbaby" might be an appropriate substitution.

Visit only as often as you are comfortable and allow your mother-in-law's participation in your baby's life at the level that feels right to you. With your husband's support, your mother-in-law will come to accept her natural place as a grandmother. And in time, you will feel increasingly secure in your position as a mother.

Remember, too, that your mother-in-law is adjusting to sharing her only child with his new family. No doubt her tenacity to "live vicariously" has much to do with her loneliness in her own marriage, however you cannot change this for her.

Although there may be some reaction from your mother-in-law as she adjusts to grandmotherhood, she will most certainly get over any feelings of rejection if you continue to include her in your life. Send her cards, invite her to visit you and the baby even though she falls silent. Expect this but do react to childish behavior. Consider her frailty, but do not take your cues from her. Act with the maturity of your new identity as mother and treat her with patience until she comes around. It is unlikely she will continue to "cut off her nose to spite her face," once some time has passed.

Placing Love In Equal Relationship To Work

Two currently powerful cultural forces that inhibit a healthy balance in family relationships are the devaluation of caretaking and nurturance in our society and the primacy of work over priorities of nurturing. The pressure to put the needs of a work schedule over the needs for caretaking drive many couples towards a detrimental imbalance in the first year of their child's life.

For example, mothers can experience their needs and their children's needs as repetitiously secondary to the father's work schedule. Unconsciously, the expectation that the wife defer to her husband's needs, which place work *above* nurturance, can leave a couple feeling estranged from one another. The following diagram illustrates the potential cultural force towards this imbalance and the ensuing shift contributing towards a weakened couple's bond and an increasingly remote paternal-child relationship.[10]

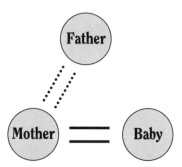

Figure 1. Unbalanced system

In Figure 1, primacy of work is favored over the primary task of establishing nurturance and bonding in the first year. Overspecialization of roles can result in economic provider (often father) becoming peripheral to the emotional life of the family. Intimacy suffers in the couple's relationship and generational boundaries may blur as the mother becomes closer to the child than to her spouse.

The following question and answer illustrates the overload of responsibility for caretaking that can occur in unbalanced systems. The birth of subsequent children introduces new stress that must be integrated. A weakened marital bond and a father who becomes remote to the emotional life of the family can dilute family cohesion and eventually undermine stability as responsibilities for caretaking and nurturance grow.

Mom on double-duty when dad is away

Dear Dr. Gayle,

We have been happily married for almost nine years and have two sons ages four and two. Our youngest has Down Syndrome and so there are some added stresses there. My husband is also in the military and is away a lot, so I end up having to arrange all the doctor and therapy sessions plus running a household without an

---

10. J. Bradt, "Becoming Parents." In M. McGoldrick & B. Carter (Eds.), *The Changing Family Life Cycle: A Framework for Family Therapy* (New York: Gardner Press, 1988). Bradt writes about gender forces for balance and imbalance in the family after birth of a child.

*extended family nearby. When he comes home I expect him to jump
back into our routine and help but he doesn't and it really frus-
trates me since I do double duty while he is gone. Any suggestions?*
                                                                    Janice

Dear Janice,

It is critical that you and your husband stay connected in caring
for both of your children, even when he is away. Particularly with
the added care required for your youngest son who has special
needs. Your husband should be involved in planning treatment programs with the doctor and therapist so that your relationship supports you even when he is out of town. You should not be alone with
the emotional caretaking responsibility for your children, even if
you are the one who provides the transportation to appointments.

Although many couples do specialize in different areas of care,
both should be equally knowledgeable about the schedules the other
keeps in maintaining responsibilities. Without this knowledge,
spouses may take each other for granted and drift apart, letting the
stresses come between them.

There is also a tendency to devalue the work of caretaking children
and household chores because these responsibilities are unpaid. The
addition of a second child alone creates a significant increase in the
primary nurturer's workload. Moreover, you have a child who
requires special care. It may be necessary to get extra help to come in
while your husband is away. He could take responsibility for setting
this up. You will feel appreciated and cared for by him if he does
make special arrangements in his absence so that things go more
smoothly for you. Talking every day by phone is also advisable with
young children so that the trips do not cause disconnection between
family members. It is important for children and spouses to feel that
when dad is out of sight, he is by no means out of mind! It takes an
extra effort to remain in touch when a spouse travels for business.

When your husband comes home from being away the whole
family is vulnerable to feeling disjointed and let down. Be aware that
these transitions are stressful on families, and it is essential that the
two of you recognize and plan for a smoother way to adjust to being
back together again. Some time to catch up with one another and
adapt to one another can ease these transitions. Your husband needs
some time to adjust to being home. You need time to adjust to his

presence. And the children need some special attention from dad as well. Talk about adopting a ritual that will slow things down when he reunites with you. Sharing stories, having a special dinnertime together soon after his return can go a long way to getting reconnected as a couple before getting mired in the ongoing family schedule and responsibilities.

Talk with your husband about your feelings. Take some time together as a couple to review the path you have traveled together as a family these past four years since you've become parents. You have been through a lot together. How has your relationship changed since you became parents? Perhaps it is time to reignite your relationship and equalize some of the workload the two of you share. It may also be time for you to ask yourself what you need, too. Are you getting time for yourself, to develop your interests? What can be done to lighten your load? Are there any support groups in your area for parents of Down Syndrome children?

Without the help of an extended family network, you will need to create your own network of supportive friends, parents and professional helpers. Reaching out for help and connecting with others in your community will also help ease your frustration with your husband.

In another example of potential imbalance, both parents may be working, and despite the need for focus on the developmental task of bonding and establishing emotional connections and knowledge of the baby, both parents focus primarily on career during the first year of a child's life. This can result in parents who uphold their own bond, especially through the activities of shared work schedules, however the baby suffers a weakened bond with both parents.

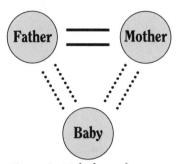

Figure 2. Unbalanced system

The following question and answer is an example of this situation.

Balancing work and caretaking goals in the family

Dear Dr. Gayle,

My husband and I are in desperate need of advice. My husband is away seven days at a time at work and is home seven days at a time. We just found out that he will be away fourteen days at a time after the first of the year. My mother has always kept our daughter, who is now one, since she was six weeks old, and I had to return to work. Our problem is, my mom is acting like it will be big bother for her to keep our daughter now that my husband will be away for two weeks instead of one. She says this will interfere with her and her husband's relationship.

Our daughter has never been left with anyone other than my husband or my mom for her entire first year of life. I do not know what to do. How traumatic will it be for her to go to a sitter or day care at her age? As much as I wish I could stay home with her, we cannot do without my income. What can I do to make a transition to a sitter or daycare less traumatic for our daughter?

Corkie

Dear Corkie,

Your daughter has been fortunate to have loving care from her grandmother consistently in her first year of life while her parents worked. No doubt your mother's loving care also gave you tremendous confidence in leaving your newborn, beyond what a babysitter or daycare center could have offered you. She is irreplaceable in her unique role in your family.

It is understandable that your mother must set limits around her needs and relationship. She has a life of her own and providing ongoing primary care for your daughter in a more continuous fashion has led to overload of your extended family system. The good news is that your daughter is one year instead of six weeks old. And it is possible for her to adjust to a new daycare situation.

However, before arranging for extra care, talk with your husband about any possibility of delaying his new schedule. Do not automatically presume that decisions about work must take precedence over caretaking your daughter. Consider the possibility of rearranging your own priorities. Your mother has stretched herself to meet your needs as a family. Perhaps you could consider stretching your own parameters to maintain your current arrangement with your mother. In fact, grandma may be suffering from the devaluation present in our society around caretaking children. She may even feel that she is taken for granted.

If change in your husband's work schedule is tied to a promotion, can he forego the advancement for six months or one year, when your daughter will be old enough to benefit from peer play in a small quality daycare? Is it possible for you to adjust your work schedule in the upcoming year to maintain the care schedule your mother can currently provide for your daughter?

Your arrangements for the care of your daughter have been exceptional this year. Put priorities of care above others. Do not overlook possibilities to choose to make the maintenance of your current daycare schedule a priority in this next year.

Parenting and marital bonding in a balanced system

In a balanced system parents devote their attention to bonding and getting to know their baby together. In the first year of life, an effort is made to share nurturing and caretaking activities that help a parent get to know their child. Even when one partner specializes in providing financially, both are involved in responsibilities and equal decision making about caretaking and about their shared economic future. *There is however an awareness of this first year as a very special year that establishes the foundations of trust in relationship. And there is concerted effort to protect the work of caretaking children as a primary value despite the pressures of society to do otherwise.*

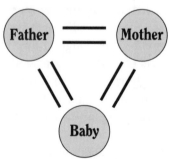

Figure 3. Balanced system

If emotional caretaking is emphasized in the first year, you and your spouse evolve together as parents. Decision making is shared. Both partners feel their needs are considered. Power is in balance and parental teamwork strengthens the couple's relationship. Knowledge of the child through first-hand nurturing experience develops simultaneously for each parent. Generational boundaries are intact.

The primary task of early family development is one of nurturance. As women become mothers and men become fathers, it is necessary to take time and energy to focus on emotional bonding and caretaking. Too often in our society the anxieties caused by this transition make us vulnerable to solving this anxiety by putting energy into work and accomplishments, instead of the emotional work of bonding. It is a cultural stress that can start many young families off on the wrong track, leading to imbalance and estrangement that culminates by the end of the child's second birthday.

Foundational patterns of emotional involvement and noninvolvement have been established and are hard to recalibrate. The child learns to rely emotionally on one parent and does not gravitate towards the other, creating an ever-diminishing opportunity for building intimacy. Or a child imprints on a persistent pattern of coming second to both parents' work schedules, leaving little sense of emotional connection or importance in the family.

It is important to understand that what is important is *a healthy balance of the needs of the family in concert with the tasks of family development at any given point in the family life cycle.* Of course economics *are* important. It is not the case that one must go hungry in order to be available for emotional needs! What is meant by balance in a system is a spirit of compromise in putting the needs of caretaking first when it is possible to do so, even though it might be more inefficient from a purely economic or career stance. Even when one person primarily specializes in the nurturer role and the other in the role of economic provider, equality between partners can be maintained through conscious awareness and consideration.

The following example represents a situation in which economics is not a significant stressor. I have used this example even though it is not an average couple, in order to make the point that *even when money is not a primary issue,* new parents are vulnerable to societal pressure to make decisions based on the value of work over relationships. While this may work on an intermittent basis, when does this become habit and an assumption that work will always take precedence? When is it assumed that business deals are one-time opportunities, but your family relationships are always there?

> Bill and Ada have an eight-month-old daughter. Their daughter is at the age where she is teething and very clingy, as she has become more cognizant of the meaning of "stranger." Ada is taking a year's sabbatical from her job as a financial consultant at Bank of America. She is unsure of whether she will return full time or not. She is committed to staying home to care for their child in the first year of life. She has told her husband that she has not recovered from his first two trips earlier in the year.
>
> Bill is a venture capitalist who is currently closing a deal, working late and some weekends. He is currently the sole financial provider for the family, although he has and will most likely share this role in some degree in the future with Ada. In the midst of an already busy work schedule he gets a call regarding an incredible business opportunity that would take him to Europe for two weeks to explore. Should he go?

In the interest of maintaining balance in the family with respect to the primary task of nurturing in the first year of a child's life, it might be prudent for him not to secure this next deal, if finances would allow it. To put the task of nurturing on equal footing with economics, it is understood that there are consequences for a loss of emotional involvement and participation in the family, particularly when the couple's relationship is already stressed. To repeatedly put emotional needs second to the importance of the most recent business deal, will create a legacy of estrangement, loss of intimacy in family relationships, and undervalued, undernurtured children to some degree. The results of this choice will vary according to specific situations and personalities, *but there will be a cost.*

It is often too easy to imagine that there is no cost to such a choice when we live in a society that worships material goods and career achievement over the feminine value of nurturance and love. We forget that relationships matter, and that without them we lose much of the human value of life itself.

However, for our couple, Ada and Bill, the most important factor is not necessarily what decision is made but the manner in which needs are considered, how agreements are made and upheld, and whether or not the decision for him to go or not go is one that both parents decide together. Teamwork in decision making and compromise will make this decision a family event in which *relationships matter*. Compromises on either side can occur, as long as they are discussed and the decision is made jointly, rather than in default to the primacy of economics or career. The following is a list of suggestions for engaging in teamwork as a couple and ensuring that both parents feel equal power and consideration in the decision making process:

1. What are the ways that the primary nurturer is recognized, appreciated, and valued? (For example, phone calls when away, special time off from nurturing when he returns, returning favors involving caretaking responsibility, verbal expressions of appreciation, including making time for family to come first unequivocally when scheduled.)

2. What are the ways economic providers are recognized, appreciated, and valued? (for example, verbal expressions, consideration and responsibility for financial planning, accommodating work schedules when deemed necessary by both spouses.)

3. What are the ways that the economic provider is connected to emotional family life? (For example, activities scheduled around family needs on weekends and evenings, conversations and involvement in household duties and joint decision making around child rearing, child development and household concerns.)

4. What are the ways the nurturer influences decisions, including economic ones in the family? (For example, joint decision making about career goals balanced with family's emotional needs and development.)

In the first year of a child's life, it is essential to slow down. This is an adjustment, not unlike getting caught in a traffic jam. If you change your pace, put yourself on "baby time," you will enjoy the music on your radio or tape player, rather than fume at the driver in the car in front of you. These are special months with your baby and they will never return. And they are formative in the development of a healthy sense of self-esteem for your child. This year will impact your child profoundly for the rest of his or her life.

The true resolution to the dilemma of balancing emotional needs and economic/career needs is to place love and caretaking in equal relationship to work. In the first year this could mean:

1. Consider a loan for staying home with your child in the first year, or spending more time at home than the office. Calculate what you would need to do so. Remember, we take out loans for new cars, furniture, computers, so why not a parental-child development loan? The time your child is young is time-limited. They will be older, less in need of you, and you will feel freer to pursue other things. There is a time for every purpose, and we sometimes forget we are only talking about twelve months, not the rest of our lives.

2. Keep in mind the family life cycle and where you are on it when considering choices involving how much time to be away from your family. Some periods of time, such as the first three years and adolescence may be periods in which your child's needs for your involvement are greater than others. There will be time for other pursuits in the future. Find a healthy balance.

3. Remember that appreciation for the role your partner is playing in the family will go a long way in helping you feel connected, even when life is stressful.

4. Remember that men and women are different. Women experience both biological and cultural expectations to nurture, while men feel pressured to provide security by performing well economically.

5. Specializing in emotional caretaking or economic providership weakens a system. Interchangeability of roles, at least to some degree, is desirable and strengthens a system not only in times of crisis or disaster, but also in stable situations.

It is important that we protect our family relationships in the first year of life. The intention to make decisions in favor of the essential task of nurturing and bonding will pay off in the long term love and quality of family life in your future. Tremendous changes in personal identity and couple's relating bring conflicts to the surface at this time. Family bonding is the first order of business!

FIVE

Communication and Conflict

Lessons in Life and Love

Effectively communicating with other family members
is not a luxury, but a basic emotional need. [11]

We marry our partners with the best of intentions. Still, learning the lessons that love has to teach us is not always smooth sailing. The ability to see the problem is one thing, while the capacity to make a change can feel "out of reach." When communication breaks down, spouses are vulnerable to disconnecting from one another at the very time they need each other the most!

Mistakes happen in life, and the potential to learn and grow from them is our biggest ally against future heartache. "Getting to the bottom" of a traumatic event in marriage requires our best efforts to use communication to rebuild trust and prevent future disconnection. Increasing our capacity to express our needs when in conflict or under pressure is a key factor in avoiding "acting out" feelings in a way that damages relationship. In cases like the following, deeper understanding and communication are essential to rescue the marriage.

Recovering the relationship after an affair

Dear Dr. Gayle,
*   I am in the process of getting over the knowledge that after*
eleven years of marriage my husband had an affair. I now can go

---

11. G. Peterson, "Communication and Problem Solving." From the *Making Healthy Families* series on www.askdrgayle.com.

*back over a two year period and see where it went wrong. I was
going through the process of bereavement over my father's death.
This took me a long time to get over. My husband and my father
didn't see eye to eye. And my husband didn't really know how to
help me in my bereavement, so I was left to my own ways. He felt,
and was, neglected, various arguments occurred over this point, but
I couldn't do much about it.*

*The opportunity for an affair was open to him at work and he fell
into it. We had a few very bad months. I believe we hit rock bottom
but are slowly climbing our way back up to the top. I still love him.
We have one son aged eight years and I cannot just think of me. We
do talk and communicate, even to the point of checking if he has
any threats made, as the girl in question acted very wild when he
finished the affair. My main problem is that I visualize them together, on a daily, hourly basis, even on the morning of my birthday! I
have such a pain still inside of me. He refuses now to answer any
more questions that I might ask. He says it won't do me any good
and only drags up the past.*

*We must try to put it behind us. He is full of regret, remorse for
his actions. He continually states his love for me and is very attentive and I know he means it. But how can I stop thinking about it? I
think I am going mad!*

Debra

Dear Debra,

You are not going mad. You are grieving your husband's betrayal!
But questions you need answered are not the details of the sexual
affair, as much as the motivation for his behavior. Except for clarifying issues of safe sex, details often become overly focused upon and
can lead to unhealthy obsessions with a life of their own. What is
more important is to focus your energy on understanding the emotional meaning of the affair in the context of your marriage.

Your husband broke the rules of your monogamous agreement.
He has broken your trust, and you have every reason to feel angry
and sad. Accepting these feelings and working through them
includes understanding what was truly going on for him when he
chose to so jeopardize his marriage. Only through understanding
the meaning of the affair will you be able to determine whether you
may be able to regain trust in him for the future.

You believe that his motivation has to do with your preoccupation with mourning your father's death. Though his reasons by no means validates his destructive acting out in your relationship, it would be critical to explore this aspect in depth. In this way the two of you will be taking responsibility for the gap in your marriage that might allow other people to come between you. And should this kind of gap present pain in the future, communication in place of dangerous acting out behavior will be more likely to occur.

It is the responsibility of both of you to create the connection that is lacking in your relationship rather than ignore it. Perhaps you were too quick to accept that your husband cannot help you in your bereavement. Your self-reliance, or in his perception, your dependence on your parents, may have left your husband feeling like he was peripheral to you instead of your main support. The silver lining in your situation may be that the obvious symptom of infidelity is blatant enough that neither of you can ignore it. In some way it may present the opportunity for focusing on your relationship and bringing you closer together. Clearly this has already occurred with your alliance against the other woman, and this is how it should be if the priorities for the marriage are basically sound.

The "other woman" in this case does not seem to represent any desirable replacement of you in your husband's mind, but may symbolize the predator of disconnection that you and your partner were falling prey to in your own intimate relationship. Without attention, this gap may have caused your marriage to atrophy and die a slow death over time. Your love for one another, your desire to remain as a family unit, his deep remorse and your belief in his genuine regret for hurting you are all reasons to consider remaining in the marriage.

Do not get seduced away from the problem by having an emotional obsession with the affair itself! Express your anger and hurt. You might want to create a ritual that includes making a fire and burning the pain, sharing it with the flames themselves. From the ashes may come the possibility for a renewed relationship with your husband. Expect a change from your husband in how he expresses his dissatisfaction in the marriage. Ask him for clarification regarding his acting out behavior. What would he have done differently, looking back on it? Instead of having an affair, what did he need to express to you about his own needs in the marriage? Is he talking to you and are you listening?

The overriding danger is that without a change in your ability to connect and communicate with one another, the two of you are vulnerable to using the affair as a continued source of distancing—perhaps one that replaces the gap left by the separate grief you experienced with your father. The rift between your father and your husband may have left you with conflict about your closeness to your husband. The distance between you and your spouse may have set the conditions that are ripe for affairs. Your best insurance as a couple is to build a bridge to one another.

Make this an opportunity for self reflection. Look deeply and honestly at your own intimacy issues. Have you been available to the marriage? Are you willing to depend on your husband for your emotional needs? Does anything keep you from making him a significant source of nourishment? He may need to feel that he is important to you and that you need him. Is he there for you when you do reach out? Determine together what kind of bond you would like to have with one another, and what may have kept you from forging it.

Make your relationship the main focus. Do not allow jealousy the power to ravage your life or to undermine your self worth! If your husband's behavior can be understood and does not represent a *pattern* of infidelity as a response to stress, it is unlikely to occur again. Contain the jealousy fire and like any fire deprived of its oxygen, it will eventually die out. Instead, direct the wind bellows towards the marriage relationship!

We are more likely to avoid "acting out" our feelings and needs through behavior that damages relationship if we take time to consider our communication patterns and how they contribute to, or detract from, successful conflict resolution and ongoing dialogue. Communication tools that promote rather than inhibit discussions is what the rest of this chapter is all about!

Feelings are physical

Although most of us are aware that *communicating* is an important element of relationships, we do not realize the full impact it has on our emotional and physical health. Patterns of ineffective communication can be passed down through generations when we grow up in families that have poorly developed communication skills. Research on heart disease[12] reveals that an inability to communicate can contribute to large and rapid fluctuations in blood pressure, which can ravage an already weakened cardiovascular system.

Psychologist James Lynch describes the concept of a "communication membrane" that exists between people in a family. The more able family members are at identifying and expressing their feelings, the more quickly their blood pressure returns to normal when emotional excitement occurs. However when we are unable to express our feelings or feel "understood," our blood pressure can become volatile because emotional release is not achieved. We can become literally "trapped inside our bodies," unable to express ourselves. Dr. Lynch calls this "alexithymia," which translated from Latin means "no words for feelings." The inability to communicate our feelings is physically as well as emotionally distressful.

A child's self-esteem develops in relationship to the people who love that child. *Being understood* is a primary and validating experience we all need in order to develop a solid sense of ourselves in the world. However, in some families, even naming the feelings a child is experiencing may be difficult, leaving him or her vulnerable to alexithymia in adulthood, ill equipped to sustain meaningful relationships.

Throughout our adult lives, our sense of self-worth is linked to our need to *commune* with others, to feel understood. "Commune" is defined in Webster's dictionary as "to converse together intimately, to have spiritual intercourse with." Effectively communicating with other family members is not a luxury, but a basic emotional need. The ability to negotiate our needs in the family and our capacity to solve problems is also a function of our ability to identify and articulate feelings. If we fail to develop a healthy "communication membrane" in our families, we are vulnerable to increased stress resulting from misunderstandings and fractured relationships.

While recent popular books attempt to separate connecting from problem-solving, the two remain inextricably intertwined. Being capable of having discussions and dialogue about differences releases stress and continues efforts towards successful negotiation without alienation. Most researchers agree that the ability to remain connected is the most critical aspect of successful marriages.

12. J. Lynch, *Language of the Heart: The Human Body in Dialogue* (New York: Basic Books, 1985).

The following question and answer illustrates the confusion that can occur when research is presented in an effort to divide and conquer, rather than integrate.

Confused by marriage research on conflict negotiation

Dear Dr. Gayle,

I recently read that a new "scientific" approach to marriage found conflict resolution not important to having a good marriage. Can you explain? I am confused, as I have always heard that solving problems was important in marriage. We are in marital counseling, but should I be concerned about working things out with my spouse when we have different points of view on a matter? And what if our couple's therapist is heading us in the wrong direction, in light of this new research?

Jim

Dear Jim,

Research by John Gottman describes three types of marriages and seeks to identify what contributes to successful conflict regulation in these different marital styles. In his book, *Why Marriages Succeed or Fail*, he writes, "If there is one lesson I have learned from my years of research it is *that a lasting marriage results from a couple's ability to resolve the conflicts that are inevitable in any relationship.*"[13]

But in his book, *Seven Principles for Marriage,* Gottman emphasizes, *"Successful conflict resolution isn't what makes marriages succeed."*[14] No wonder you are confused! Gottman claims to offer a new "scientifically based" model for couples. Yet, his findings are not altogether new, his presentation is often contradictory, and his research is not based on clinical trials. Still, he offers couples some good suggestions for stabilizing their marriages.

We must be careful not to throw out the baby with the bathwater!

I attended Dr. Gottman's advanced training for professionals,[15] and I am more clear than ever that being concerned about resolving conflict and how you approach your spouse about problems in your

13. J. Gottman, *Why Marriages Succeed or Fail* (New York: Simon & Schuster, 1995), p. 28. Gottman's emphasis.

14. J. Gottman, *Seven Principles for Marriage* (New York: Crown Books, 1999), p. 11.

15. Gottman Institute training seminar, San Francisco, California, June 1999.

marriage are both critical to a healthy partnership. His research reinforces the findings of others, that what creates connection over disconnection in relationship is important. Communication that encourages positive connection during and outside of conflict, predicts greater marital stability.

Gottman's recent definition of "conflict resolution" appears to be "all or nothing." In earlier research on conflict resolution, researchers differentiated between affective and instrumental problem-solving in families.[16] Gottman throws both of these dimensions of family life together. All types of conflict that generate ongoing discussions or arguments he labels as unresolved, even though couples may experience varying degrees of compromise, improvement or resolve in their experience of these issues over time. Gottman appears to have changed the terms of his own definitions. He labels these ongoing discussions that keep open the opportunity for change, as "conflict regulation" instead of "conflict resolution." Hence, your confusion.

Dr. Gottman generates contradictory statements that serve to single his work out above all others in the name of "science." But he could just as easily present his new information in the context of past research and creativity already available in the field.[17]

Still, this new research spawns a creative approach to helping couples communicate effectively, and is a valuable contribution to the field. He makes the point that up to sixty-nine percent of arguments in a marriage focus on ongoing differences that are not immediately solvable. Like others, Gottman encourages communication that maintains connection over disconnection. Communication that decreases negativity and increases positive responses during conflict is critical. This focus allows couples to continue discussions about differences rather than get alienated over problem areas of the marriage.

Like most family therapists, Gottman believes in the "emotional

---

16. N. Epstein, D. Bishop, C. Ryan, I. Miller, & G. Keitner, "The McMaster Model View of Healthy Family Functioning." In F. Walsh (Ed.), *Normal Family Processes*, 2nd edition (New York: Guilford Press, 1993).

17. Stoking controversy is one way to refute all previous relationship gurus. But a deeper look at Gottman's research and his criticisms create more questions than answers. Because his research is not done with control groups, but "innovatively" as he describes it, it may prove difficult to legitimately compare his findings to that of other controlled studies.

bank account" in marriage. This concept emphasizes the fact that we "cut our partners slack" when we have a greater percentage of positive to negative interactions. Specifically, his research shows happy couples have a ratio of five positive interactions to one negative! And though he belittles the use of "I" statements, saying they are impossible to do in an argument, his own solutions include a "soft" approach to dialoguing about conflict. And many of his examples of "soft start up" contain "I" statements.

Gottman also criticizes the "active listening" technique found in many books on marriage, because he states it does not increase empathy by itself. Yet, he does recommend it in conjunction with behavioral approaches and in times when a partner is distressed about something outside of the marital relationship, such as work or other friendships. So if you have been practicing the use of "I" statements or active listening, do not throw them by the wayside! They remain viable tools for helping you stay connected, and help you return to address conflict when it does erupt.

Gottman ridicules Harville Hendrix's focus on childhood wounds[18] as significant to a good marriage, yet he believes in revealing the "triggers" in arguments that are related to childhood pain. So do stay tuned to your childhood experience when your emotions negatively charge your interactions with your partner. It is still thought by most researchers and therapists to be significant!

What is helpful is to remain connected through conflict. Recognizing the fact that some arguments in your marriage will not completely resolve will allow you to pay better attention to how you are treating your partner, rather than simply what is being said.

Although Gottman's work can be useful to couples, his books are peppered with admonishments about misguided therapists and ineffective therapeutic interventions, which are often contradictory. He describes himself as a researcher, not a clinician. And his clinical strategies are deduced from his research on what predicts divorce or stability, not on clinical effectiveness. (Still, it's enough to make you distrust your therapist unless he or she has the Gottman stamp!) The unfortunate result may be to deter couples from getting professional help to save a troubled marriage.

---

18. H. Hendrix, *Getting the Love You Want* (New York: Simon and Schuster, 1991).

Marital therapists have been aware of the connection between communication and the affective dimension of relationship for a long time. Gottman's findings add to this body of research.[19] If you think your marriage is in trouble, do not delay. Marriage counselors have been focused on helping you talk about your conflict regardless of whether you reach complete compromise, long before Gottman came out with his new model! Do not shy away from consulting with a competent therapist when needed.

Be aware that there will be problems you will continue to be in conflict about in your marriage, and that keeping the dialogue going and *maintaining positive connection is success* by itself. Dialogue keeps you connected so that empathy can develop around conflict and there is always the potential for resolution to occur over time. Sometimes resolution evolves through an understanding of the emotional meaning of your spouse's position, rather than a behavioral change. When we deal with problems without alienating our partner, we are able to hold the lines of communication open and keep alive the possibility of continuous long term shifts in the marriage. These shifts can, in fact, result in resolution, acceptable compromise or a better ability for tolerance (through understanding) over the long haul.

Stop short of adopting an attitude that conflict resolution is not important in your marriage! Instead, pay attention to how conflict is handled.

The following guidelines are elements of communication that researchers have found help you connect with your partner, rather than become alienated or disconnected in times of conflict. These categories are described below in light of Gottman's work with couples, on which he bases his predictions for divorce.[20] This represents the heart of his research, which is both useful and significant to the health of your marriage.

1. *Stonewalling* or withdrawing from an argument cuts your partner off. Instead, attempt to soothe yourself. Even if you need to take a

---

19. Dr. Gottman's work restates what previous research has shown contributes to healthy family relationships. Characteristics of healthy families that promote connection over disconnection, such as warmth and humor, have already been identified. It is not surprising that Gottman finds that these processes exist within healthy marriages.

20. J. Gottman, *Seven Principles of Marriage* (New York: Crown Books, 1999).

walk, in order to come back later and continue the argument when you are calmer. Likewise, if you do "blow it," use apology to repair the damage! The antidote is to get back into the conversation. Connect rather than disconnect!

2. *Criticism* is defined by Gottman as specifically putting your partner down, rather than offering a legitimate complaint that stops short of assigning negative attributes. Complain about not having dinner on time, for example, but use a softer approach, "I am really upset that we are always waiting around for dinner until you are ready. It really bother me." Instead of, "You always hold dinner up. You think the whole world revolves around you!" The second comment criticizes the person, rather than complains about the situation.

3. *Contempt* goes even further in damaging the connection and so reducing the possibility of having a discussion or dialogue that could result in some understanding or even compromise. The antidote is to increase appreciation.

Contempt goes beyond criticism in that it passes judgment on character. For example, one husband in my practice told his wife, "You're not doing your part. I initiate talking to you about feelings, but because I don't do it at the right time, or in the right way, you do not respond, like I never do it good enough." So far, so good, but he went on to say, "You don't care about this marriage or me. You are not committed. You are irresponsible. I want to see some commitment out of you for god's sake!" His wife grew quiet, while just before she had been the one to bring up the issue as a complaint.

In this case, I was able to successfully point out to the husband that he did not even believe what he just said! He has often appreciated his wife for her consideration and commitment to himself and the children. He realized this was true, and was able to soften his approach. But it was an eye opener for both of them to observe how their discussions got derailed.

Contempt can be toxic if used a lot in the heat of conflict and can stop your partner in his or her tracks. This is particularly true if one partner came from a family where conflict was avoided and the other from a family where conflict (even insults) were common and even part of rapport. Still, a more volatile style of relating must include a good ratio of positive appreciation during times of low conflict, in order to maintain a quality relationship.

4. *Defensiveness* can also preclude connection during a discussion. It is often the case that there are two openings for a response to our partner and we choose the one least likely to succeed. A rush to defensiveness shuts down connection and discussions may falter. Sometimes it is better to try the road less traveled, even if it is not as familiar as your defense. The following example illustrates this opportunity.

One of the wives in my practice offered a complaint to her husband that included responsibility on her part: "What you say is true, I do need to consider the effect that my sporadic work schedule has on you and the kids. Maybe I could practice this week getting up earlier so I could get to work sooner and be home at a reasonable time for dinner. But could you do your part in finding out when the kids are scheduled for soccer practice? You said you would do it, but never gave me that information." His response began, "I help a lot around the house, more than most men do. You need to take responsibility for getting home on time." I stopped him and pointed out how he had gotten derailed in defending himself, rather than continuing on the bid for a solution his wife had offered. He was able to get back on track and create a joint approach to their problem.

Physiological flooding and "I" statements

Physiological "flooding" refers to the fact that when we are upset our hearts race and we find ourselves unable to process new information calmly in the heat of an argument. James Lynch found this in his research with patients suffering from cardiovascular problems and related this physiological flooding to his concept of the "communication membrane" between people. Gottman's claim that "I" statements are difficult to use is accurate, if you expect to instantly be able to use "I" statements in the initial stages of an argument. (See page 96 for a full description of the "I" statement.)

We learn in a specific emotional state and we must relearn our responses within that same emotionally charged state, if we are to change our behavior. Learning theorists call this "state dependent learning."

Arguments with our spouse present opportunities for working through our beliefs at an emotional level, and "I" statements are useful tools that you can turn to for regaining your physiological calm. They represent part of a learning process, rather than an end product. Instead, they contribute to self-soothing when used to organize and separate your own thoughts and feelings.

Lynch's research found that naming and validating your own feelings allows you to calm down and successfully return to complete a discussion. If you have no words for feelings (alexithymia) you are quite literally trapped inside your body, as Lynch puts it, unable to release feelings through expression, therefore caught in heightened physiological arousal. *"I" statements provide an avenue for calming yourself because they allow you to identify feelings and express them.*

Strategies for returning to an argument, such as a walk around the block, when your heart rate has returned to normal, are essential for working through some of our most heated disagreements in marriage. As you calm yourself, make use of the "I" statement as an aid in helping you organize your feelings and thoughts into words that communicate your experience, without attacking your spouse. And do not be too proud to offer an apology to repair damaging statements you may have made!

Physiological calming and apology make "I" statements useful rather than useless. Through this process, you will likely build a greater capacity for a clean complaint when under pressure, instead of a disparaging attack. And whether you actually always begin your statements with "I" is not the point, but that you communicate your vulnerability, "I felt hurt when you didn't listen," or, "You didn't hear me. That hurt." Both get the message across, without criticism. Use the style most natural to you.

"I" statements are not solutions by themselves, but they offer a tool on the bridge towards emotionally retraining yourself to be non-defensive towards your partner in your approach to problems. You may find that you drop this technique for different language, once you have achieved mastery in calming yourself enough, so that you are less defensive during your marital arguments.

Family researchers agree that family communication either strengthens or inhibits family bonding, and leads to or discourages potential for problem solving. Numerous studies using biofeedback research with couples in dialogue show us that how couples communicate impacts their physiology and their ability to relate around conflict. Healthy families solve problems through relating rather than controlling.

Family researchers have known for over a decade that warmth, humor and appreciation promote joy and connection in families, while discounts, sarcasm or other "put downs" result in disconnection and depression. Be concerned about your spouse's views and work to discuss differences without attacking character in the process.

Listening and empathy

Below is an exercise in *listening and empathy*, the first step towards healthy communication. Without an ability empathize, you will not be able to sustain an emotional connection with your partner. The following discussion and exercises are intended to help stimulate reflection on patterns of communication and problem solving you learned in childhood, and to develop your current family's "communication membrane."

Exercise: Exploring your childhood experience

Ask yourself if you were listened to as a child in your family, and if other family members listened to each other or not. This will give you an understanding of your own trust in being understood and the pressure you might feel around communication that is rooted in the past.

Remember, it is never too late to develop skills, or *take the time* for listening that we did not learn or experience in childhood. Life is for learning. And now it is your turn as parents to decide what kind of family atmosphere you want to develop!

Rate your overall childhood experience of feeling "listened to" in your family on the scale below. You may also rate your childhood experience as it relates to your relationship with your mother, father, or other family members separately, if you wish.

1	2	3	4	5	6
Almost always	Mostly	Usually	Sometimes	Seldom	Almost never

If you have been "listened to" in your childhood, you are more likely to be able to listen to others. Still, under stress, we can abandon our best tools and resort to blocking rather than hearing what others have to say. If you feel you did not develop your ability for self expression, do not despair! It is never too late to develop your "communication membrane." Begin with the exercise below.

Developing Your Listening Skill

Family researchers have identified six areas of family communication,[21] however *listening* to emotionally laden messages without automatically blocking the flow of a discussion is primary in laying a founda-

---

21. D. Olson, "Circumflex Model of Marital and Family Systems." In F. Walsh (Ed.), *Normal Family Processes*, 2nd edition (New York: Guilford Press, 1993).

tion for solving problems. This is especially true during emotionally heated discussions when conflicts arise. The more you practice, the easier it will be to express yourself in a way that is non-blaming, and to listen to your partner's experience without blocking the flow of productive discussion. Keep in mind, however, that this is a process that builds tolerance for feelings over time, allowing you to remain increasingly calmer during heated discussions.

It *is* natural to become reactive in the course of family life. However being able to get back on track, without losing large amounts of time to polarizing or even hurtful discussions, will help you solve problems more effectively. And it will help you free up love for one another, following a short-lived but appropriate release of anger. If couples can express anger and resentments to one another without getting stuck in blaming or punishing, love is preserved and intimacy blossoms!

Just as importantly, couples who are able to *recover and successfully repair* painful disagreements and misunderstandings fare well over the years of relating because they stay connected and in dialogue with one another rather than becoming disconnected.

Listening includes the ability to be attentive to the other person's experience of what is being discussed. It also means being able to understand and *empathize* with their experience, *even when you do not agree*. Showing empathy is crucial to your partner's ability to hear your side of the discussion when it is your turn to express yourself. This exercise also gives you and your partner a tool to help you *slow down an argument* so that you can successfully carry important discussions to a point of mutual understanding. This is the first step in developing a capacity for self-soothing during an argument, which increases the potential for finding acceptable compromises.

Use the "I" statements to address particularly emotionally charged topics in your marriage. It is when our discussions get "heated" that we need to be heard most. Still, it is when we are emotionally upset that we communicate *least* effectively! This exercise will help you begin to express your strong feelings in a way that will give you an opportunity to carry your discussions through to completion, rather than miscarry them prematurely.

Exercise: Using "I" statements to avoid blaming and attack

Using the following sentence, fill in the blanks with your appropriate feelings, the description of behavior you are responding to, and your emotional interpretation of what the behavior means to you.

I feel _____ when you _____ and I imagine _____.

When you fill in the blank for "imagine," you may find that your feelings are partially rooted in past childhood experiences, which may color the way you are receiving your partner's message. This exercise offers an opportunity for clarification, including the possibility of separating past emotionally charged wounds from distorting your present interactions.

Example: I feel anxious when you swear and I imagine you are about to lose control of yourself and hit me. Or: I feel tense when you swear and I imagine you will withdraw from being affectionate to me the rest of the evening.

Your partner then should reflect back to you an accurate understanding of your feelings, without defending or explaining himself before he or she connects with you around being understood.

Example: You feel anxious that my swearing will result in my hurting you physically. Is that right? You feel afraid that my swearing means that I won't be loving to you the rest of the day. Did I get it?

When you use this method of communicating around emotionally-charged topics, you will be more likely to be understood because you are eliminating blaming your partner for how you feel. You are expressing your feelings without attacking the other person. This makes it easier for your partner to understand your feelings *when they are different from their own.*

Using "I" statements also allows you to validate your own feelings, increasing your ability to calm yourself. *This capacity for self-soothing in your marriage cannot be underestimated!* It eliminates the pressure for two people to see things exactly the same in order to feel connected or loved. Space for two people to experience the world differently decreases the possibilities of misinterpretation. And this kind of connecting allows people to reflect on the source of these feelings, sorting out what percentage of their feelings belong to their present partnership experience, and how much of it may relate to past childhood relationships. Because there is more space for feelings, the understanding can evolve more smoothly.

For example: " I know you've never hit me. I guess your anger triggers my experience of being hit by my brother when I was a kid."

When clarifications like the above can happen, partners will be more able to increase their capacity for receiving messages that carry strong emotions (including anger) from their partners, without overreacting. The more we build tolerance for feelings, without responding with defensive blocking techniques such as withdrawal or blaming, the greater our ability is for closeness and intimacy. Trust is built through an experience of safety in being able to express powerful feelings without disconnecting from those we love.

Daily practice

Set aside time for relating each evening with the goal of increasing your listening skills and using your "I" statements. Choose a topic that you feel needs attention. You can take turns, or alternate days of being the listener with your partner if you like, so the exercise is easy to do. Even if you think you are too tired, you may find that receiving empathy can be rejuvenating. And being able to connect as the listener may give you a feeling of accomplishment and maturity that deepens your appreciation of not only your partner, but yourself!

Speaker: I feel _____ when you _____ and I imagine _____.
Listener: Reflects back what you heard your partner say
Speaker: Tell the listener if he or she "got it." If he or she missed a piece, repeat the above statement and try again, until you feel heard.

You will both feel successful when understanding has been achieved. There is no other goal but successful understanding of the speaker's experience. Do not proceed to change roles until understanding has been accomplished.

"I" statement exercise: Goals and trouble-shooting!

Listener: Remember the goal as "listener" is to truly understand, not necessarily agree. Do not get into a discussion about your viewpoint during this exercise! This will likely cause you to undermine your ability to simply reflect and understand your partner. Just see if you can accurately reflect your partner's experience. If you succeed in doing so, you have created an empathic connection!

Speaker: Remember the goal as "speaker" is to communicate your experience, not present fact or lay blame! Do not attack. This can happen if you slip in a "you" in the first blank. For example, "I feel like you always...," or I feel that you are...," represent common mistakes made when first doing this exercise. Be aware that you are to put words to a *feeling* that is your own. For example, "I feel angry, hurt, belittled when...," *not* "I feel that you are angry, mean, nasty to me when you...." You will sabotage your opportunity to be heard if you express your feeling as a statement of blame against your partner.

Be direct and clear in your communication. Use the "I" statement exactly as it is presented without distortion. Remember, too, that one goal of using the "I" statements is for self-soothing. So journaling in this form can also be quite helpful!

The following question and answer illustrates the importance of developing your "communication membrane" from the start of your relationship, before destructive patterns set in to roost.

The difference between "having an opinion" or being "opinionated"

Dear Dr. Gayle,

I wish that my fiancé was more sensitive to my opinions, views, and feelings. When I express myself about an issue, he tries to correct me or make a better point of it. After some time of arguing, I tend to give in to him because his point seems better than mine.

I feel so misunderstood because I believe that I have understood his views, opinions and feelings more than he understands mine. I have told him that I feel its not fair that he always has to make a point out of an issue. I wish we could just appreciate each other's views and opinions. Am I wrong in this? Does it have to do with me not feeling understood in the past?

Diane

Dear Diane,

The health of your relationship depends on feelings of fairness and mutual respect. How you handle differences is pivotal to having a future together, regardless of your shared similarities or divergent perspectives.

Regardless of your past, your experience of your fiancé is a valid one for you. And feeling understood is one of the key elements to any successful relationship. Though your beloved may not agree with you, it is important that you feel he can empathize with you most of the time. But you must be clear about the difference between needing him to agree with you and feeling understood.

Reflect on whether or not your fiancé is "opinionated" or just having an opinion. To be opinionated means that the person has an opinion and his view is the only "right" one. If he very often invalidates your opinion because he believes his perspective and feelings are the only ones that should be considered, then he is missing the value of differences in a relationship. Consider also the reasons for giving up your opinion. Have your views and feelings been altered by a fresh perspective which you decide to incorporate, or do you just feel worn down?

Let your fiancé know how you are feeling. Discover what the meaning of these discussions holds for your relationship. Is there some way to share your *feelings* about your views and opinions separate from the point you are trying to get across? Focusing on the process of how the dynamics of the discussion feels to both of you is far more important than settling the content.

Healthy relationships allow for differences in points of view without diminishing the good feelings of love and respect that flow between you. Differences are inevitable in any relationship. Consider just the fact that one of you is raised as a female and one of you as a male. This alone can create totally different experiences and perspectives of the world! The richness of your relationship is developed through sharing the very different perspectives that each of you brings to the table. Though your fiancé may never experience things in exactly the same way as you do, it will benefit him to be curious and interested in understanding the world through your eyes to better know and appreciate you.

Listen to your instincts about what you need in your relationship. You are right to believe in appreciation of differences rather than winning an argument!

Problem Solving, Communication, and Emotional Connection

Families may become dysfunctional when problems cannot be solved and increasing emotional disconnection results. Establishing a well-functioning "communication membrane" which allows us to receive and send messages smoothly when things are going well, and encourages us to remain in dialogue when things are not going well, is not just about physical or emotional health.

Regulating conflict in a marriage depends upon the quality of emotional connection present in your relationship. The overall atmosphere present in a family is directly related to whether communication *facilitates* or *blocks* the potential for conflict resolution. All researchers agree that the manner in which you communicate affects the quality of your relationships.

The capacity of family members to resolve problems contributes to an overall spirit of harmony or dissonance present in the home. Attention to family atmosphere is important because high and consistent levels of tension related to unsolved difficulties is thought to be the single largest contributor to maladjustment in children.[22]

Contrary to popular belief, neither dissatisfaction reported in a marriage nor frequency of disagreements spawn failed marriages. Instead, styles of communication that inhibit problem solving and positive emotional connection spell trouble. A legacy of unresolved conflict may be the writing on the wall that precedes a consult with a divorce attorney, if you and your partner are not able to successfully regulate the conflict that is inevitable in family life.

Some family researchers have found the strongest predictor of divorce to be the inability to solve problems.[23] Others, such as Robert Levenson at the Institute for Personality and Social Research at the University of California at Berkeley[24] emphasize the ability to regulate emotions and having a "wide emotional zone" in the marriage to be the most important dimension for a successful marriage. He describes happy couples as "good" listeners and emphasizes the overall quality of the emotional connection between partners to be predictive of happiness and stability. He cites an attitude of disgust between partners to be the most reliable predictor of divorce. Clearly, the summation of research points to the link between a couple's ability to handle conflict and their capacity for accepting the expression of a full range of emotions in themselves and their partner.

Effective conflict regulation goes hand in hand with respectful and

---

22. N. Epstein, D. Bishop, C. Ryan, I. Miller, & G. Keitner, "The McMaster Model View of Healthy Family Functioning." In F. Walsh (Ed.), *Normal Family Processes*, 2nd edition (New York: Guilford Press, 1993).

23. E. M. Hetherington, T. C. Law, & T. G. O'Connor, "Divorce: Challenges, Changes and New Chances." In F. Walsh (Ed.), *Normal Family Processes*, 2nd edition (New York: Guilford Press, 1993).

24. Reported in an interview with Robert Levenson in the East Bay Express, volume 21, no. 40, July 9, 1999.

loving attitudes in marriage. Successful negotiation may be immediate, or it may take the form of ongoing discussions about differences between the two of you that change in nature over the course of your marriage. Continuing to discuss differences between you with an effort to positively connect, empathize and understand can yield satisfactory compromise, tolerance or adjustments that adequately insulate your marriage. Positive interactions in marriage buffers conflict and tension when it occurs. Remember that healthy families have a positive to negative ratio of five to one in their *daily* interactions!

A common pattern that creates distress in a marriage is one in which one spouse confronts conflict and the other blocks communication through withdrawal, sulking, stonewalling, flippancy, discounting, or other methods of conflict avoidance. Communication that relies heavily on blaming, placating, whining or sarcasm to express feelings leads to protracted discussions with less probability for reaching solutions. This is because these approaches cause your partner to turn away from you rather than towards you, emotionally. The marriage is damaged when we do not feel respected by our partners.

It is easy to intuitively identify when we are having difficulty being understood or getting our point across. Similarly, we can often feel when we do not connect with another person's interpretation of an experience. What is more difficult to understand is the relationship between our own communication and the potential for solving problems and remaining connected when conflicts are not immediately solvable.

One way to know if your communication is effective in the family is to take note of how, or if, problems get discussed, and if they do what percentage of time a resolution occurs. It is also important to note the quality of your experience, as *conflict that is negotiated with great pain will be likely to be avoided*, while conflict that is resolved with positive feelings will make problem solving a more likely possibility in the future.

One team of family researchers[25] at Brown University suggests that there are seven steps to making certain that problems get resolved:

1. Identify the problem.
2. Communicate with appropriate people about the problem.
3. Develop a set of possible alternative solutions.

25. N. Epstein, D. Bishop, C. Ryan, I. Miller, & G. Keitner, "The McMaster Model View of Healthy Family Functioning." In F. Walsh (Ed.), *Normal Family Processes*, 2nd edition (New York: Guilford Press, 1993).

4. Decide on one of the alternatives.

5. Carry out action required.

6. Monitor to guarantee action is taken.

7. Evaluate effectiveness of your decision making process.

If communication skills are poorly developed, negative processes such as blaming, condemnation, and withdrawal may be prominent. It will prove difficult to get past the second step of conveying your description of the problem to someone else without losing connection and ongoing discussion. Likewise, unresolved conflict could be expressed in a miscarriage of action once it is decided (fifth step). However, if family members gestate a decision through to the final step of self-reflection, they are more likely to give birth to a feeling of team spirit, particularly if each felt respected in the process.

The following question and answer illustrates how destructive relationship patterns can develop in a marriage. Solutions to problems can become stymied with patterns of communication that miscarry plans rather than facilitate them. Strain on the relationship, more often than not, ensues.

Following through on agreements in marriage

Dear Dr. Gayle,

I just finished reading your article on "communication." It helped me pin-point the step I feel our problem solving falls apart. We get to step 4, deciding on alternatives, but decisions don't get implemented. How do I get past this with my husband? I try repeating myself on several occasions, but this gets old and becomes unproductive. He resorts to calling me a "nag." But he never gets beyond what we discussed and into the actions he agreed to do to carry the plan to completion. Any suggestions?

Devoted and out of energy

Dear Devoted and out of energy,

Your husband is avoiding immediate conflict by saying "yes" but doing "no"! Your relationship is suffering from an inability to keep agreements. Agreements are the basis for trust in a relationship. Each time an agreement is broken, the foundation of trust that the relationship is based upon is eroded. This is damaging to a marriage and often the reason cited for eventual divorce.

Ask your husband why he continually pretends to make agreements that in the end he does not follow. This kind of disappointment weighs heavily on the relationship and no doubt costs him your affection and tenderness as well. Is this really what he wants? What is he getting out of this behavior? Is it worth the cost?

Take time to explore with one another how conflict was negotiated in your respective parents' marriage. Was conflict resolved effectively? Did each spouse have equal power in decision making in the family? Our first role models for relating to a spouse are forged in childhood. If our dads acquiesced to mom's wishes, only to frustrate her with disappointment later, what was being expressed and what was the result? Was this a passive way for him to express anger? Was mom the one left with all the angry feelings? Did they covertly agree that it is safe for mom to express anger in the family and unsafe for dad to do so?

Sometimes patterns of gender interaction are based upon reactions to particular male and female figures of the past. If there was an abusive father, for example, the next generation may spawn a passive son who refused (was afraid) to deal with conflict because it involves expressing angry feelings. Instead of developing skills for safe and direct expression of anger or his own needs, he may avoid conflict in the short term, agreeing to anything in order to "keep the peace." His spouse may be left expressing unproductive, unrelenting frustration due to repeated broken agreements. A pattern can develop in which a man may avoid expressing his needs because he is afraid of his own anger more than his wife's "nagging." This example may or may not relate to your situation, but represents one possibility to consider.

And what part may mom have played in this? Was she unwilling to experience her husband's anger or needs directly? Sometimes couples create patterns that reinforce gender roles of childhood without realizing it. Ask your husband to interpret the meaning of his actions. Is he attempting to frustrate you? Is he afraid of displeasing you for some reason if he says "no" to you? Explore your own contributions to the failure of your agreements. Do you insist on getting your way through emotional blackmail or are you interested in hearing your husband's experience and needs? Did you come from a family background that respected and included men's needs or ignored them in the negotiating process?

So, what does this kind of passivity in follow through mean in your marriage? If you are unable to get a handle on completing the negotiation process, seek couple's counseling to explore deeper issues that are seriously sabotaging your happiness. Your feelings of being out of energy are a sign that you may be "giving up" quietly. Statistics show that depression in women is more a function of marital unhappiness than it is for men. Pay attention to what "out of energy" means for you. An ongoing undercurrent of unresolved friction deteriorates your own self-esteem as well as the marriage relationship.

Though your devotion may maintain the marriage, over time you may find yourself mired in a depression which takes the place of angry disappointment. Ask for your husband's help in creating a marriage that gives you energy rather than tires you out!

Exercise: Rate your level of conflict resolution

What is the rate of successful conflict resolution in your marriage and what is the quality of your experience? Do topics of discussion reach closure, particularly when action needs to be taken? Pay attention to how you make decisions in the family and how this process feels to you and other family members.

Ask yourself and your partner to reflect on the following two questions. Write down your first response after reflecting on the question, then come back again to this question in a week, two weeks and four weeks. Take the average of your responses after one month's observations.

1. What percentage of problems reach successful compromise in your marriage? Rate it below.

Level of conflict resolution:

0%	20%	40%	60%	80%	100%

2. What is the quality of your experience around problem solving in your relationship? Rate it below:

Quality of the experience:

1	2	3	4	5

1: extremely painful/not "worth it" and would like to avoid this process
2: painful and exhausting but would do it again reluctantly only if absolutely necessary
3: somewhat difficult and time consuming, but happy with the outcome
4: difficult and very rewarding experience
5: stimulating and bonding experience

The rate of successful resolution that is carried through to completion builds trust and self-esteem in family relationships. A persistent miscarriage of plans or compromises that are reached only after great anguish result in distrust of the process and decreased energy for dealing with life's problems. This kind of family atmosphere can become a breeding ground for depression or other disturbances in both physical and mental health.

Communication under pressure: Conflict and compromise

Conflicts are not only inevitable in the natural course of family life, but they are necessary for growth. It is the way we express ourselves and listen to our partners (and children) that determines our capacity to successfully negotiate with our loved ones when conflicts arise.

Skillful communication prevents misunderstandings and keeps your partner apprised to the emotional changes and development that happens on quiet levels inside each of us every day. But with busy schedules, it is often difficult to carve out enough time for the discussions we need to have together as a couple to resolve problems, much less to keep each other informed about our changing perceptions, experiences and growth! So it is inevitable that we sometimes depend upon "heated" discussions with our partners to inform us about what is going on inside.

We all have the ability to destroy our relationships. No one is immune to destructive patterns of communicating when under stress and we all use them at some time. The key to health is not perfect communication, but an awareness of when we express ourselves in destructive ways and what patterns each of us have a tendency to "default" to in times of stress. A marriage that becomes laden with a legacy of unresolved problems is vulnerable to increasing negative feelings, eventual break-up and/or "deadening" of the passion and marital bond.

Avoiding conflict by withdrawing from marital discussions is a common, but deadly tactic many spouses use in their marriages. The following question and answer illustrates how patterns of avoidance can develop in a marriage, the potential impact on children, and the eventual emptiness that can result when withdrawal from conflict is a repetitive, long term coping pattern.

Living separate lives

Dear Dr. Gayle,
   My husband won't talk out any problems. He won't argue with me, he just walks out. I think he feels as long as nothing is said,

there is no problem. My husband and I spend a lot of time in differ-
ent parts of the house and have almost no shared interests. He lets
me do anything I want, buy anything I want, and is very generous
in many ways. Maybe you are by now asking... what is the problem?
Well, it just seems as though there should be more to life than this!
We are married, and we have one son, age twenty-one, who lives
with us. But it seems we are living separate lives. Any suggestions? I
am afraid I may want to leave the marriage.

Kay

Dear Kay,

Successful negotiation is a vital part of a healthy intimate relationship. Your husband is avoiding negotiating with you. But you
and your husband created this pattern of avoidance together over
the years. It is probable that neither one of you had experience that
caused you to believe that a couple could successfully resolve conflict without destruction! So you may have colluded to side-step
tense interactions, which set up a pattern of separate living. What
you thought was in the best interests of the marriage in keeping it
safe from conflict has actually contributed to loneliness and dissatisfaction. Often it is more painful to experience loneliness *with* someone, rather than loneliness resulting from being truly alone.

You may have mistaken "getting your way" about small things,
for having true satisfaction in your marriage. Obviously this is not
the case. The amount of personal space your husband affords you
may have felt pleasant to you when you were younger, but now you
crave intimacy rather than freedom from conflict.

It is possible that you were initially attracted to your spouse
because of the very traits that disturb you now. Did you come from
a family in which marital conflict was upsetting to you as a child? If
so, you may have chosen your husband for the peace and calmness
his avoidance of conflict meant to you in your younger years
together. Or you may be following the role model of one of your
parents in recreating a similar pattern of avoidance in the marriage
that was also true in your parents' relationship. Patterns in your
husband's family may also contribute. He may be either modeling
or reacting to similar patterns of dealing with conflict that he experienced in his childhood.

Both you and your husband have neglected the relationship to some extent by not developing shared interests or activities. Perhaps this was satisfactory to you when your child was growing up, as it gave the two of you a focal point to share in the family. However, now that your child is an adult, you and your husband are facing your relationship and reevaluating what is there. It is natural for you to do so at this time. It is also important to assess whether your adult child is being held back from leaving the two of you because of an unconscious responsibility to hold your marriage together. Sometimes only children or youngest children who do not leave home as adults feel that their role in the family is to keep the parents' marriage together. This kind of subliminal pressure to keep the family intact can keep grown children from developing their own lives.

Your marriage needs development at this stage! Let your husband know that you love him, but that your needs have changed in the relationship. Acknowledge your shared contribution to developing patterns of communication and interaction that created distance instead of closeness over the years. And point out to him that the two of you are at a crucial stage in your marriage because you no longer are raising a child together.

Begin to focus on your relational connection and address the elements from your family of origins that have influenced your behaviors with one another. This can become a time of tremendous growth. You have lived many years together, sharing life side by side. This certainly accounts for something! You are no doubt deeply bonded and may be very committed to each other. So it is now time to really get to know the other again.

Focus your energies on forging new patterns that include the ability and tools to successfully negotiate. Communication will allow you to have the tension in the relationship that promotes connection rather than separation. When you are no longer afraid of conflict, you will find that your partnership warms up.

Working through conflict with respect allows you to unleash passion safely. And this is the key to closeness and intimacy. Develop your skills for dealing with the expression of anger in your relationship and you will find that your feelings of warmth, affection and love are also released in the marriage. Right now you are maximizing peace at the price of deadening the marriage. You need to come to a middle ground where tension is tolerated and can be transformed rather than avoided.

Seek support in the form of marriage seminars or group support for exploring intimacy in your partnership through community resources. Make your marriage the central focus. Develop activities and explore new interests together. Perhaps you may once again find each other, and your child may find his own living quarters!

It is our ability to communicate effectively under pressure that will make the difference in our lives and relationships. In order to increase our tools for communicating more effectively, we must take an honest look at our own *discussion-busters.*

The following exercise will help you change your own personal patterns that destroy empathy and connection during marital discussions, and will facilitate new responses that will sustain your most intimate relationships.

Exercise: Identifying your discussion-busters!

How did your parents resolve conflict? Can you identify any patterns that might have been used or learned in your childhood experience that are not satisfactory?

Attack-withdrawal/withdrawal-attack syndrome: Did one partner withdraw from discussion repeatedly? If so, the other may have attacked in an attempt to continue the discussion but to no avail. Or the attack could have come first, with the withdrawal reinforcing an unsuccessful and furious pursuit. What did your parents demonstrate to you in their marriage? What do you do in your marriage when under emotional pressure?

Blow-ups as a way to stop discussions: Did you learn, either by parental example or deference to your own angry outbursts (as a child), to gain control of a situation by becoming emotionally "explosive," contemptuous or in any other way, intimidating?

Placating to stop discussion: Did you learn to say "yes" to keep the peace in the short term, only to renege on your agreement by doing "no," causing greater distress and broken promises in the long run?

Discounting, teasing, whining, flippancy, sarcasm, or nagging: Did you learn to block discussion and consideration of your partner's viewpoint through discounting, teasing, or repeatedly flippant or sarcastic remarks? Did you to learn to "nag" unsuccessfully rather than present your point of view with self-respect and an expectation for full discussion of the problem?

We all learned some form of unsuccessful communication and usually we resort to only one or two primary culprits. What are yours?

Consider your own patterns and the patterns present in your relationship. Ask your partner to do the same. Can you identify patterns that block discussions in your marriage?

Tendencies and patterns I resort to when under stress:_____

_____

_____

_____

_____

Patterns that block discussions and resolving problems in our marriage: _____

_____

_____

_____

Exercise: Overcoming destructive patterns

Once you have considered the communication you may "default" to when under pressure, develop strategies that help you *change these self-defeating behaviors as they occur*.

Research in learning shows that we often develop our behaviors within highly aroused emotional states. Researchers call this "state dependent" learning. When we are not in these highly aroused states, our reasoning can prevail. It is when we are in the charged emotional experience that we find ourselves acting differently than we want to act or behave!

It is crucial that we re-learn these behaviors in the highly aroused state, if we are to succeed in communicating effectively under stress. Therefore, it is necessary to give yourself "cues" to help you begin to change your learned behavior while you are upset.

Develop your strategy now! If you usually walk out of the room rather than express yourself with "I" statements, for example, consider:

Strategy # 1: Take ten deep breaths and stay in the room rather than withdrawing in a 'huff." Remind yourself that you are safe and you can *take your time* to calmly express what you feel. Use your "I" statements now!

Strategy # 2: If you do walk out in a "huff": Come back to the room as soon as possible and try again. Your partner may appreciate your return, if it is a new behavior to him/her during an argument. This change may open the door for more productive discussion.

Strategy # 3: If you have not been able to return to the discussion, promise yourself that you will after you have had time to calm down. Remind yourself that your goal is to return to it. If at all possible communicate this to your partner: "I am too upset to talk right now. I need to discuss this with you when I am calmer."

Strategy # 4: Apologize when you have behaved or communicated in any of the ways that you have identified as destructive or blocking to your partner. Keep it brief and simple: "I am sorry for discounting your experience. I am working on being a better listener. That was an unfair tactic."

Personal strategies for change

Consider your personal patterns that stop or block continuous and successful flow of productive discussion and compromise. If you attack, or "blow up" rather than withdraw, consider taking a walk around the block and coming back to the discussion when you are able to calm down and use "I" statements, listen to your partner, as well as be heard.

If you say "yes" to avoid short term discomfort but do not follow through on your promises, develop a strategy to anticipate and remind yourself of the problems you will experience in the future by not doing what you say. Develop written cues as reminders and place them where you can refer to when tensions rise. Use them to reflect on what is realistic before making your next promise.

If you discount your partner's feelings or viewpoints, develop a strategy for refraining from doing so to get your point made. Develop written cues to remind you to listen and empathize rather than dismiss your partner. Be willing to use written reminders to short-circuit sarcasm and develop alternative verbal expressions that require a compromise be discussed and achieved, to replace ceaseless and ineffective "nagging."

Write down your personal strategies and written cues for change. (Personalize the ones suggested above, or customize to your needs.)

_____

_____

_____

_____

_____

_____

Remember to apologize

Genuine apologies help you to change! And they can feel good to you as well as your partner. A sense of mastery and self-esteem will replace self-defeating patterns of "being right." Try it. You will not be disappointed! Taking responsibility for your mistakes and correcting them actually gives you the feeling of being "in control" rather than "out of control" of the situation.

The link between intimacy and equality in marriage

Family communication either strengthens or inhibits affection, a key factor in a satisfying marriage. Researchers[26] describe communication to be the most pivotal dimension in family functioning. Communication that relies heavily on blaming, placating, whining, or sarcasm to express feelings leads to protracted discussions with less probability for reaching solutions and less "warm fuzzies" between spouses.

It is easy to intuitively identify when we are having difficulty being understood or getting our point across. Similarly, we can often feel when we do not connect with another person's interpretation of an experience. What is more difficult to understand is the relationship between our process of decision making and affection in marriage.

Control over finances is one hot area of conflict that can illustrate the decision making process and its impact on intimacy. Partners must feel that decisions are made fairly and that they each hold equal power in the relationship, or the affection in the marriage will suffer.

---

26. D. Olson, "Circumflex Model of Marital and Family Systems." In F. Walsh (Ed.), *Normal Family Processes*, 2nd edition (New York: Guilford Press, 1993).

Decision making power and intimacy

Dear Dr. Gayle,

My husband and I have been married for over a year now. We have a beautiful baby girl who is nine-months-old. I earn four times my husband's salary and it bothers him. Recently, I deposited a large amount of money into my father's account and did not tell my husband. He later found the deposit slip. He was upset that I did not ask permission to give my dad the money. I don't understand why I need to consult with him about how I spend my money, when I earn my own salary. What do you think?

Marietta

Dear Marietta,

The good news is that you are aware of how your husband feels about the fact that you earn a greater income.There is no doubt that traditional gender roles have defined men as being the "major bread-winners." No wonder he is sensitive! But no matter which spouse earns more, marriage involves sharing equally in the family's decision making processes. Do not shy away from talking about money. It is not a matter of "permission", but negotiating how the joint funds will be spent and how you will handle your financial decisions together.

You may be jumping to conclusions to assume that your husband wants unilateral control over whether you give your father money. Naturally, this is not a viable solution in a marriage based on equality. It is more probable that your spouse feels disrespected as his opinions were not included when you made this decision. Consulting one another about financial decisions shows respect. When both partners feel equal in the realm of decision making, the respect they communicate is most often reflected in the quality of affection they feel in their marriage.

Women have righteously complained about the tendency of their husbands to assume unilateral control of financial resources in the family because their husbands bring home the paycheck. Feminist family therapists have pointed out the fallacy of relegating women to non-decision making status merely because their work at home is "unpaid". Similarly, because your husband earns less then you do, is no reason to keep him out-of-the-loop.

Couples may consider making a budget, and rules, for monthly joint expenses. Naturally, contributions to the joint account would be based on equitable percentages that reflect differences in salary. After these expenses, and any savings they agree to deposit are satisfied, couples may agree to consult one another on any transaction that exceeds 100 dollars, or whatever amount they feel is significant enough to warrant joint decision making.

If a spouse feels "cramped" by this agreement, the couple could consider making an agreement for more separation around finances. For example, after monthly joint expenses were paid, each could be free to spend or save according to their own desires. This kind of negotiation allows for individual choice and freedom in money matters, but does not side step coming to an agreement about how decisions around money will be made.

Consider that your husband is responding to an inequity regarding the power to co-make decisions in the family, rather than attempting to block your ability to help your father or simply control you. Develop a strategy for dealing with money that reflects equitable sharing of finances and treats both of you respectfully when it comes to making decisions about your resources. You will feel more love flow between the two of you when you both feel a sense of equality in your decision making together.

Five More Elements of Healthy Communication

Your ability to listen and to express yourself in a non-blaming manner (using the previous exercises) makes you eligible for succeeding at integrating the next five ingredients researchers have identified for healthy family communication!

1. Speaking for yourself and not others

Children whose experiences are constantly explained by someone else may not develop their own sense of what their feelings or opinions are, much less be able to express themselves in the world. A developing sense of self includes speaking for yourself and not others, unless they are truly unable to do so (i.e., too young or too sick). Though children may not always be able to express themselves clearly, they will develop their ability to do so if given the opportunity.

Valuing the expression of feelings, however, does not mean you are always in agreement. Nor do feelings negate consequences or discipline when it is required. However speaking for others can also contribute to putting others, such as children, in the middle of marital conflict. When this happens, family communication can become particularly distressful.

> Example: Dad: "It's cold in here. Put this shirt on Sam."
> Mom: "It's not cold in here. Sam doesn't need that shirt."
> Sam (age twelve): " I don't want that shirt. It's ugly! I'm fine. Leave me alone!"

Children are less likely to become entangled in disagreements between parents if parents speak for themselves and request the same of their children.

> Example: Dad: "I'm cold. I'm going to get myself a shirt. Do you need one, Sam? How about you, Honey?" (directed to wife)
> Sam: "No thanks, dad. I'm fine."
> Mom: "I'm not cold either. Thanks."

Discuss with your partner: Did family members speak for each other in your childhood? Do members in your current family speak for themselves most of the time, ("I feel" vs. "You feel") or is it common practice to assume you can represent others' experiences in the family? Research on communication shows that when members commonly express feelings for others in the family, information is likely to be distorted and individuals experience difficulty being autonomous.

2. Personal sharing

The ability to share feelings of resentment as well as love and appreciation are examples of honesty and intimacy in the family. Feeling safe enough to share things that may be troubling requires that families do not expect perfection in people. Being human means that people may experience "unpopular" feelings in the family. But being able to express them will help ease the pain. In this way, families act as shock absorbers for one another. If self-disclosure is practiced, a family can be a safe place to retreat from the world, temporarily, while recovering from life's ups and downs.

Discuss with your partner: To what degree did you feel it was safe to express feelings in your family as a child? Evaluate how easy or difficult it is to share unpopular feelings with one another in your present family.

Together you set the climate for family intimacy and sharing. This is your chance to decide what kind of family atmosphere you want to create!

3. Clear messages

Whether a message is clearly communicated depends on how direct the communication is and if the verbal and non-verbal communication matches.

Example (indirect): "It would be nice if sometimes a person were able to do something in this family without criticism."

The above message is indirect in many ways. It lacks clarity about *who* is sending the message, *to whom* the message is being sent, *what* it is that is being criticized, *by whom*, and *what exactly is being asked for*. Indirect messages tend to be dead-ended because it takes so much energy to ascertain what is being said and what should be responded to. These communications rarely lead to anything other than frustration.

Example (direct): "I feel hurt when you criticize my cooking every evening. Please tell me what you want to eat." It is much easier to understand what the message is when it is clear and direct. The likelihood of some level of resolution of conflict between people increases.

Non-verbal tone that does not match the content of the message can also be confusing, particularly to young children who understand tonality but don't yet fully comprehend the meaning of words.

Example: Did you know I get (giggling) really angry when you (giggles) embarrass me by calling me names in front of your family?

Even for adults, the nonverbal tone communicates a much weaker message, one that is not meant to be remembered, or taken seriously.

Example: I feel really *angry* when you call me names in front of your family. It *embarrasses* me! A natural emphasis of tone on "angry" and" embarrasses" congruently communicates to the right hemisphere of the brain (which picks up tonality) that these feelings are important, to be taken seriously and remembered.

Sarcastic humor and criticism can also be frustrating and damaging when used as a "default" manner of communicating in a marriage. The following question and answer illustrates this.

If he loves me, why does he put me down so much?

Dear Dr. Gayle,
   My partner constantly makes fun of things I do. He asks me a question that requires an explanation. When I try to explain, he

makes fun of me and says I take a simple question and make it difficult. He asked me why it would take two days to set up my computers. He has no clue about computers. So I started by saying that first they have to come in and set up the equipment. He said I should have used the word "installed." I then was going to say how they have to download the software, and make sure all the equipment works. But as usual, he never gave me the chance. He started laughing at me, saying I was making a mountain out of a molehill. I got angry and slammed a pop can down and told him to stop "putting me down." This hurts, as I was often criticized by my parents growing up.

I love this person a lot. He treats me special in every other way. But I feel inadequate when I communicate with him. I don't know how to tell him sometimes his "kidding around" hurts my feelings.

Madeleine

Dear Madeleine,

It can be difficult to pierce humor when it is used as a defense. Your husband may have developed his humor to protect him from feelings of inadequacy. Putting you down may also be something that was done to him by his parents. But this is no excuse for continuing to make himself feel better at your expense!

You have taken the first step by being aware that you feel devalued when he uses sarcastic humor. Let him know there is a difference between laughing at someone and laughing with them. Tell him that while you do love him and appreciate the ways he does show his caring for you, that this is one style of communication that is damaging your affectionate feelings towards him.

The joining of two individuals in a long-term relationship requires that you develop your own customs and rules about family interactions. Naturally, since both of you come from different childhood experiences, you have internalized ways of relating that may have worked in that family, but do not work for the two of you with each other. You must come up with acceptable compromise based on your unique differences in order to forge a new "culture" of your own if your relationship is to succeed.

Ask your partner where his patterns of humor come from. Did they exist in his family? Or did he begin this way of putting others down as an adult? Let him know that you feel particularly vulnerable to "put downs" because of earlier abuse, as well. Ask for his sensitivity to this issue. Also ask for his feedback about anything that he feels you put him down about in any way. Let him know that you are willing to look at your own behavior and caretaking his needs, too. And continue to work on strengthening your own self-esteem and communication skills to increase your own resiliency.

If your partner truly wants to "kid around" ask him what effect he wants to have on you by doing so? Perhaps he will begin to see that the effect he wants is not what he is getting!

Exercise: Communication patterns

Consider and discuss the following questions with your partner:

1) What was the communication like between members of your family in childhood?

2) Was it direct or indirect? Clear or ambiguous?

3) Did nonverbal and verbal communication generally match, or were there incongruencies, double messages?

4) What was the role of sarcasm and criticism?

Explore your experience in your present family. If necessary, you can research this by listening closely during the next week and writing down your observations about your family's communication patterns.

4. Completing discussions

Researchers found that completing discussions on a topic during a conversation contributed significantly to healthy family communication.[27] Discussions that allow for democratic expressions, opinions, and sharing *while staying on track* enable children to learn the skills necessary to set and achieve goals. Critical thinking is a process that is learned in the family setting.

Distractions that block follow through on a topic can take a variety of forms: irrelevant asides, changing topics midstream, and interrupting the flow of discussion are all potential contributors to fuzzy thinking and potentially ineffective problem solving. However, a very interactive family may interrupt without damage to critical thinking and problem solving *if they get back on track* and carry a topic through to some sense of completion. Interruptions that add to the information needed or

---

27. L. C. Wynne, J. E. Jones, & A. Manhal, "Healthy Family Communication Patterns." In F. Walsh (Ed.), *Normal Family Processes,* 2nd edition (New York: Guilford Press, 1993).

develop a topic may be invigorating as long as these interruptions are not a result of one person dominating the discussion.

Topic changes or interruptions that are *in the service of keeping one person center stage* in the family result in one-sided discussions that may meet the need for attention of one family member to the exclusion of staying either on the topic or allowing other members a chance to express themselves.

Pay attention to discussions in your family. Ask yourself and your partner the following questions in relation to childhood family discussions and your own present family's debates:

1) Do topics reach natural closure or are there abrupt changes in topics that disrupt continuity?

2) Is there equal air time for all members who have something to say about a topic?

3) Do people disrupt the flow of conversation through topic changes? Distractions? Asides that pull attention away from completing thoughts or establishing a plan of action?

4) Do interruptions abort continuation or closure on the topic, or does someone bring the topic back for completion?

5. Respect and appreciation

The more each person feels like he or she matters, the easier the flow of communication in a family. To treat one another with respect for feelings, even when we disagree has clearly obvious benefits. However, it is less obvious whether, for other reasons, people feel unimportant in the family. Younger siblings are often the most vulnerable to feeling unimportant in a family because of their developmental limits.

For example, everyone else can do certain things like ride a bicycle, except for three-year-old Sam. His older sister Sarah, who is six, has already been to kindergarten and knows hundreds more things than he does. It is very easy for a younger child to see himself or herself as not being as valuable a contributor to the family. It is important to identify ways he or she is unique even though she is unable to do as many things as the older members in the family! And it is important to take time to listen to youngsters who do not yet have the vocabularies or speed in self-expression that their older siblings enjoy.

Families with one girl and three boys, or one boy and three girls may find that the odd-sexed sibling feels left out, instead of special.

Even moms who have a husband and three sons may feel left out in this way.

Ask your present family members about their sense of importance to the family. Respect for their feelings about their role in the family will be validating. Also ask yourself whether you felt you were an important member of your family in childhood?

Summing it up

When the "communication membrane" is healthy between family members, relationships are more likely to flourish. There is a smoother flow of emotions, which may also allow our love to be more fully expressed and received. It is my hope that this information will assist you on your journey as parents, with one another and with your children. As parents, you are the leaders and the best source of authority on your own children and their needs. You are in the best position to know what really works. Whatever your childhood experience, you are the parents now! It is your turn to decide what kind of family you want to make together.

A heightened capacity to speak directly, clearly and without blame will help you resolve problems as they happen. Meeting conflict with an ear that can really "hear" and heart that can "listen" leads to deeper and more rewarding relationships. Although research can point the way, it is up to each one of us to develop our family "communication membrane."

Sex and Healing in Marriage

What is the value of sex to a marriage? Although men and women may answer this question differently, most agree that sex is a critical element of a good marriage. However is it the quality of the sex rather than frequency alone that matters? And how does our early learning about sex contribute to the quality and pattern of sexual relating we develop in our marriages?

What is a "normal" sex life?

Dear Dr. Gayle,
  What would you consider to be a "normal" sex life in a marriage?
                                                              Robbie

Dear Robbie,
    As with most things in marriage, the definition of what is "normal" is left to the partnership between two people. Marriage is about meeting one another's needs. What is acceptable to one person might not be to the other. A marriage may be generally considered functional if both partners are satisfied with it.
    Often, the quality of sex in a marriage is more important than frequency. Again, if both partners enjoy and feel satisfied by their sexual connection, then it is functional for them. "Normal" sexuality could be defined in context of a person's capability for physiological orgasm. But what is normal sex for one couple would vary not only throughout the course of their own marriage, but in contrast to other couples. For example, it is normal—due to biological changes and environmental stress—for parents to have less sex in the months after a child is born.

Many things, including hormonal, environmental, and emotional stress, affect sexual expression in a marriage. Remaining connected on an emotional level may be reflected in an easy negotiation of sexual needs, while emotional disconnection or alienation can quickly lead to sexual disinterest by one or both partners.

Be aware that introducing the concept of "normal" may not prove to be a very useful approach in marriage. A partner who is accused of being "abnormal," often because they are not meeting the sexual needs of a spouse, is likely to feel judged or inadequate. This kind of approach usually drives a lover away, rather than increases interest in meeting the needs of his or her partner.

Sex is a vulnerable part of a marriage because sexual appetites differ and spouses depend on one another to meet sexual needs. This is a part of monogamy that partners must take seriously, particularly if one has a much greater sexual desire than the other.

It is up to both partners to address individual styles and desires. Talk with your partner about your feelings and needs and what your vision of sex is in your marriage. Then listen to your partner's opinion. While the presence of sexuality in a marriage is an important part of your relationship, the negotiation for when and how these sexual needs are met must be defined by the two of you.

Cultural programming about sexual intimacy

There are many obstacles that can act as potential roadblocks to rewarding sexual intimacy in a marital relationship. One primary theme is the cultural programming most of us experienced from childhood that clearly makes all sex "naughty." Regardless of our participation in the "sexual revolution," early associations can haunt us, particularly when we marry. I remember the first time I found out about sex and the fact that my parents had "it" with each other. I was appalled that they would do such things to one another with such private parts of their bodies (heretofore used only in the bathroom as far as I knew). I was ten years old and took the first opportunity to tell my younger nine-year-old cousin. She immediately revoked such illicit behavior from her own parents' bedroom with the declaration, "My father would never do *that* to my mother!" That stopped our discussions on the topic for some time.

Desensitization, then, is the first order of business for many of us before we can even begin to explore our sexuality. How we relate to our own sensuality is oftentimes through unacceptable fantasies, which although in conflict with our morality, match the cultural messages we absorb growing up.

During the course of marriage therapy with a couple in my practice in their sixties, the husband shared his experience of growing up male, which included the belief that when women said "no" they meant "yes." To be a successful male in his teenage years meant to "score" with a woman sexually. However this put him in great moral conflict. His wife of forty-one years shared that she learned being a "good" girl meant always saying "no" to her sexual feelings. This put her in conflict with her developing sexuality.

Throughout their marriage, which included growing both of their careers and raising their three children, sex became conflicted territory between them. She felt oppressed by his sexual overtures and he felt rejected by her. By sharing their experiences of growing up male and female, they discovered they had been set up by their cultural upbringing to be at war with each other sexually. They had never worked out a way for her to say "no" to sex without his experience being one of major rejection. Nor had she taken responsibility for *initiating* sex in the marriage. Talking about their adolescent years helped him take her refusals less personally and helped her to begin relating to her own sexual desires, causing her to become increasingly proactive in their sexual relationship.

They were also able to identify what contributed to her being turned on sexually and ways to accommodate one another when one was turned on and the other was not. Each sympathized with the formative conditioning their partner endured, that had been placed between them in their marital bed. They were able to find new approaches to one another in the bedroom that allowed for renewed romance, and greater freedom of expression to respond sexually to one another. Sharing their adolescent experiences with each other was one step towards desensitizing their early gender conditioning.

Sharing your sexual history with your partner

Schedule some private time with your partner to share your sexual experiences and feelings growing up. How did you first learn about sex? What were your initial feelings when you did? When and how did you first experience orgasm? What are your sexual fantasies? Have they changed over the years? Are you comfortable with them or not? Take turns sharing. Listen with compassion to your partner's experiences and stories. Explore stereotypes, whether each partner can say "yes" and "no" to sex without serious repercussions to the relationship, and how each takes responsibility for initiating conditions that promote and encourage sexual satisfaction in the marriage.

Shedding light on sexual thoughts, feelings, and fantasies helps you take charge of defining your own sexual relationship. Sharing responsibility for clarifying and developing conditions that promote romance and sexual satisfaction can strengthen your marriage. Simply taking time together to share in this way creates a space in time that says your relationship is meaningful. Attention to your marriage in this way helps give it priority in the midst of busy lives and schedules that can otherwise obscure the nourishment that a couple needs from one another. Your relationship is the foundation of your family. It is well worth the time and energy!

The following question and answer illustrates the way unrealistic expectations for mutual "instant arousal" can dampen sexual passion.

Sexual arousal begins internally

Dear Dr. Gayle,

I have been married for ten years. We have three kids ages nine, seven, six. My husband is the only man who ever made me have an orgasm. He was my fourth lover. When I first started having orgasms it would happen about every two-three days. Over the years it has dribbled to almost none. I usually only want sex about every two weeks to maybe once a month. But at that point I'll want it every day for about two maybe three, then I go back to not wanting it at all. My husband is thirty-four and he wants it anywhere from once a day to every other day. I'm only twenty-eight and I'm lucky if I want it once a month. I'm tired of making excuses. I seem to have more trouble having an orgasm as well as losing my sex drive. I feel badly because my husband is sweet to me and puts up with my shortcomings.

April

Dear April,

Perhaps the loss you are experiencing is related to your image of yourself as a sexually attractive woman, or "good" wife rather than your sex drive itself. There is nothing wrong with fluctuation in sex, or wanting more or less sex than your partner. In addition, the pressure you are feeling about sex may contribute to decreased desire.

There is a lot of hype and misinformation about sex in our culture. Commercial advertising and movies promote the idea that people are ready to be sexually active at any minute. Any variation or change in sexual activity is often experienced as a loss. Sexual appeal is projected onto the objects we buy as well as our relationships. For example, when I bought my black jeep, to my surprise, a colleague of mine described it as "sexy"! Our world inundates us with the suggestion that sexiness should be ever-present in our lives or something is wrong.

Often cultural biases acquired when we are young lead us to believe that the "other" is responsible for our sexuality. Contrary to popular belief, (or the beginning stages of falling in love) others do not "turn us on" sexually. We, in fact turn ourselves on through accessing our own desire, bringing positive sexual feelings to the center of awareness. This takes time (maybe ten minutes or less) but is a necessary precursor to physiological readiness for sex.

Naturally, when arousal happens quickly it feels as though someone else is responsible for our sexual response. Yet, it is the responsibility of each partner in a marriage to know how to access their own sexual landscape and bring it forward to the relationship. Clearly, partners influence one another. But accepting responsibility for self awareness is crucial to success in any area of marriage, and sex is no exception.

Let go of guilt. Instead, begin to explore the nature of your own sexuality. After three pregnancies, you may still be reclaiming your body as your own. Particularly if you have pressured yourself to keep up with your husband's rate of sexual desire.

You and your spouse are different. He has not experienced the pregnancies, the hormonal changes that you have. He has not shared his body in this way. If he is not the primary nurturer in the family and you are, then he does not have the daily physical contact with children that you may experience. These are just some of the things that may absorb your creative energy, causing you to desire sexual activity less. Also, your husband may not feel the societal pressure that a woman feels to be sexy in order to feel valued in the culture. Although he, like you, may experience cultural pressure about his sexual adequacy if he takes the difference in your sexual arousal personally.

It is natural for your sexual desire to ebb and flow, as you have described. It is unrealistic to believe that two people would not experience differences in their desires for sex. Lovemaking is an intimate activity requiring synchronicity of energy that is not always matched by your partner. More often than not, one partner is sexually aroused before the other. Sometimes a lover is sexually primed, physically and emotionally, while the other has not even thought about sex! Unfortunately, possibilities can be stymied when partners expect instant availability, rather than an invitation to *become* sexually aroused.

Sexual arousal begins internally. Heart rate, hormonal surges and other physical excitement follows a familiar, if not conditioned, pathway of sexual arousal in the limbic system of the brain. By the time a spouse has made a sexual overture to a partner, he or she has already experienced body changes. Their partner, however, may have other things on his or her mind. The initial overture can be perceived as a pressure if she or he expects (or is expected) to be instantly responsive sexually. This can lead to feelings of intrusion instead of invitation.

Realistic expectations can prevent the interpretation that lack of immediate sexual response is a personal rejection. When a sexual overture is registered as an invitation to become aroused, there is more likelihood that sexual lovemaking will occur. With the understanding that two partners may be differently primed, the invitation from one to another can be considered! "Consideration" time allows for the partner who has not been thinking sexually to entertain the possibility (without pressure) and trace the biologic responses in their internal landscape of the body that creates "turn on."

The fact that you have orgasms with your husband means that you have passion for him and you are orgasmic. You may have only had orgasms with your husband because he is the first man you trusted enough to let go. Trust is an important ingredient in intimacy. However, it is critical for a woman to know and relate to her own anatomy for orgasm, independent of a partner so that she can guide her spouse in pleasuring her more effectively.

Women are often not encouraged to understand their bodies, therefore they may depend on their husbands to develop their relationship to orgasm or other sensual, sexual pleasure. Although it is true that relationships are the vessel to contain our development, it is also important that we understand and relate to our sensual nature independently. Lonnie Barbach's book, *For Yourself: The Fulfillment of Female Sexuality*,[28] as well as the chapter on women's sexuality in Karen Johnson's book, *Trusting Ourselves,*[29] are good resources for deepening your relationship to your own sexual nature. Dr. Johnson makes the point that although boys handle their penis from a young age, a girl's genitals are not as immediately available for exploration. Masturbation may come more readily in a boy's development and is often supported by his friends. Girls, on the other hand, are not encouraged to develop their relationship to sexual pleasure. Yet without exploring what brings pleasure independent of a partner, it is difficult to take personal responsibility for sexual responsiveness in the marriage.

Explore your sensual and sexual nature and become aware of your personal biological rhythms. Invite your husband to join in your sexuality when you are ready to share, and interpret his overtures as invitations to do the same. You might also benefit by sharing your sexual histories and development with one another. Beginning to talk about sex will help defuse guilt. By opening an avenue for communication, you will no longer be avoiding the subject, but moving forward together. And in some cases, it is the communication itself that becomes the foreplay!

The Healing Potential of Marriage

Marriage is a matrix for healing past wounds as well as a crucible for ongoing nourishment and growth of both partners. We all come to our relationships with yearnings based on unfulfilled childhood promises. Sometimes we are aware of these unmet needs and their effects on our present relationships and other times we are not. When these hidden desires can be understood, it may be possible for the marriage to meet our needs rather than frustrate them.

The nature of such healing when it occurs creates powerful and lasting bonds. And in some ways all marriages are based on each partner's ability to recognize and meet needs of vulnerability in the other. If we can identify

28. L. Barbach, *For Yourself: The Fulfillment of Female Sexuality* (New York: Anchor Books, 1976).
29. K. Johnson, *Trusting Ourselves* (New York: Atlantic Monthly Press, 1991).

with our partner's fears, hopes and doubts it is easier to empathize and offer realistic support and comfort. But to be able to give support to our spouse we must also be able to accept our own vulnerabilities with compassion.

An elderly friend of mine lost her mother when she was two years old. She and her older sister spent eight months in an orphanage until her father could find another wife to raise his children. The early wound of maternal loss left her sensitive to abandonment and rejection. By early adulthood she was ripe for what Wallerstein and Blakeslee define as the "rescue marriage."[30] The man she married was the youngest of eight children in a family raised by his mother when his father abandoned the family for another woman. The fit was a good one. She needed a man who would not leave her and he needed to be the committed family man his father never was. The healing that evolved for both was deep and lasting. And their mutual affection outweighed the inevitable disappointments in one another.

To some extent we all marry for reasons of rescue. Hope and desire to heal old wounds is hidden in our hearts, if not our minds. Sometimes the agenda of the heart is realized in a relationship. Other times it is not and history repeats itself causing old wounds to fester and reopen.

Particularly in stepfamilies, where previous divorce creates an aftermath of loss and disappointment, stepmothers and stepfathers are catapulted into the role of "rescuer" whether they like it or not. Minimally, the mother or father hopes for a more satisfying relationship with the second marriage partner in ways that the former marriage failed. In more extreme cases, abandonment by a biological parent sets the scene for a child's testing the relationship with the stepparent in extreme and sometimes puzzling ways. Sudden outbursts by a child can be of surprising intensity when charged with pain from the relationship with the biological but absent parent.

Working through issues of trust and security is difficult when previous pain plagues new relationships. However, when partners are able to develop trust and be there in ways that were not experienced in the past, relationships are fortified in gratitude and appreciation which is rewarding to all. As my friend, now in her late seventies, after over fifty years of marriage put it, "He loved me, and I needed that!"

The success of the "rescue" is founded to some extent in the conscious awareness of vulnerability. It is only with this awareness that we

30. J. Wallerstein & S. Blakeslee, *The Good Marriage* (New York: Warner Books, 1996).

can separate our feelings of past pain from the present when it does get stirred up. And we can appreciate our partners when they are able to come through for us. Because we know our needs and accept them, we can recognize when our yearnings have been fulfilled.

Too often, our unconscious, unmet needs come out in behaviors our spouses do not understand. When this happens, it can be important to look at your marriage as a container for growth and healing, rather than get mired down in disappointment. The following question and answer illustrates this choice in marriage.

He has a new baby and a good wife, so why is my husband depressed?

Dear Dr. Gayle,

I am a new mother. I am one of those young mothers who although always wanted children never really thought that I would be somebody's "mom." My husband is ten years older than me and had just gotten out of a very depressing, bizarre, unhealthy relationship when we met. The woman he was involved with had a eight-year-old son when they met . He maintains that he stayed in the relationship because he didn't think she was a good mother and grew very attached to the child. Ten years later he was saturated with her "problems" and separated from her. He said he always wanted children of his own but never believed he could or would be able to have them. Well now he has a new healthy nine-week-old and is depressed most of the time.

What could he possibly be depressed about? He has his own child, he has a sane, drug free, intelligent wife, he has a nice new home, he knows that his son is being well cared for. Whenever I question him he cannot provide any answers; sometimes he doesn't answer at all. I am a no-nonsense type of person and I fear that I will one day walk away from him for my own mental health and the mental health of my son. What should I do?

"Worried"

Dear "Worried,"

You are right to be concerned about your husband. He is expressing symptoms of a depression rooted in his own childhood. His attraction to his first relationship was to save the little boy with whom he identified. Now that he has separated himself from this role in his previous relationship and found a more healthy situation, he is left to face his own depression.

Your loving care of your infant son provides a stimulus for your husband to get in touch with his deep neglect. It is likely that his relationship with his own mother resembled the experience of little boys he tried to save. Now it is time for him to rescue the little guy inside! But he will need your help and possibly professional help to do so.

Remind yourself of what qualities you fell in love with when you met your husband. Remember that he is still the same person covered in a fog of depression. Realize, too, that he has learned to walk away from the unhealthy situation in which he was entangled. Give him credit for recognizing the emotional bankruptcy of his role in his previous relationship. But require that he seek help for finding the answers to your very important questions regarding his happiness. Let him know that you love and care about him, but that his depression is deadening the relationship.

Your husband's current crisis stems from some sense of neglect or abandonment that was real for him in childhood, maybe even as early as infancy. Coming to terms with his childhood relationships to his parents is essential if he is to have energy available for bonding with his own son. Finding his place as a father and husband holds promise for being exactly "what the doctor ordered." However the prescription is not as simple as you expected it to be!

Your adjustment to motherhood is quite stressful by itself. You are no doubt experiencing great disappointment in your partner's ability to nurture you through this period. You will need support of friends and perhaps other new mothers to help you process your disappointment. Without appropriate support, you will be prone to feelings of abandonment and likely to project this disappointment onto the marriage.

This is a formative transition in your family's development. If your husband does not treat his depression, you may find that you feel you have two babies on your hands. Each day this experience persists, your resentment grows and the marriage is being damaged. Hope can be gained from taking action. You may experience great relief, when your husband acknowledges his problem and seeks competent treatment. Passivity, on the other hand, will almost certainly assure that your desire to leave will become a reality.

Your husband's healing requires his acceptance of his problem. If he takes responsibility for his own "rescue" this time, he has a great family to support him. This much he has changed! Joining a father's group can actively support his involvement with his son. And finding a place by your side as a partner may come more quickly with both group and individual support.

Be patient. Your marriage can become the healing vessel necessary to help both of you find the answers. Be firm in your need for him to seek treatment, but do not reject or punish him. And take care of your needs for support and companionship. Join a new mother's group, seek out friendships, and establish family goals with your husband. Imagine a possible future together in which you tell the story of how you successfully addressed this first hurdle together. The key to your family's development will lie in your ability to help one another, as well as take responsibility for self-healing. Teamwork is not always easy, but it can result in feeling bonded in response to problems, instead of alienated.

Look on this year as a journey in your family's development. Going up a steep hillside can be difficult, but putting one foot ahead of another inevitably results in progress towards the top. You may reach the top by the time you celebrate your son's first birthday, or you may be half-way or three-quarters of the way there. This first year as a family may represent the first major challenge for growth and a time of healing in your relationship. You owe it to your son, and each other to develop the kind of family you want. See how much can change in the next year, when you work at it!

Exercise: Recognizing potentials for healing

Discussing the following questions can be a start towards developing or recognizing potential in your marriage for this kind of healing. If abandonment pain is identified in either you or your spouse's past history, the resolution of this wound will play a part in determining the success of your marital relationship. Explore the element of rescue present in your marriage. The potential for realistically meeting security needs in the relationship will be critical to cementing your bond with one another. Or potentially breaking a relationship, if abandonment patterns repeat.

Take time to sit down with your partner and ask the following questions of one another:

1) Is there a history of parental abandonment in your childhood, or spousal abandonment in a previous relationship? If so, how do you see

these past wounds affecting you in your current relationship with me? When you feel this past pain is triggered in our marriage, how do you want me to respond?

2) In your experience, what is the greatest strength I bring to our marriage? The greatest weakness?

3) How do you need me? How do you think I need you?

4) What are your greatest dreams and aspirations? For the relationship? The family? Yourself? Your greatest fears for our marriage?

5) Do you feel the two of us are a good match? How so? And how not? What do you need from me for it to feel like a better match?

Generally, if your partner's needs are in line with the kind of person you want to be, it can be a good match. If not, can you see yourself changing to meet your spouse's needs? Will such change benefit you in your development? Clarifying deep and primary needs in the relationship can help build a marriage with potential for powerful and profound healing for both of you.

SEVEN

What Is "Good Enough" Parenting?

Attunement and Self-Esteem In Child Rearing

Raising children is one of the prime tasks of a marriage. Raising them well should be a motivating factor that informs all of our decision making while our children are growing. But no parents are perfect! Finding the balance between meeting our children's needs and our own, appropriately, is a continuous adjustment.

"Good enough" parenting

Although we all love our children, researchers[31] [32] who study infant and child development document that children need something more in order to develop a true and solid appreciation of who they are in the world. With greater understanding of what contributes to healthy development in newborns, infants, and children, it becomes clear that adequate "attunement" is also desirable.

To "attune" to our child means that we attempt to respond to his or her needs, particularly emotionally, resulting in the child's sense of being understood, cared for, and valued. Depending on the age and development of the child this means different things. Attuning to a two-

---

31. D. Stern, "The Early Development of Schemas of Self, Other, and Self with Other." In J. Lichtenberg & S. Kaplan (Eds.), *Reflections on Self-Psychology* (Hillsdale, N.J: The Analytic Press, 1983).

32. M. Mahler, F. Pine, & A. Bergman, *The Psychological Birth of the Human Infant* (New York: Basic Books, 1975).

year-old child in the midst of a temper tantrum will include not only responding with appropriate limits, but understanding what the emotional meaning of the outburst might be. Is he or she tired? Angry? Hurt? Challenging limits to get clarity? In contrast, attuning to a newborn's wails will always be an attempt at primary soothing, as limit-setting of any kind would be inappropriate. To determine the "attuned" response, we must seek to truly understand the nature of the experience of the child and his or her needs, even though they cannot always tell us. The job of parenthood can be a highly challenging one!

Yet, if we can maintain a clear vision of our goal, to be as attuned as possible, we will inevitably learn more. If at first we do not succeed, sooner or later we will come to better understand our children and be better able to meet their emerging needs. With practice we will become better parents and gain a clearer vision of what we believe will make a difference in our children's development.

Still, the world is not a perfect place and we cannot be perfect parents. Though we will often meet our children's needs, we will sometimes frustrate them. Ideally we can provide a matrix in which the frustration itself becomes a tool for building strength of character. Psychologists have termed this "optimal frustration." The key here is to determine what amount of frustration is overwhelming and will result in a breakdown of a healthy sense of self for the child, and what is benign or even advantageous to work through with appropriate emotional support. This balance creates the essence of the "good enough parent."[33]

The dilemma of "good enough" parenting is at the heart of parents' questions about many things. One common example revolves around how to get a child to sleep through the night. What is too much crying and what is not? How soon should I go to him or her in the middle of the night? Again the answers to these questions depend upon your child's unique set of needs as well as your own. It also depends on your family's style and values. In her book, *The Sleep Book For Tired Parents*[34] Rebecca Huntley offers various strategies for walking this line of maintaining empathy and attunement to your child's needs while taking care of your own.

The following question and answer illustrates the struggle to find the right fit between parent and child.

33. D. W. Winnicott, *The Family and Individual Development* (New York: Routledge, 1989).
34. R. Huntley, *The Sleep Book for Tired Parents* (Seattle, WA: Parenting Press, 1991).

Helping toddler to sleep alone

Dr. Gayle,

I cannot get my fourteen-month-old son to sleep in his own bed. My husband and I have tried everything, but when I put him in his bed he screams until I can't stand it anymore. When he is with us, he stays up until at least one in the morning. This is putting a strain on our marriage, not to mention my nerves.

Ann

Dear Ann,

Your son is in need of your guidance. If your son still naps, consider decreasing his daytime naps, so that he becomes more tired at the end of the day. It would also be wise to initiate a bedtime ritual that allows him to adjust to a nightly separation from you.

Talk to him when you put him down to bed. Review what his activities were during the day. Rub his back, read several books, and sing a goodnight song while putting him to bed. It is important that you do not let his crying disrupt your calm. Instead, repeatedly tell him he will be fine, and explain to him where mommy and daddy are sleeping. You might want to give him a cuddly toy animal.

If he is sleepy enough, he will be more likely to succumb to your reassuring voice and gentle, but firm, persistence. Take turns putting him to bed, so that he can experience both mom and dad as his primary nurturers at bedtime.

You might also consider whether he is getting enough of you during the day. Does he spend time with you on a daily basis, or does someone care for him other than yourself? If he is crying because he misses you, consider spending close time with him before putting him to bed each evening. He will learn to count on this period of time as his and be more willing to relinquish you at bedtime.

If he is with you most of the day, rest assured that his crying is a sign that he is attached to you, and naturally orients himself to be in your presence. It is his job to cry (survival instinct), and yours to establish limits that you can live with, and help him adjust to, over time.

Be prepared to stay in his room up to thirty minutes the first night, before his crying truly subsides. Patiently wear him out with persistent reassurances and cooing. Absorb his screams, neutrally and calmly. In other words, *find your own sense of centeredness* inside. This is necessary in order for your child to sense that he is indeed secure in separating from you at night. Children often pick up their parents' inner calm—or inner exasperation!

Consider returning in the night to reassure him with your presence, if necessary. He will eventually learn that his own bed is a safe and secure place. But do not underestimate the quality of your own internal resolution in calming him.

Keep in mind that your most effective allies in parenthood are patience, calm and determination. Learn to answer his tears with these qualities, and you will develop the skills you need to help him "let go" and trust the guidelines you establish for him, now and in the future.

Learning from our mistakes

As parents, we all naturally fail at times. But if we are committed to parenting as important work, we will be able to correct our mistakes and learn from the experience. Children do not need "perfect" parents. However children do need parents they can trust to reflect on their actions and attempt to repair misunderstandings when they occur. This working through is an act of attunement and strengthens the bond between parent and child.

It is essential to remember that our failures can in part create the healthy disappointments that children must work through to gain strength. However, these are the inevitable failures that occur, *despite* our best and determined efforts to be attuned and to provide the most optimal environment we can for our children. Therefore we will not have to concern ourselves with perfection. Thankfully, we can narrow our focus to being the best parent we can along this path of family-making we have all chosen, and turn our attention towards a deeper understanding of what it means to be attuned to our children. Then we can rest assured that our natural failings will be enough to provide our children with some appropriate frustration along the way!

Even when we are doing our utmost to be sensitive to our own child's feelings based on our memory of our childhoods, and our child-rearing philosophy, we as parents may still misunderstand our children. Let's take a look at some of the most common ways that this can happen.

Healthy attunement or over-identification?

Our ability to attune as parents depends not only on the child, but on his or her stage of development and on the emotional legacy of accurate understanding we received from our own parents. The ability to attune also depends on the personality and temperament of the child and how easy or difficult it is for us to relate to a particular child, given our own individual personality traits and family upbringing. Giving nurturance to a child includes identifying with the infant and later, the developing adolescent, enough to have empathy for their situation in the world and the control they have or do not have over it. It is sometimes easy for us to identify with wounds we had as children that we swear we will not do to our children. However, often we can over-identify, and actually be out of attunement with our children, in an attempt to heal personal wounds from our past.

Projecting our own childhood experience is a common pitfall conscientious parents fall into when they have difficulty separating themselves from their own offspring, who have not experienced the same childhood wounds. There can exist a subliminal drive to re-experience childhood through our own kids, but this time to have it "right." In an attempt to heal past pain, we may unwittingly project it onto our child's behavior because it "looks" similar to our pain, although the meaning for the child may be entirely or significantly different. In such cases, parenting reactions that originate to answer our childhood pain miss the real needs of the child who stands before us, *a completely different person with a different set of experiences*.

Naturally, it is true that we can repeat traumas to our children (such as child abuse) when we are unaware of our own pain. The old adage of "what was good enough for me should be good enough for junior" reflects the attitude in which these painful legacies are passed down through generations. By not identifying what was painful to us in childhood, we are more likely to repeat the damage. However, as parents become attuned to their childhood experience, they often try to heal their own early developmental wounds in ways that are inappropriate for their children. The following case illustrates this potentiality.

A thirty-five-year-old mother complained about her four-year-old child's persistent tantrums. Sally was a stay-at-home mom who spent most of the first two years at home caring for Elia, and had put him in very part-time daycare in the last two years. Though he spent plenty of time with her, he seemed extremely unhappy to be separated from her, though he played very well and happily once she left. Elia would not let her leave him without major distress and had difficulty sleeping at night, crying profusely to have her stay with him in his room. No amount of being with him or attempts at soothing activities or objects satisfied him or caused him any greater ability to fall asleep on his own. Sally and her husband were desperate for sleep and to answer their child's needs. Yet no matter what they did to comfort him before bedtime, he screamed and cried relentlessly for one of them to sleep with him each night.

Sally had experienced very little emotional attunement to her needs as a child, particularly around getting appropriate help and support from her parents. She had been left to fend for herself in many ways, including being given money to go out and buy herself a wardrobe at age ten. She was told that she was indeed loved, but both of her parents worked outside the home full time once she began school, and did not have time to attend to her needs, particularly with the trouble her older brother was causing them.

Her mother left her cakes and other sweets to show her affection, and Sally ended up battling bulimia in her later adult life, partially an expression of the anger she could not express directly in her role of "good girl" in the family at the time. She resented being forced into independence at such an early age, and felt sadness and anger at not having received more guidance as a child. Instead, she had been lost in the role of the "good" child, while her parents spent most of their energies dealing with her older brother who earned himself the role of "trouble maker." Sally had worked through these feelings with her mother to a great extent, and enjoyed a positive relationship with her as an adult. Still it was hard for Sally to observe the way in which she had projected her own unmet childhood needs onto her son.

Sally and her husband Sam finally sought some brief-term counseling for their son, frightened that he was in some distress that was not being resolved. Following a thorough evaluation, their counselor assured them that their son was actually quite independent and capable when he was at preschool. He had no trouble traveling a distance to the bathroom facilities by himself. He could be with friends or play by himself with ease. Elia was clearly not in distress of abandonment!

Sally came to understand that she had projected her own intense fears regarding any distress that her son might have, to such an extent that he had learned a pattern of getting what he wanted by increasing his demands; this indeed became distressful, as his parents were unable to assure him that he in fact would be just fine in his own bed. He had somehow internalized the idea that he should never be left by his mother, or left alone at night. Although most of his development progressed smoothly, transitions involving separation became highly charged between mother and son.

Throughout Elia's life it had been difficult for Sally to differentiate normal stress from distress when the two of them separated. Naturally, this became more problematic as her son grew older and needs for dependency and developing independence clashed. Both mother and son were caught in confusing normal, healthy separation with abandonment. Elia's father, who was not in a primary caretaking role and had his own abandonment issues, was not able to intervene effectively to break the pattern of over responsiveness that Sally showed Elia at these times, and it had grown into a vicious cycle; a virtual battle of wills with enough drama to wrench the heart of any parent. But within a short time, when her son learned his parents would not respond to his demands because he really was okay, he was able to sleep peacefully by himself, and the extreme tantrums upon separation diminished.

Attunement to Elia, who had not suffered forced independence too early, meant a *genuinely* confident and realistic expectation that he would be able to soothe himself and fall asleep on his own. Elia needed his parents to guide him in this way, but it had been difficult for Sally and Sam to separate *normal* stress of inevitable separations because of Sally's fears, based on her own consistently unmet needs as a child. With the guidance of a counselor she did answer her own need for reassurance, which she could then pass on to her son with confidence.

The realignment of the couple's relationship was also helpful, as both parents learned and bonded from the experience of helping their son enjoy more independence. It left more room for couple's relating. And Sally learned to rely on Sam to help her sort through her feelings as a parent, while Sam learned that he had much more to offer as a vital part of the parenting team!

Whether we seek professional help along the way or not, most of us have come across these times in parenting where we identify our unmet childhood needs in the cries of our children. Getting help to sort things out with a spouse, a friend, a relative, or a professional means you are answering your need to reach out and depend on others. The following questions can help you reflect on the role your own projection of childhood pain may have in a situation, and assist you in sorting out what you believe is healthy attunement to your child, rather than a wish or desire to heal your own "inner child."[35]

Ask Yourself

1. In the present situation, do I feel overly charged about how my child should feel?

2. Does it remind me of anything particularly painful that happened to me as a child? If so, is my child experiencing the same intensity of this feeling as I did in childhood?

3. Do my child's previous experiences in this area equal the deprivation or pain of my childhood experiences at the same age? Or is it milder or not comparable? Do I know the range of what is normal distress in this situation or am I confused by the reminder of my own pain?

4. What is the meaning of this experience to my child and what does he or she need?

5. How is my child's experience different than mine? How is it similar? Be sure to include an assessment of your child's particular temperament compared to your own, in answering this question.

Contrasting previous experiences of your child to yourself at that age, the availability of support experienced as a child compared to your child in the present situation, and the particular *meaning* the event has for your child can help you sort through your past, finding the most accurate attunement to your child.

As research on patterns of child abuse bears out, parents are less prone towards repeating abuse when they have become aware of their own past hurt. *But we must go beyond simply identifying our childhood pain to be truly attuned to our children.* When we respond to children as if they bear our own scars we fail to see them in their own right. The child's needs can become distorted, leaving him or her vulnerable to misattunement, as in the above example. Finding a neutral

---

35. John Bradshaw has various books and tapes on this topic, available from The Center for Recovering Families in Houston Texas.

path, one that is not reactive but truly thoughtful and aware, is some-times the hardest one to walk.

Empathy and reflection of feeling

Children need our accurate reflection of their feelings so that they develop not only words to express feelings, but ways to understand themselves and their experiences. Reflecting to young children, or older adolescents, that they are angry, disappointed, or matching their delight and enthusiasm about something they have done, is a necessary part of their development. When traveling through times of stress or change, or when facing failure or disappointment, children need to feel that their emotions can be named, reflected back to them, and accepted as natural and understandable events. It is through this process of naming feelings that a child grows a sense of self. The following question and answer illustrates how important it can be to understand the emotional mean-ing of your child's misbehavior.

Four-year-old lying about misbehavior

Dr. Gayle,

I have a four-year-old son. Please help with the situation we are dealing with. I woke up this morning and went into his room where he had been playing, presumably for some time while my husband and I were sleeping. There was black fuzz all over his floor and when he caught me examining it, he proceeded to explain that somebody had gone into my room, taken a pair of scissors and cut the ears and tail off his stuffed dog. He then pro-duced the earless, tail-less dog; divulged the hiding place of the scissors in question (his hamper); and revealed that the ears and tail had been thrown away.

I explained that somebody had broken the rules of the house by taking the scissors and ruining the toy, not to mention that an innocent toy had been ruined. My son offered several more possible suspects, the bad kids at school (I explained that there was no one else in the house); a plastic hamburger meal toy (I explained that the toy is not real and can neither walk into my room nor use scis-sors). I then asked what should happen to somebody who did these things and my son said they should get a time out. I asked again who somebody might be and my son very discreetly pointed to him-

self and began to cry because he didn't want a time out. I hugged
him, told him I loved him but that he still needed the time out
because he broke the rules. I told him I was very proud that he told
the truth and that I knew it was hard to do. He stayed in time out
for about two and a half minutes.

I feel a little frustrated. We know so much more about child rear-
ing than our parents did but it feels like I have less answers. I also
have concerns because my son is the product of a former marriage
to a man with severe emotional problems. He is my only child so I
don't know what's "normal."

Ella

Dear Ella,

Your son's behavior is normal! Not only did he tell you the truth,
but his actions were relegated to his own property. Be careful that
you do not project your ex-spouse's emotional problems onto your
son. Seeing him through a lens of anxiety could distort your ability
to respond to his needs.

Most children do experiment with lying at some point and four
years old is a common age for this kind of behavior. Children are
becoming aware of the world they live in and their ability to manipulate it. Your son's behavior gave you an opportunity to teach him
values, which is your job as a parent. You were kind and loving, but
firm. He no doubt got your message!

But, do take into consideration two important pieces that you
may have missed and may be interrelated. These are: 1) your associ-
ation that he would somehow be emotionally ill, like his father; and
2) exploring the true meaning of your son's behavior.

The intensity of your concern about lying for this first time
offense suggests that you may be susceptible to viewing his behavior in all "or nothing" terms that are based on your fears about his
father rather than your knowledge of your son. The scenario
would look like this: You might begin to see his behavior as
"good" or "normal" only if he follows strict and narrow guidelines.
Any deviation from being "good" could become overly charged
with anxiety that he is like his father. You would be vulnerable to
overreacting when your son does need special attention, or when
he does make mistakes. Your anxiety could cause you to be
unavailable to him for problems that will inevitably arise through-

out childhood. And he could reflect your anxiety by refraining from asking for your help when he needs it. Over time, a pattern of lying and deception could develop from your fears, if your anxiety overrides your ability to separate your anxiety about your ex-spouse from your experience of your son. However, do not despair, I do not think this is the case at this time! I am merely playing out the potential for your consideration.

Become curious about the meaning of your son's behavior. By focusing only on the act of lying and "the rules" you may miss important information about his emotional or intellectual life. Could he be expressing anger or feelings of hurt? Children express feelings through play. What might be your son's real reason for wanting to cut off the ears and tail of his stuffed dog? It is possible that he has feelings coming up about his father at this time, and this might be an opportunity to address them, rather than to be afraid of these issues.

Feelings about his dad will no doubt surface at some point and helping him to resolve them will be a natural part of his development. Also consider the possibility that his behavior was more investigative in nature. Your interpretation that he "hurt an innocent toy" may or may not be in line with his real intent. What if he was practicing surgery on his own toy? Or practicing manipulation of future artistic forms? His behavior could represent an early interest in science or even art, though it would be too early to know for sure.

Consider, too that he may not have interpreted the house rules to include that he could not experiment with that which was his. There could be contradictory messages to sort out here. I remember my own daughter mutilating her Barbie doll because she wanted to see what it would look like with a hair-cut. She felt it was hers and that she had a right to change her hair-do! And finally, is there any possibility that he might want to repair his dog? If so, helping him to sew the ears and tail back on (if at all possible, and if they could be found) might be appropriate consequences to include, particularly if he responded positively to the idea of reparation.

Naturally, rules are important and need to be upheld. But also allow yourself to be interested in who your child is and what he is trying to express. Do not narrow your focus to crime and punishment, without fair investigation into meaning and intent! Though the intent may not change the consequences, it will shed light on understanding your son's uniqueness. It is possible that your innermost fear about your son replicating his father's behavior may have distracted you from what otherwise may have been a very natural curiosity into his motives.

This incident of misbehavior created an opportunity for teaching values of honesty, clarifying rules, and getting to know your son better. You are capable of loving consequences and clear boundary setting. Both of these are qualities essential to good parenting. (And you are conscientious to boot!) Future opportunities will arise for value clarification. And when they do, consider adding an element of curiosity about what makes this little guy tick to your parenting formula!

Attunement to others

Through all of the attunement we are working towards in our relationships with our children, it is essential that we assist them to develop an awareness of others' needs and feelings as well. To be capable of relating is necessary not only to survive in the world, but to do so in a way that brings us happiness and connection to one another instead of loneliness and alienation. Teaching our children about the value of human relationship and caring values is traditionally saved for daughters in our culture. However, an increasing number of men who write and speak about fatherhood[36] are expressing the need for human nurturing as a necessary part of men's development as well.

Sons as well as daughters benefit from an understanding of feelings and relationship. And your feelings as a parent are no exception to the rule. Though you as parents are the leaders, this does not mean you do not have feelings and needs, too. Allowing your children to appropriately give and care for you should also be a factor in the equation. One child may be easier for you to parent than another. There are no perfect children. As with any relationship, some of us are better or worse matches for each other. Striving for balance and learning, with humor by our side, may be our best allies in walking the path of the "good enough" parent.

---

36. B. Linton, *The Developmental Stages of Fatherhood*. Unpublished doctoral dessertation, Columbia Pacific University (1992). Dr. Linton is also the founder and developer of The Father's Forum in Berkeley, California, where he conducts fathering groups. See www.fathersforum.com.

Parental influence and peer pressure

Peer relationships are a crucial element in your child's development. But they do not replace parental influence; rather, these relationships interact with the ongoing nature of the parent-child bond! As a parent, you are like the sun, always constant though periodically out of sight as the world revolves. Your child's experience of peer pressures and influence cycles like the moon, waxing as your child grows towards pubescence and waning at the approach of high school graduation. Remember, however, that the moon depends on its relationship to the sun for its very light! What your sons or daughters experience in the world will be filtered through their primary parent-child relationships, for better or worse.

Parents serve as a young child's first and major reflection of who they are in the world. A strong psychological foundation early in life buffers later insults to self-esteem that inevitably occur on the playground and throughout a child's interface with their peer group. Likewise, a faulty self-image acquired early in life creates greater vulnerability to outside devaluation when it occurs. A child with a poor psychological foundation will incorporate self-doubt more readily in negative social situations. When a child has been inadequately nurtured in the early years the likelihood is greater that detrimental peer interactions can become a central organizing theme in a child's identity rather than a transient phenomenon.

A child requires nurturance and protection throughout childhood. If the family is an effective source of protection, parental influence will be powerful. But like any long-term relationship, your connection with your child must remain "current" throughout childhood and adolescence in order for you to effectively guide him or her through periods of development when peer pressure *is* high! The fact that peer pressure exists is not a "problem" by itself, if your family atmosphere promotes three basic elements.

First, children need to experience *both* a sense of "belonging" in their families, *and* an experience that they are valued for their individuality, or how they stand "apart." The security of belonging to a family group provides natural "immunity" against the propensity to adopt peer groups and values blindly (such as gangs) to answer the basic human need to be included and protected. And a home environment in which it is safe to express differences sets the stage for meeting the need to be unique and special. These two elements are a must in your family's atmosphere.

Promote a safe atmosphere for expressing "unpopular" feelings and topics. Stay connected with your youngster through discussion that allows for radical ideas, even though you do not believe in them yourself. Make room for differences and, yes, undeveloped "opinions." This allows you to share your worldly experience and perspective with your young ones without "shoving it down their throats." Although your child may not believe what you say at that moment, he or she is quite likely to consider the validity of your viewpoint at a later time because of your ongoing relationship!

Keep lines of communication not only open, but vibrant! Developing avenues of shared activity and predictable family rituals (like eating dinner together) allows you to remain a strong influence over time. Keep in mind that peer influence measured at age twelve may well undergo a complete shift by seventeen years of age. Your continued respectful involvement in your child's life in the form of shared activities, ongoing family rituals, and proactive guidance can make a big difference in who he or she turns to in times of stress or crisis.

The third element that will fortify your ongoing influence in your child's life is flexibility. As a parent, you must adapt to your child's expanding and changing interests. This means that it is not enough to "check in" with your twelve-year-old about life at school, but develop meaningful activities that can be shared throughout your child's development. This could mean learning about things you have absolutely no inclination towards, except that your child loves it! The nuances of skateboarding technique could be the farthest thing from your mind, but seeing the world through your child's eyes will keep you conversant and connected.

Be willing to stretch your interests so that you develop shared activities together. This allows you to "hang out" in a way that can allow you to become an invaluable resource when "troubles" arise in a child's social life. When the opportunity does arise, be a good listener. Do not try to "fix it." Instead, allow your child to express feelings and support him or her towards making decisions that answer essential needs. Sometimes it just helps to know that a competent adult had similar feelings of inadequacy or jealousy when her or she was in the sixth grade, too!

Remember that no child skates through childhood unscathed. Healthy family relationships and processes provide resources for a child to overcome negative influences of all kinds and to triumph over adversity. It is your job to hold a broader perspective for your child, which will be appreciated over time. Your child will respond to your influence because he or she has the experience that you have his or her best interests at heart! Trust is the key here.

It is through all of our relationships that we learn who we are, who we are not, and who we want to become. If we have prepared our children well, it is because we have helped them understand themselves and cope with a taste of the good and the bad of life's smorgasbord. But there is one more thing. If we are trustworthy in our efforts to support our children's growth and we genuinely know and love our kids for their strengths and their weaknesses, they believe in us. If they believe in us, and we believe in them, our love has the power to move mountains!

Common parenting challenges

Specific questions arise in the early years of parenting that give us cause to wonder and struggle with what is right for our children. The questions and answers in the following section relate to common parenting challenges.

Getting kids to listen: Four easy steps

Dr. Gayle,

I am the mother of three children, ages two through nine years. I have great kids, but they often do not listen to what I tell them to do. Things can get so chaotic that it drives me crazy. What can a mother do?

Kim

Dear Kim,

Your dilemma is a common one in this day and age. Our parents' generation was very adult centered. Children were to be seen and not heard. The pendulum has swung, but it need not go overboard. It is possible to empower your children and still retain parental authority.

You have done a good job of listening to your children. Now it is time for them to also listen to you. However, do not mistake establishing your authority to mean you are authoritarian. You have clearly established a democratic atmosphere that has given your children a voice in the family. But your leadership is required. The following guidelines for discipline will help you clarify who is in charge in your family.

1. *Communicate your expectations clearly.*

Pitfall: Some parents express what they want their child do by including a child's feelings as a part of the communication. For example: "Let's get in the car. I know you want to go to grandma's, don't you?"

Say, instead: "I want you to get in your car seat now. We are going to grandma's house."

2. *Accept your child's feelings, but reinforce your expectations.*

Pitfall: Expecting your child to show enthusiasm or contentment about doing what is required.

Instead, be willing to reflect your child's negative feelings about doing what you require, but do not negate what you expect. For example: "Grandma is waiting for us. You must get in your car seat. I know you are sad about having to leave your friends right now. You will be able to play again another day."

3. *Communicate and deliver consequences.*

Pitfalls: Many parents resort to yelling, instead of communicating and delivering consequences in a matter-of-fact tone. Or they do not follow through on consequences they communicate because they threaten inappropriately in the heat of anger.

Instead, accept complaints, but clarify what will happen if they do not listen. For example: "If you do not get in your car seat by the count of three, I will put you in myself." Or, for an older child, "If you do not do your homework, you will not be able to watch your TV program." Be sure you make appropriate consequences that you are willing to deliver. Then, follow through! (Note: Yelling is not a viable consequence, and only leads to escalation.)

Expect to follow through on your consequences *before* your children will listen. It will take one, two, or three times for your child to know that you mean what you say, especially if you have been resorting to whining or complaining instead of being authoritative (which we all do at one time or another).

*4. Separate your child's behavior from his or her self-esteem. Label
a behavior "bad," but not your child's motives or character.*

Pitfall: Confusing behavior with character labels. For example:
"No hitting! Only bad boys hit."

Instead, "Hitting is a bad thing to do to others. You must learn to
use your words." Or to an older child when addressing a bad mistake: "You are not a thief. Why in the world did you steal that lipstick?" Separating behavior from action allows children to learn
from their mistakes, rather than be condemned by them.

It is our job as parents to guide our children. We must be willing
to accept anger and other negative feelings when we set appropriate
limits. As long as your expectations are reasonable for your child's
age, you may successfully adopt the role of benevolent dictator when
necessary.

As parents you have your children's best interests at heart. You
have raised them to give you their input. Pat yourself on the back.
They will feel empowered to express themselves and be able to influence the direction of their destiny in their adult lives.

But do not stop short of taking charge. Your calm leadership is
necessary to create a stable environment. Children and parents
flourish in an atmosphere that promotes order over chaos.

Love and discipline

Dear Dr. Gayle,

*My six-year-old is getting to be impossible. I've set limits with
her and rules for our home and she refuses to adhere to them,
almost as if she is a spoiled brat. When I give in and let her receive
some positive reward, later it's like dealing with a spoiled bear.
Instead of appreciating the quality time with friends or family, she
acts like a spoiled brat, like I don't let her have any fun or rewards
or treats. At this point I want to cancel her birthday party. I don't
know what to do with her any more. It seems like I can't make her
happy no matter what I do or say. I'm at my wit's end!*

Susan

Dear Susan,

It is realistic to expect your daughter to follow appropriate house
rules. It is not realistic to expect that she not be unhappy when she
does face consequences for breaking the rules, whether it be in front

of others or privately with you. You are giving her mixed messages when you set rules only to give in because you do not want to be the "heavy," or perhaps you do not want the effort that setting limits requires of a parent. Either way, you need to ask yourself what you can do to change the situation. You are the parent. She is the child. You are in charge! What skills do you need to develop in order to deal with your own frustration at this point in your development as a mother?

The fact that you are feeling so negatively about your daughter runs the risk that she will internalize your belief that she is a "brat." This will not build her self-esteem or help her delay gratification, which is at the heart of the self-discipline you want her to develop. Instead, believing this label may cause her to develop more problem behavior that fulfills your expectations of her. Begin to see your daughter's behavior as separate from her core self. She may in fact be a very loving and sensitive girl that is having difficulty following rules. Labeling her as a "brat" is a reflection of your frustration in dealing with this part of parenting that is so difficult for you. Take responsibility for what she has to learn from you, and ask yourself to go the extra mile, before you expect her to do so.

Healthy communication between you and your child means that you can accept her feelings, but have expectations for her behavior. Separating feelings from behavior is important for all family members. This means that you can accept your child's anger and sadness when you do set limits. And because you are the parent you know you are acting in her best interest in the long run. You can delay your immediate desire for a happy, smiling child and realize that she needs you to love her by setting limits and carrying through. Accept her sadness and her anger when you discipline her. This will communicate love. But do not shy away from your responsibilities to help her learn self-control.

You may be placing your own self-esteem in your child's hands, and then perceiving her as "bad" or "spoiled" when she acts differently than you think she should. Your own need to make her happy may in fact be a reflection of wanting her to behave in ways that are only positive, and do not cause you to be the "bad guy" yourself. If you are placing your self-esteem as a mother in your child's hands, you may be colluding to feel close to her by pleasing her, rather than accepting the boundaries of the parent-child relationship. It is your job as a parent to accept her unhappiness when she bears the consequences of breaking rules. Giving in to her leads to more of the same behavior you already dislike! Without setting consistent limits, your daughter learns to manipulate others in ways that will frustrate her in being able to make and maintain enduring relationships in the future.

First, it is important that you clearly establish what is expected of your daughter, including the consequences, which should be appropriate to the infraction. You should not only be absolutely ready to carry out the consequence when your daughter does misbehave, but you should expect it to occur! She will test what you say, and it may take three or four times before she believes that you are serious at this point, and that she can trust you to mean what you say. Do not threaten her with the fact that you are ANGRY. This will only lead to spiraling emotions on your part, which leave you feeling guilty later. Instead, communicate consequences and follow through on them. Your anger is not the consequence, the consequences are!

Secondly, when you do discipline your child, it is critical that you do it in as calm and neutral a manner as possible. No matter what you are feeling inside! It is okay to feel angry, but do not make an issue of your anger. This will simply lead to your feeling out of control. Simply follow through on the discussion about rules and consequences. Do not retaliate in anger, even though you may feel an urge to do so. Develop self-control and enough emotional separation from her that you see her as the child. You can remind yourself that this accounts for her immature behavior. See yourself as the adult who does not indulge your feelings but who accepts her need for your discipline as part of your parental role.

And finally, develop tolerance for her emotions, but do not accept her acting out behavior. Likewise, accept your own feelings, but do not act them out on her! Canceling her birthday party sounds like an idea that arises out of angry retaliation, rather than a calm, natural, or appropriate consequence that has been communicated in advance of the infraction. If this is the case, do not do it. Instead, calmly reflect on the fact that you are a great mother, but that this is a particularly difficult part of parenting for you. Realize that as much as you love your child, you are tempted to model the very kind of behavior she is showing. Giving her treats may be your way of being close to her, making up for being angry at her, or solving a situation quickly by getting her to behave in the moment, without anticipating the future. Canceling her party because you feel angry and hurt by her misbehavior sounds excessive. These may be signs that you do not follow through on calm limit setting yourself, but have a tendency to resort to emotional extremes in acting out your emotions, without separating feelings from behavior. This is what your daughter is doing, too. She may also be resorting to manipulating you in the moment because she cannot tell whether you mean what you say, or are just acting momentarily out of anger. If you are acting out your own anger in these ways, she quickly learns that when your guilt sets in, it is another story.

Remorse and guilt may then be acted out as well, by giving treats to make up for an inappropriate outburst, for example. In such a situation, anger and guilt become an endless cycle. The child receives confusing messages: "I am very angry at you and so I will punish you"; and later, following drama and tears, the guilty message, "I am sorry for being so angry with you and of course I will not punish you now because I feel differently." In this case, the punishment is an extension of the feeling. And because feelings change constantly, so do the rules! Consequences should always be independent of whatever feelings you are experiencing towards your child in the moment. Then you can be assured they are not excessively punitive or, alternately, too permissive. She can become confused as to what the truth is if feelings become confused with actions.

Trust will be established when your child experiences your feelings as separate from the consequences for breaking the rules. Then she knows the rules are always the same no matter what mood you are in at the moment! The result will be a calmer child, as she does not have to constantly figure out what the real limit is today. You will feel more in control. And she will have the security that comes from consistency and trust in what you say.

It is wiser to allow yourself the feelings of anger, which will pass, without acting them out in the situation, but calmly delivering consequences as previously discussed and seeking satisfaction from the fact that you are in charge and can set limits with your child. Perhaps this will feel empowering enough to you that when your anger passes and her tears dry, you can calmly reinforce the rules and continue a loving relationship. Sometimes it helps for a mom to be able to say out loud, "I love you and I am angry at you for not following the rules we talked about. You will have to go to your room for a time out, as we discussed." Be clear with yourself that you love her *even when you are angry* and you will be less likely to feel guilty.

It is a source of security for children to rely on their parents to set and carry through on appropriate limits. Children feel loved because they feel contained by their parent's ability to model control where they have not yet learned self-control. By experiencing your clear and matter-of-fact limit setting, your daughter internalizes an ability to set her own limits as a future adult and gains a capacity for self-discipline. Setting clear and consistent limits will help your daughter feel secure in your love, despite the fact that she is expected to learn self control!

Reflect on the way you were disciplined, or not, as a child. Sometimes, when we come from families where discipline was too extreme, we err by not setting limits for our children as an overreaction to inappropriate limits in our childhood. Or, our own experience of discipline may have been equally inconsistent and did not allow us to develop self control in dealing with the limit-setting responsibilities of parenthood. If so, we will pass this lack of control onto our children if we do not develop in ourselves what is missing.

Often, the missing link is realizing that you can love your child even as you are angry; and that feelings are separate from actions. Do not try to control your daughter's feelings. Instead, accept that she is sad and angry at you for setting limits, but you still love her even though you, too may feel angry at her behavior.

And remember, you are not alone! All of us mothers continue to grow and develop throughout life. There is no such thing as a "perfect parent." Your own desire for help and ability to reach out to learn from others when things are not working well, is a sign of strength. Seeking help when you need it is a wonderful legacy for your children.

When potty training is a must! An innovative program

Dear Dr. Gayle,

My child is now three years old and she still displays no interest in potty training. We've tried the rewards, praise, and even stickers,

*but nothing has worked. In fact, she usually fusses about sitting on
the potty chair and says she doesn't want to. What is the best
method of encouraging her interest and accomplishing the goal? It
will soon be a problem at her day care if she is not trained like the
others in her age group.*

Sheryl

Dear Sheryl,

Consult with your pediatrician to rule out any physical problems
that might cause her to "fuss" about using the toilet. If there are no
medical reasons for her reluctance, your little girl may need an extra
"push" to use the toilet if your circumstances require it. It may be
time for communicating your expectation with more conviction,
and in a way that peaks her interest. You may also need to motivate
her with a reward program that will better inspire her performance.
Read on for details!

First, communicate to your daughter that it is one of the rules of
the daycare that all three-year-olds must use the potty, and so you
are going to help her learn how to do this. Let her know that her
body is equipped with sphincter muscles that help her control when
the pee and poop is held and when it comes out.

Secondly, get creative! Draw her a picture of the bladder and
how it works, or use a small balloon filled 1/4 with water, using
your fingers to demonstrate how we can use our sphincter muscles to "hold on" and "let go" of urine at will. Show her how difficult it can be to hold pee when the fluid brims to the top, but how
much easier it is when we empty our bladders when they are less
than half filled, such as, every two or three hours. Ask her if she
can tell when her bladder is "this" full or "that" full, engaging her
in considering the physical cues that tell her it is time to use the
potty. Captivate her interest in how the body works, but don't stop
there! Make it clear that you believe in her body's ability to learn
this process because she is now three and her body is ready to use
these muscles.

Finally, consider a reward that works for your child. It may be a
little known fact that many parents resort to candy reinforcement
for toilet training. There is no need to create an on-going pattern
of using food for reward, but at this age, many children do
respond to candy, when other non-food rewards, such as "stickers"

have languished. Lollipops, held on a stick, hold great appeal to children of this age. Perhaps it has something to do with the still powerful "sucking" reflex that brings such pleasure. When other reinforcement has failed and potty training is necessary "potty pops" may do the trick!

The "potty pops" program was inspired by my grandson who was sporadic in his potty use until he was consistently rewarded with a small lollipop immediately and only after successfully using the toilet. His mother found them superior to other candy alternatives (M&M's or jelly beans) because the lollipops were often licked only a few times before being discarded, so he was not eating as much sugar. Ideally, these rewards would be small, flat lollipops (for safety from choking) and vitamin enriched. I eventually trademarked the concept in hopes of providing a smaller, safer lollipop than those on the market, and a more nutritious alternative for parents who felt comfortable with this approach.

Feel free to adopt or create a similar program, substituting with your own resources. Instructions for use of this approach to potty training appear below.

Dr. Peterson's Potty Pops (TM) Program [37]

Introduce the use of the toilet to your two- to three-year-old in a positive manner. Tell the child he or she will receive a potty pop after each use. Do not give potty pops at any other time or for any other reason except after successfully using the toilet. Give them consistently after each use for up to three weeks. After this initial training period, give potty pops only as asked for by your child. Toilet training will become a learned, conditioned reflex that is generalized and potty pops will no longer be necessary for reinforcement.

Best wishes for an enjoyable and successful potty training experience!

I can't get my four-year-old out of my bed

Dear Dr. Gayle,

I am a divorced mother of two (son, four and daughter, two). My son has been sleeping in my bed for over a year now. I don't remem-

---
37. Dr. Peterson's Potty Pops Program copyrighted 1999 by Gayle Peterson.

ber exactly how it started, but he became terribly frightened about sleeping by himself. So much so, that bedtime became a very traumatic experience for both of us.

I have made several attempts to have him sleep in his own bed, moved it in with his sister, put his bed in my room, etc. I feel terrible when people ask me about where he is sleeping, but I'm not sure what to do. I don't want him to be traumatized about going to sleep.

Any suggestions? Should I aggressively pursue getting him into his own bed? Or will he eventually go there himself?

Cindy

Dear Cindy,

It may be likely that your son began sleeping with you as comfort you sought when you were going through your divorce. Particularly if it was traumatizing to you, your son could have sensed your needs, merging with you as a source of mutual soothing through the transition. Although this can be comforting in the short run, it can pose long term difficulties in adjustment and adaptation when continued. Whether his fear is based on trauma or manipulation, it is important to help him gain a sense of mastery about his ability to sleep on his own at this point, for his sake as well as for yours.

Setting limits can be difficult when you feel guilty. At this point, it may be more the case that your son is manipulating you than that he is truly traumatized. He needs to know that you believe in his ability to sleep in his own bed, and that no amount of crying will make you change your mind about his capacity to develop this independence.

Because he is your first, your bond to him may have a special quality of closeness. He is the child who helped you forge your motherhood. If he began sleeping with you at the time you separated from your ex-husband, he may also be filling in for the loss experienced at that time. Remaining in your bed gives him the message that he is important because you need him for comfort. He needs to know that you do not need him in this role. It is not his job. His ability to sleep on his own will be in his best interests when he wishes to do a sleep-over with a friend or go on a camp outing. Helping him develop the ability to self-soothe is critical to his development. It also gives him a secure place in the family as a brother. Sleeping with you elevates his position in the family, separating him from his sibling connection.

It is important that he be able to sleep in his own bed because it is in his best interests, because his sister does so, and because you may want an adult partner of your own at some point, too. Should you remarry, your son would then be set up to feel rejected by you, causing difficulties with future stepfamily formation, as well.

Talk with your son about what will help him to sleep in his own bed, like his sister does. Let him know you believe in him, and you expect it of him. Establish a plan with him that helps him master his fears. A night light and a new special stuffed animal friend may be useful ways of helping him develop his confidence in himself to sleep in his own bed. Assure him that you know he will be able to do so because he is becoming five years old in the next year! Express certainty that this will help him adjust, and that he has the capacity to conquer his fear.

If you remain uncomfortable and unable to hold these limits with your son, seek professional guidance to explore what, if any, other events may be at the heart of his fears. Review any life events that could be the trigger for such fears when they began one year ago. Explore any possibilities that some traumatic event that you are not aware of (sexual molestation, getting lost) could have been actually traumatizing to him and pushed below his awareness. If this was the case, play therapy would be therapeutic in helping him feel safe again.

Your love for your child will be expressed in your clear boundaries and sensitive assistance. Your guilt will be resolved by addressing this problem and taking charge of the situation. Besides, why should you feel guilty when you are asking all the right questions?

Preschooler's love affair with opposite parent

Dear Dr. Gayle,

Our son is almost three years old. His father is very good with him. He takes him to the park and plays hockey with him. In general, when time permits he tries to spend as much time with him as he can. However, my son is quite often hostile to him. I don't quite understand this. When my husband tries to dress him, he screams "No mommy do it." When he asks him questions sometimes, he just tells him to "Go away." Is he jealous of my husband? Is this normal?

*Do children grow out of this or is there some way we should be
dealing with this. My husband finds it very frustrating and so do I. I
don't want to be the center of everything all of the time.*

Margaret

Dear Margaret,

Your son is at a stage in which he is having a "love affair" with the
opposite sexed parent. The healthy and natural resolution to this
"oedipal complex" (as it was named by Freud) is simply that he
comes to understand that he gets to have both mommy and daddy,
and that he can have a wife of his own someday!

Clearly, your son is not trying to make you his wife. He is however competing with dad for your attention during this period. This
classic phase can be interpreted to be a developmental working
through of two of the most powerful emotions we will ever experience: love and hate.

In short, he is experiencing a crisis that, if resolved, results in
deep ego strength. D. W. Winnicott, the famed child theorist, calls
this stage "the first maturity," which occurs between two and five
years of age.[38] He describes it as a developmental crisis that is meant
to prepare the child for handling the intensity and ambivalence that
is life. The drama of competition with the father allows the child to
experience two of life's primary emotional forces. He learns to handle strong feelings by integrating rather than disintegrating in the
face of conflictual feelings. If this period is handled without rejection by both parents, he learns to internalize mother's love, which
actually frees him to identify and associate with his father in some
important ways.

Do not get lost in too much interpretation! The important concept is that dad not take the rejection of his son personally. Your son
needs to feel that dad can tolerate the rejection without losing his
father's love. Your husband can take comfort in the fact that he is an
adult and his son is a child. You are clearly supportive of your husband, and your empathy can go a long way in creating a buffer for
dad's natural reactions. Support him, but share the emotional meaning of this stage and its resolution as a higher purpose in raising
your child together.

---

38. D.W. Winnicott, *The Family and Individual Development* (Routledge,London,1989).

Your son is doing his job in using dad to represent an emotion that he must come to terms with if he is to function well in the world. It will also help future stages (such as adolescence) if he experiences a taming of this very primal force. It is the father's ability to absorb his son's aggression that allows the child to develop internal strength and stability. If your husband did not experience this with his own father, or felt serious rejection from his dad, this stage could be more challenging for him. And he may need greater support in resolving his own issues with his father so he can remain loving and nonreactive to his son's behavior at this time.

Your job is also to remain tolerant and neutral to your son's clinging. Be clear that daddy is an available and acceptable resource. Do not give in to his demands for you to do everything for him. Be loving and firm with limits and reflecting that dad is a source of nurturing, too. But do not shame or rebuke him. You must absorb your son's expression of dependency without reacting with rejection. If you succeed in this, he will internalize your love and be more capable of independence in the future. Simply accept his feelings as normal. Be clear that you and daddy love him and can equally address his needs, but accept that he wants only you and for daddy to disappear. (But not really!)

When this stage resolves you will have one very calm and confident child. This will be his first experience with resolving the conflict of having strong, competing emotions. And he will have won! If he wins, you all win. He will be capable of expressions of love to you both and he will learn that this is a family in which conflicting feelings can be expressed and resolved. A sense of well-being is the result of experiencing love and hate in a family that is able to contain and transform these primal energies, without making anybody go away. Somehow, this tempers the polarities of the primary forces inherent in life and renders us more capable of experiencing the ups and downs of living with less distress and more equanimity.

And by the way, you should also congratulate yourself on the stable and nurturing environment the two of you have created in order for this natural crisis to emerge. Your son must feel that you are safe people to express these strong feelings to you rather than repress them. Now it is your job to prove him right!

Can parents "spoil" a baby?

Dear Dr. Gayle,

My daughter is eight months old. Everyone always told me that you can not spoil a child under the age of one. I seem to think that my daughter is spoiled. I can't ever get anything done during the day. She always wants to be right next to me. When I try to put her in her playpen she screams. So, I try and hurry what I have to do and rush to pick her up. I feel like I am deserting her. I don't want her to feel like I am not coming back for her.

I am a new, single parent and don't know what to do. Should I still be allowing her to sleep with me? I don't mind but everyone I talk to says that she should be sleeping in her own bed. If I let her stay how and when should I start to put her in her own bed?

Jessi

Dear Jessi,

You are by no means spoiling your eight-month-old baby when you sleep with her or pick her up to carry her around with you during the day!

Young babies need to feel physically attached to their primary caretakers in order to develop a sense of basic trust and security in the world. Over the next two and a half years your daughter will develop what is known to child psychologists as "object constancy," which means she will be able to feel your caring for her, even when you are not there. However, developmentally, that is yet a long way off!

Do not despair! Simply lower your expectations of what must get done in your day. You can continue to do the daily chores that need doing, but your pace will be greatly reduced by doing them with her very close by. This is not a punishment. It is parenthood! And though it seems as if it will go on forever, it does not. Your child will develop into a self-assured toddler, and then a small child, incrementally, but inevitably, by age three years. If you devote your attentions to satisfying her needs in the first year, you will succeed at helping her to develop basic trust. Through the next two years, if you work to meet her emotional needs and set appropriate limits, which cause her to master her sense of independence, you will have the ability to do your work increasingly separate from her.

But you are not an endless nurturing source, I know! You do have needs of your own, and single motherhood without many friend-ships may be weighing heavily upon you.

Seek out a mothering group with other mothers, some of which are also single. Develop a support network for yourself so that you are able to pursue some of your own goals. Whether you take a class, date, or develop an involvement in community projects, you need more val-idation and companionship than your baby alone can give you.

Connecting with other single moms will lighten your expecta-tions of yourself in these early developmental years with your baby. You will see other moms struggling to get things done and meet their child's needs for closeness. Take the time you need away from her to recharge, so that you have greater patience for her dependen-cy when she is with you.

And remember, these early years will never come again. You have a right to enjoy the closeness she seeks with you now, for she will not always want you this close. Before long, she will be seeking her own friendships and activities independent from you. Childhood yields to adolescence, which gives way to adulthood. Slowly but surely she will need her separation from you. Enjoy her need for you now, for it will gradually disappear. Like time-lapse photography, we need to imagine a sense of ourselves in time. Imagining her growth over the next seventeen years is crucial to keeping a sense of change and growth alive, in order to appreciate the moment!

And if you do the job well, she will choose to be connected to you in her adulthood, when love and friendship with you is an indepen-dent choice.

Guidelines for helping children recover from loss or trauma

Dear Dr. Gayle,

My six-year-old is bright and a sensitive boy. But he seems to give up and cries easily. When he was three, his sister was born, followed a week later by the Northridge earthquake, which destroyed our community and greatly damaged our condo. A year later my wife was diagnosed with multiple sclerosis, and has relapsed frequently with severe bouts of blindness, double vision, vertigo and weakness. At this time she is hold-ing her own but she is now blind in one eye and it's permanent.

I try to be sensitive to his needs, but sometimes I am over-whelmed myself. I have tried to instill confidence in him and sup-

*port, but I feel that I've failed him. I want to help and get help for
him but don't know what to do next.*

Gary

Dear Gary,

You are doing a wonderful job as a father! You not only appreciate
your son's intelligence, but have concern regarding his difficult experiences of the last three years. Your sensitivity to your son's needs
and intent to support him are signs of courage and good parenting
on your part. You are entering a phase of healing, following disequi-
librium. This represents a new phase in your family's development.

Given that you have been in a position of "holding it all together"
it is likely that you need to attend to healing and recharging your
own emotional batteries at this time. This will help you to have
more of a buffer when your son breaks down and cries easily. Keep
in mind, too, that the good news may be that he *is* crying right now.
It may be that it is the first time that multiple crisis have abated and
the environment is settled enough that he can begin to grieve and
feels safe enough to "fall apart."

"Falling apart" is necessary to some degree in order to reorganize
the psyche after significant experiences of loss or change. Personal
identity is shattered to a degree and must be resurrected. You have
all come through multiple traumas any one of which would have
caused great emotional upheaval in your family. Any family would be
reverberating in the wake of such enormous change. The timing of
subsequent losses following the momentous change of adding a second child to your family did not allow for a "breather." But now it is
time to turn your energies towards healing.

Check into public or private community programs in your area
that may still exist that center on healing the trauma for earthquake
victims. Several community programs sprung up in the San Francisco
Bay Area, following the Oakland firestorm of 1991. Art and gardening
projects helped bring many families together to recover. A ceramic tile
project in which each family produced a tile of their experience of the
event is now a public piece of work displayed at the Rockridge Bart
(Bay Area Rapid Transit) system in Oakland, California. The artwork
helped to bring people together to share, grieve and re-integrate a part
of their lives they had lost. Community gardens also helped many people express the pain that words alone could not contain.

Your family might benefit greatly from family counseling focused on recovery from the enormity of change and loss you have all experienced these past three years. Enrolling in community art programs or finding some avenue of emotional expression to release the pain, will help you to grieve so that you can develop greater strength from your experience. Naturally, child therapy aimed at working through these issues in play therapy can also be highly productive for your son.

Plan on devoting the next year to recovery. Talk with your wife about the possibility of having a family meeting simply acknowledging and reviewing the last three years. Perhaps each of you could start by simply drawing something that expresses your feelings about this period of time. Take turns sharing your drawing and what it represents. Rituals like this can bring you closer and open up avenues for processing the experience together as a family. Go slow, do not rush the process. Simply express one feeling each, listen and accept each member's feelings without recrimination or "fixing." Later you might want to take a trip to the site of the old house, followed by a positive experience of walking on the beach and throwing something that represents your pain into the ocean with a wish for the future. If the thought of this kind of processing through ritual or talking together brings up intense anxiety, seek professional family counseling to resolve your own feelings as a couple before attempting to support and guide your children.

This time period has represented half of your son's life and your entire daughter's life span. However, that will not always be the case. As years pass, this time period will be significantly less overwhelming. Healing will take place gradually, but as the trauma of the past is mastered, strength and depth of character will replace the emotional fragmentation your son is now displaying when frustrated.

Research on recovery from trauma suggests three guidelines for families:[39]

1. It is critical for parents to share grief with their children in a manner that allows them to feel the healing power of the family group but does not burden them with resolving parental pain.

---

39. F. Brown, "The Impact of Death and Serious Illness on the Family Life Cycle." In B. Carter and M. McGoldrick (eds.), *The Changing Life Cycle* (New York: Gardner Press, 1988).

2. Open communication that allows for a full range of emotions (anger, grief, relief, despair, guilt) facilitates adjustment to change. This includes acceptance of differences in how individual family members grieve and what they feel. For example, it is common for men to grieve miscarriage differently than women. Pressure to feel the same feelings their wives do inhibits adjustment. Acceptance of the range and differences in feelings promotes healing.

3. The power of rituals to carry the pain and grief are impactful for working through healing.

Research on families of holocaust victims[40] revealed to us that it was the families who talked about the past that were capable of transforming deep levels of despair into future capacity for coping, living and loving. Children who came from families in which their parents did not express and continue to process the tragedy as it came up in family life, experienced greater degrees of dysfunction, particularly depression. Repression breeds depression. Expression is the antidote to dysfunction following trauma.

Do not be afraid of your son's emotionality. The fact that he is showing it to you means he feels safe to let down his guard. He needs to fall apart a bit, be safely held in his sorrow, and gradually build his confidence and ability to cope with daily stresses. Play therapy can provide a safe and healing framework for such release of emotional tensions and re-integration.

"Healing" literally means to "make whole." It derives from the old English "hoelan," which means to synthesize or re-integrate. Any kind of artistic expression can prove highly valuable for processing deep loss and change because, at first, our experience may be too deep for words. Putting poetry, drawings, gardening, or music to our feelings can help us cope with them. Eventually feelings that are released give birth to new thoughts and perceptions that allow for a stronger sense of self.

Consider constructing or getting professional help creating your own meaningful family and/or personal rituals during this next year. Congratulate yourselves on how well you have coped through enor-

---

40. J. Herman, *Trauma and Recovery* (New York: Basic Books, 1992).

mous change! Cry together, laugh together, and have joy together. Future years will serve to show you the value and strength of family healing. Make this process one that brings you closeness instead of distance. But do not forget your own need for support and healing. Through taking care of yourself you will gain the strength and patience to better serve your son.

Part III

Crisis and Transformation
on the Family Life Cycle

===== EIGHT =====

Raising Adolescents
The Transformation of the Family

The presence of adolescents in the family precipitates a transformation. No longer children, and not yet adults, teens waver betwixt and between, as they prepare to leave home and establish independent lives. Unlike younger years, teenagers are making choices that will have an effect on the rest of their lives. The stakes are getting higher. The protected period of childhood is fading quickly.

The new family system is no longer just about caring for children, but also subject to new and independent ideas, styles, and philosophies for living brought home by their budding teenager. Adolescent development pressures the parent to evolve toward a new understanding of the differences of individuals in the family, especially where poignant issues of sexuality, career choice, and academic and social achievement are concerned.

Parents, too, may be experiencing pressures of their own involving identity. Mid-life issues may arise, and new career choices may loom for parents as they look ahead to the rest of their lives after their children leave the nest. Couples' intimacy issues reach a peak of intensity at this time, if marital conflicts remained unresolved while the children were growing up. And as if that were not enough, parents may be experiencing the stress of dealing with aging parents of their own! Unresolved dependency needs from childhood can surface for parents who have functioned well as providers for younger children, but are reminded of their own freedom looming at the horizon. The need to focus on their own growth and development as adults can become salient at a time when they are "sandwiched" in between the needs of the younger and the older generations simultaneously.

Family life evolves in a kind of "pressure cooker," which can make it hard to see the special and unique challenges of parenthood during this period. The following question and answer illustrates the changes parents must make in parenting during this time, and the way we can may experience difficulty changing "gears" as adolescence arrives on the home front.

Changing the parent-child relationship

Dr. Gayle,

I would appreciate some advice on a parenting style that hasn't worked. My wife and I have been married for fifteen years. We have two boys, aged fourteen and eleven. We both have been extremely tolerant of all needs and desires of our kids and now it has come back to haunt us. Our fourteen-year-old spends hours each day on the phone with his girl friend and then actually visits with her daily. He's constantly in his room with the door closed talking on the phone. His interaction with us leaves us feeling suspicious and frustrated. Neither myself or my wife have invoked much in the way of limits or consequences.

I have been a stay-at-home dad since 1989 and am just now re-entering the work horse. As of tonight, I have removed the phone from his room and insisted that he go outside to try to get a life. He's into bicycle road racing but procrastinates excessively about training. I don't care if he races bikes or counts the rocks in the driveway, I just need some guidance on how to get back on track as a parent.

Phil

Dear Phil,

You and your children are going through changes! Be compassionate toward yourself because you are losing the earlier years of closeness as a parent to younger children, especially since you stayed at home with them during that time. Your children, too, are developing their own separate identities, which is the central task of adolescence.

Adolescence itself is a transformational stage in any family. And many parents hit their own mid-life transitions at this same time. No wonder you are feeling alienated and tossed aside. But do not take it personally! It does not mean that you have done it all wrong in the past. It is simply a time to reassess your roles as parents in your children's lives. What do they need from you now? What do they no longer need from you? Becoming teenagers is wrought with the incredible complication of hormonal change. Their young bodies are steeped in hormones, causing physical changes that could be overwhelming by themselves alone, not to mention the considerable psychological adjustments that are taking place. It is a period of intense self-absorption and selfishness. Some psychologists jokingly refer to this developmental stage as "healthy narcissism."

Adolescence is a time when the search for identity becomes a more separate and independent endeavor. The need for parental attachment does not disappear, it merely changes. Adolescents are seeking out the company of peers, and doing the hard work of trying to find a place for themselves in the world, socially and eventually economically. These are big pressures, and they are intuitively aware of the upcoming future prospect of having to survive on their own, away from the family. This is both terribly exciting and enormously frightening on a subliminal level, to parents and children alike! But do not let your fears for his future well-being cloud your view of him. Often parents project negative images of their children based upon their fears of the transition that lies ahead, without taking into account that the teenager is still in development for this launching. Teenagers are "beginning adults" in a manner of speaking, and your role becomes more one of guidance than of protection. This means that you are in transition in developing new skills and parameters to guide them on their journey.

You have raised them and enjoyed a primarily unambivalent attachment to them in their younger years. Perhaps you are feeling a bit rejected by them. But be careful you do not retaliate or punish them for their development. It is their job to grow away from you. And if you have done your job well, they will do so.

Their growing independence does not mean, however, that they do not need you! They simply need you in a different way. Continue to develop your relationships with your sons. Take them out individually to spend time together. Perhaps playing basketball or some other activity can provide a touchstone through the teenage years for connection and sharing their lives in a new way. Work to forge a new kind of relationship instead of throwing in the towel or overreacting in a rejecting or demeaning way. If you are concerned about your son's direction or how he is spending his time, tell him so. But

be careful not to do it in a destructive way that shames or infan-
tilizes rather than opening up opportunity for your guidance and
suggestions. Telling him to "get a life" communicates your frustration and lack of belief in him without offering any guidance. It is a
put-down. Taking his phone away does not address the problem. It is
infantalizing rather than limit-setting, and reduces him to a child's
position, rather than helping him learn the requirements of a being
a beginning adult in the family.

Instead, seek to involve yourself in one of the activities your son
enjoys. Learn more about him, what makes him tick. Become interested in really grasping the man he is becoming. He needs your
help, not your criticism at this time. Begin to see that your son is
passing through a period in which he needs to learn how to become
a man. You can help him with this. Consider that you are apprentic-
ing him to manhood, now. He needs you to help him grow into the
unique man that only he can become. Search yourself for obstacles
that might be in the way of your relating to your son, based on your
own relationship to your father. Did you get the relationship with
your father that you needed when you were a teenager? Did he help
you find your own answers through your teen years? Or did he just
tell you what to do? Did you share activities that gave you ongoing
contact with your dad on your terms as a developing young man?
Did he assist you towards manhood and leaving home by guiding
you, but not overshadowing your growing need for independence?

This is a critical period of continued availability and nurturance,
and setting limits, guidelines, and conditions that help your son
continue to develop into manhood. If you have not needed to set
many limits up until this time, you are fortunate. You enjoyed a
harmonious relationship with your children. But today is a different
story. Their development calls for a new approach. Perhaps you
could benefit from reflecting on how and what limits are appropriate at this point in your children's lives, rather than questioning
your childrearing.

Remember, too, that *relating* to your son is also crucial. Share
your concerns about priorities in life. Develop *discussions* between
yourself and your teenager. Solicit his opinions and his thinking
about such things. This is how you will influence him at this time,
not by telling him how he should be, but encouraging him to devel-

op self-reflection, morals, and values of his own. Being the parent of a teenager requires different skills than being a parent of a younger child. Seek to develop these skills, connect to your son, and continue to parent! These conversations will prove precious as he will find them valuable resources to refer back to when he experiences himself out of balance in his life. Remember that it is your son's job to challenge you at this point in his development. Accept this, and do not shove your ideas down his throat, just describe how and why you believe a certain way. And trust him to evaluate it.

I can't count the times through my own son's adolescence that he vehemently pronounced his very opposite view from myself on a subject, only to come to similar conclusions himself one to two months later! But this kind of behavior, I learned, was key to his growth. He absorbed the information of my experience (though denying it at the time), which he later processed with his own experience to come up with an independent answer (which just happened to be the suggestion I had made!)

Don't think for a minute that you do not have a profound effect on your teenager. You, as a parent, have been and continue to be the most significant influence in your son's life. It is his job to make you feel that you are no longer significant. But do not believe it! He will consider what you say, but in his own time and with independent reflection of his life experience. And so, one of the most important skills to develop as a parent of a teenager is the ability to discuss. These discussions should have room for diverse opinions, ideas, and be open-hearted and honest without devaluing your teenagers thoughts and feelings. Share your own ideas, opinions, and why you see things a certain way. But remember, as your children grow, you do not maintain the same level of control you once had. They need to fly on their own, and you must help guide their beginning glides without believing that you can control their flight.

Your son will make mistakes. Let him know that you trust him to make decisions in his best interest. If you have concerns, let him know, but place it in context of his learning how to balance priorities and learn from consequences. Perhaps you remember teaching your boys how to ride a bike. If you used training wheels, they had to come off at some point, resulting in some inevitable falls in order to acquire independent balancing skills. You trusted they would be able to learn that, even though they fell. You held a picture of their inevitable success in achieving that balance. You believed in them to succeed.

Maintain a healthy picture of your sons, despite the difficulties. If you feel there is more need for accountability to you, discuss it with your wife. Consider what should be expected of these young men at this age and come up with a plan of implementation. Teenagers need to know that they are part of a family with certain required responsibilities, despite their self-engrossment. Adolescents want their freedom, but they still need your care.

Establish areas of responsibility (household chores, cooking one dinner per week). For example, when your son reaches driving age he could do weekly grocery shopping for the family. This combines his newfound freedom to drive with a new, more adult responsibility to the family. In this way, adolescents learn that freedom is also grounded in responsibility and discipline. And being loved and cared for in relationships is a two-way street.

Talk with your wife about your feelings about your boys growing older. How has your relationship changed? Are you grieving the closeness of your past relationship with them as younger boys? Perhaps you are missing them. Your wife can be your partner in sharing these feelings, particularly if you were a stay-at-home dad. You may be experiencing a preview of the "empty nest" syndrome. And if you have just reentered the work force, there are many changes of your own that may be clouding your parental role.

Do not berate yourself with self doubt. Trust that you have done a good job raising your sons. And realize that the appreciation for your fatherhood must come from your wife. She is your co-parent. Do not expect it to come from your children at this time. They will have plenty of appreciation for you when they mature into adulthood. But for now their job is a selfish one that includes preoccupation with themselves and separating from you. Your job is to remain connected in a new and different way to both your sons and offer guidance in the form of established structures for responsibility and accountability that will build respect into your changing relationships.

Adolescence is a transformative time for all relationships in the family. More energy is returned to the marriage, as children separate. Forging a deeper bond of appreciation for your spouse can be rewarding, as you endeavor to adjust to the needs of your teenagers.

Enjoy the changes that can come with living with beginning adults who can contribute in more adult ways to family responsibilities; and who eventually will let you back into their hearts more openly. Tolerating your teenagers needs for privacy without going away will reap the reward of closeness in a couple of years when they feel more secure in who they are. And from my personal experience the welcome back in is well worth the trouble.

Who ever said that anything that is worth waiting for was easy? When the butterfly finally emerges from its dark cocoon, lightness returns. The experience of the transformation is felt by all. Perhaps this kind of shared experience is what "being family" is all about!

Parenting during adolescence

The key emotional tasks in parenting during this stage are to navigate the adolescent's "identity crisis," and the transformation of the family system to include the child's growing independence. Parents have to adjust to their child as a beginning adult in many ways. Adolescents still need guidance and much support, even intermittently on what may feel like a younger child's level (for example, forgetting homework).

Teenagers' extreme ambivalence about their own independence and vacillation between polarities of independence and dependence make this period a stress on all families. However, the main focus should be on helping them to make their own decisions and discussing social responsibility and ethics as a backdrop for the task of establishing an identity. Most adolescents will make decisions in their own best interests, or learn readily from their mistakes if they have appropriate support and guidance. However, due to the extreme physiological, emotional, and cognitive changes that are going on simultaneously at this time, adolescents and preteens are vulnerable to symptoms of depression, anxiety, fatigue, and societal dangers. The following question and answer reflects the dangers of this period, which parents may be inclined to neglect rather than address.

Is my twelve-year-old daughter's depression serious?

Dr. Gayle,

My twelve-year-old daughter tells me she is depressed and has talked about not wanting to live anymore. She says these things when she is feeling rejected by her friends or when I discipline her.

At first, I thought this was a stage, but now I'm wondering if I have cause to worry. What are the signs, at school and at home, that we should take seriously?

Hannah

Dear Hannah,

Your daughter is at a stage when her social life is critical to her, so her feelings of rejection and not fitting in may be at a peak. But she is telling you that she is not only depressed, but having suicidal thoughts and feelings. Take her seriously!

Ask your daughter to tell you what is depressing her right now. It is likely that hormones have hit, and puberty is giving rise to shifts in her perception of herself. She may have feelings of inadequacy related to her body changes and to the physical changes of other girls in her group. For example, she may feel left out because she is not yet developing breasts when other girls are, or feel odd because she is developing breasts ahead of her other friends. She may be mourning the loss of old childhood friends, as puberty brings shifts in social affiliations that may be taking place within her group.

This is a time for you and your daughter to get closer. She needs you to guide her through this transition to becoming a young woman. Spend time with her, talk with her about what is changing at school, in her friendships, and how she is feeling about her body. Help her feel good about herself!

Let your daughter know that it is normal for friendships to change over time as people change, too. Some friendships will wane, others will develop. This may be a time to discuss whether different or new friends may be in her best interests, too. Use this period as an opportunity to help her clarify who she is and how she can become proactive in meeting her needs, rather than depressed. Perhaps she will want to begin a new interest, such as horseback riding or some other new activity that could enlarge her social circle and introduce her to new skills that could help her feel competent.

You can be the buffer for these tumultuous times. Lend her your genuine and positive thoughts about her. Let her know what you see as her strengths and talents. In short, be her friend, if that is what she needs now. But do not stop there!

Find out where her passions lie, and help her to develop them. Too often girls of this age are encouraged to give up on their dreams, instead of to move towards them. This can also cause depression. In *Reviving Ophelia*,[41] Mary Pipher discusses how girls are at risk for losing themselves because they are encouraged to define their identity by their relationships rather than their interests. Help your daughter to identify her interests and set realistic goals that make her feel successful.

Finally, do not be shy to ask your daughter what she means when she says she does not want to live. Does she fantasize ending her life? Or is she trying to express the depth of her loneliness? If your daughter continues to express suicidal feelings and depression, despite your best efforts to listen to her and help her through this period, consider a consultation with a child therapist. Be alert to the following signs of depression, which may indicate the need for professional help.

1. Difficulty maintaining relationships and withdrawing from them.

2. A reduction in the level of physical activity she engages in.

3. Suicidal thoughts and feelings.

4. Low self-esteem; unable to identify strengths, talents and interests.

5. Self destructive behavior; including frequent overeating of sweets or taking unnecessary risks.

6. Academic difficulty or lowered performance or problems at school.

7. Erratic sleep patterns; sleeping a lot more or a lot less.

Girls' social cliques often revolve around threesomes and issues of inclusion and exclusion become a major, and often quite painful, focus during these years. Try to recall your own struggles with this issue at her age. It will help her feel less alone if she hears that you grappled with feelings of rejection, too, when you were twelve.

And remind her that the fact she is depressed now does not mean she will always feel this way. Like adults, our children sometimes need us to help them see the bigger picture!

Contracting for life with your teenager

Discussions regarding safety and established guidelines for communication are paramount. Parents who are concerned about their children's well-being often agree to a policy that a teenager may call them at any

---

41. M. Pipher, *Reviving Ophelia* (New York: Grossett/Putnam, 1994).

time they are in need, with no questions asked at that time. If your adolescent does find him or herself in a compromised situation, such as being driven home by an inebriated friend, your teenager should know that it is acceptable and safe to call you for help with no questions asked that night. You and your child can make an agreement (and even sign it formally if it seems beneficial to do so). This agreement should state that safety is more important than an argument about the situation. Further discussion can take place, but safety is given priority at a time when teenagers are stepping out of the previously protected boundaries of the family system.

Tired of my son's adolescent identity crisis

Dear Dr. Gayle,

Help! I have a thirteen-year-old teenage son who of course is going through the "Who am I?" stage. My son has a terrible time in facing his chores or homework. He just started school again and I ask him to please get his homework done before chores, telephone or friend time.

When I arrived home last evening around 9:00 p.m. he was just beginning his homework. The dishes had not been put in the dishwasher, he had a water fight with the teenage neighbor and left his wet clothes lying on his bedroom floor. Now, was I wrong to get upset? At this point I put him on phone restriction. When I put him on restriction, he tells me I'm not being fair. What should I do? I'm only trying to teach him responsibility, respect for himself and others, and equally important, his education (by the way, he's an honor roll student.) This "I'll do it when I want to" attitude is truly driving me insane.

I realize the identity issue is very important, but at the same time I also believe the morals and standards are important.

Robyn

Dear Robyn,

Maintaining your perspective is crucial to raising teenagers. Since your son is on the honor roll, he is not disrespecting his education. Your problem does not reflect immorality but rather a struggle for autonomy and control. His adolescence has upset your former order in the household. Clearly, some guidelines need to be established, but being overly critical will lead to greater disharmony. And a mutual lack of respect can lead to a rupture in your relationship at a period when maintaining connection is vital to the immediate years ahead of you!

You are also witnessing the natural disorganization that comes with hormonal upheaval. Remember that physical changes are careening internally, causing excitement to erupt in your son's life. And this eruption is creating a certain loss of control over your life that you are not accustomed to! Time is an important measure of independence. We all want to be in charge of the way we spend our time and making choices is essential to our sense that we have some control in our lives.

Adolescence requires a major shift from parents. Try changing gears from being a parental authority figure who dictates rules to being a friendly authority who sets a framework for your teenager to experiment with making independent choices. Your son is at the beginning of his adolescence. He needs contact and a commitment with you that promotes his sense of autonomy in making decisions. Start with choices around his own scheduling of study, chores, and socializing. Establishing independent decision making is necessary for self-direction. It is good news that your son is not only academically, but socially involved. Your difficulties are with his choices in timing and creating an atmosphere that links his responsibilities to the family with his growing independence.

It is also important to consider that he may need more parental guidance, but in a different form than when he was younger. If he has a lot of independence in the form of being home alone or without parental contact during the day, his behavior may reflect a loneliness based on a need for more meaningful connection and discussions of such things as "fairness." By making room for discussions of ideas about fairness and other philosophical issues, rules can be established, and autonomy can take the form of passionate discourse. Allow yourself to be influenced by his feelings and needs and show him that you do respect his right to express himself and be understood. Even though you may not completely agree or entirely understand him! At least he will be aware of your effort to treat him as an equal, soliciting his ideas and opinions.

At this age, his natural outlet for not having enough parental connection might be to maximize his freedom. This could include experimenting with his schedule independently and choosing to ignore household rules. His need for parental contact in a new form may be eclipsed by his obvious motivation to belong to his peer group. But do not be fooled! Though he is vulnerable to his needs

for a peer group, he also needs your guidance to set up a different
kind of connecting with you that satisfies his needs for greater
autonomy, but honors his need to still depend on you. Tricky, huh?

Perhaps you would be wise to consider relenting on the timing of
his study schedule, and simply establish appropriate house rules. Let
him know that he does have privileges of an adult that are earned by
his taking part in the daily functioning of the family (chores). Be
specific about his phone being a result of his contributions. Do not
dictate the times of his chores. Instead find ways to allow for him to
make choices within certain parameters. For example, dishes need
to be done by 8 PM. He can do them earlier, however if they are not
done by that time, he will not be allowed the privilege of phone conversation until he has finished them. The chore becomes tied to his
responsibilities rather than to punishment doled out by a parent.

Changing gears in this way, allows your teenager to reflect on his
choices and gain mastery of his schedule. But do not misunderstand
my message. There will be a period of flux and change in your
household. You will need to tolerate not only pointing out and struc-
turing the opportunity for decision making. But you will also have
to develop some tolerance for his choices as he experiments with different times, and (as if that is not enough change for you, the parent) react neutrally to his initial cries of "injustice" when he suffers
the inevitable consequences you have described to him.

When the cry of "injustice" does echo, simply reiterate that it is
his choice to do the dishes by a certain time in exchange for the
adult privilege of talking on the phone. Maintain a matter-of-fact
tone and your stance that it is not a punishment but a consequence
of his choice of scheduling. Be sure to reinstate his adult privileges
as soon as his dishes are done without delay. This will ultimately
give him a sense that he can indeed have control!

Creating an atmosphere in which discussions can take place may
limit the amount of "acting out" behavior if such conduct is an expression of his need to separate from you. He can remain connected by
talking with you and separate by expressing a different opinion. Talk to
him about his experience of his day. Consider with him what might be
the best time for his studies. What does he think? Is it best to socialize
after school after having classroom schedules all day? Would he do better to focus on homework after dinner in the evenings? Engage him in

a discussion that includes his views, even if you do not agree with them. Realize that he is separating from you, and this may be upsetting to you. But seek contact with him that communicates respect and belief in his ability to make choices about his own schedule.

He may need your help with organizing strategies, particularly when he enters high school, at which time there will be greater impetus for new organization to succeed in a more complex environment. But for now, if he is in junior high school, he needs discussions and guidance that gradually leaves more choices to him. Expect him to try some outlandish things (including staying up too late), but trust he will create an appropriate balance when he experiences the consequences of sleep deprivation that follows.

Spend time with him doing some quality activity you can both enjoy together if at all possible. And even though you become angry or annoyed with this phase of his development, maintain the activities that bring you some time together. Even having dinner together can serve this function of sharing valuable time and letting him know that you want to be with him.

It is at this time that we as parents must show our children what we want them to value by doing it. It is very tempting to reflect annoyance, critical attitudes, and a true lack of respect for teenagers. (After all, aren't they acting like "idiots"?) Instead, try treating them with increased respect. Take the attitude that they will respond to you with greater consideration as you relate to their needs in a positive and curious manner, rather than a deprecating one.

Remember to use humor as your best ally in letting go of some of the control you enjoyed when your children were more obedient and well-behaved. You are in for a few years of ruckus in the household, but this is the price of sharing your life with a teenager. Sometimes I have found it useful to (almost) pretend that my teenager was two years old, but with a bigger body!

All teasing aside, there is some resemblance between the two periods of childhood. Both represent periods of development in which conflict between independence and dependence prevails. And though your adolescent appears to want only his freedom, he also has significant needs for guidance into what it means to be an adult.

Consider also that you may gain spiritually, from experiencing some humility during this period. Your ability to react with neutrality instead of supreme indignance will most probably prove satisfying to you in the end. It will also help you bridge the "gap" with discussions and activities that keep you connected. I often think of Martin Luther King's words, "The measure of a man (woman) is not when things are going well, but when they are not."

Adolescence challenges our growth as parents to develop into that which we preach. I found this to be a period in which I had to learn increased patience and tolerance, and a willingness to model the very behavior I wanted to imbue in my own children. Perhaps you will find some personal jewel beneath all the hard work. After all, diamonds are formed when carbon molecules are crystallized under pressure!

Many other pressures arise with the differentiating that occurs in adolescence. The following question and answer illustrates the difficulties parents face in guiding their teens through modern times for which they may feel unprepared!

Daughter does not want intercourse, but sees no problem with oral sex

Dear Dr. Gayle,

My teenage daughter told me she does not plan on having intercourse but she (and her friends) see no problem at all with having oral sex. When she told me this I was absolutely floored and didn't have a clue how to handle it or what to say. Any ideas?

Lynn

Dear Lynn,

Your teenager is ignoring the emotional ramifications involved in becoming sexually active. Her psychological readiness to share her body with a sexual partner deserves special consideration, whether she is contemplating oral sex, intercourse, or mutual masturbation! Let your daughter know that having sex is an intimate experience with both emotional as well as physical dimensions. Do not be thrown by your adolescent's arbitrary statement. She may be speaking provocatively in order to stimulate having a discussion with you on the subject. Certainly, if her concern was only about pregnancy, then oral sex might be her answer. It is your job to point out to her that pregnancy is not the only issue here!

Do not be afraid to speak frankly and directly to your daughter about sex. It is your teenager's job to challenge, and yours to answer the call by letting her know your beliefs and philosophy. Have the same kind of discussion with her that you would have about intercourse. This is an opportunity to share your values with her as a woman and as a mother.

If you truly believe that sex should be nurtured within a loving and committed relationship, tell her so and why. If you believe that trust is an important prerequisite to sexual vulnerability with another, let her know why you believe it will make a difference for her. But do not stop there!

Banish any myth that oral sex equals safe sex. Though rare, it is possible to contract HIV orally, presumably if open sores in the mouth were present. Since the mouth is susceptible to undetectable lesions, oral sex is no guarantee of safety from this or other sexually transmitted disease, such as herpes.

But physical health is not the only point. Your daughter's developing sexuality and her self-perception is at stake. How she relates to her sexuality now, will lay the foundation for how she values herself in future relationships with men. If she chooses to sexualize a relationship, it is important that it be a positive experience that increases her sense of value rather than decreases it.

Emotional health and self-esteem hinge upon meaningful relationships with others, whether they are sexualized or not. Sex is a big step that requires responsibility for another person. If trust is important in friendship, why wouldn't it be critical in a sexual relationship? Your daughter's self-respect rests upon how she perceives she is treated by others, and what she means to them. Sex can alter the definition of an existing relationship. Help her to anticipate these changes and evaluate how she might feel about having sex with someone, after the fact.

Use this as an opportunity to connect and discuss sex with your teen, rather than avoiding it. Your teenager's sexual development and interest can also bring up vulnerability for you, too. If so, sort through your feelings with your husband or a close friend, so that you can speak openly with your daughter.

If you never had this kind of discussion with your own mother, you may find it particularly awkward at first. But if you talk through your initial discomfort, you will likely find that your relationship with your daughter deepens. She might even be secretly relieved for your guidance on the subject!

Teaching values to adolescents

Learning to use opportunities for disagreement to teach values cannot begin too early. Lately, violence has erupted in our schools and researchers have linked these events to a lack of involvement and recognition of warning signs that our children are in trouble. The following two questions and answers are examples of parents' struggles through the Columbine high school tragedy in April of 1999, in which two students killed students and one teacher.

Talking to our children in the aftermath of tragedy

Dear Dr. Gayle,

My eleven-year-old is afraid to go to school. I am afraid to send her and do not know what to say to her to help her and myself deal with the Columbine High violence. What should I be looking for, in terms of stress symptoms in her and what can I do about them?

Pam

Dear Pam,

It is natural for your daughter to want to stay home with you at a time when her sense of safety has been shattered. Children can experience post-traumatic stress from identification with the students who endured the violence. And you, too, experience empathy and shock for the parents whose children are direct victims.

Staying physically close to you may be your daughter's way of coping. Your presence alone is immediately soothing, and can help her to recover her sense of security. Use the following guidelines and discussion to help you and your daughter find the path towards recovery.

1. *Expression: The first step of recovery*

Establish a safe environment for talking about feelings. Show your willingness to talk with your child about her feelings, but do not force her to talk. She will express herself when she is ready. Let her know that you, too, are stunned and saddened. Answer her questions honestly, but do not try to explain anything you cannot understand yourself. Refrain from giving false promises, "This can never happen to you;" but do convey a sense that you believe this tragedy will cause people everywhere to actively search for needed answers.

2. *Active response*

A second step in the recovery process includes being able to address or actively respond to the traumatic event. Being witness to a crime is traumatic because the witness was helpless to stop the crime. In a true sense, we are all witnesses to this tragedy, and as such need to actively respond to heal. Let her know you are deeply concerned, and will be talking with other parents and teachers about safety at her school.

Make time to consult with teachers, administrators, and other parents about addressing this tragedy. Many schools have provided classroom time devoted to talking about this event. High school English teachers are well aware that students use poetry and writing assignments to work through traumatic life processes. Art, drama, and music projects, as well as community gardens, have been utilized to recover from crisis. Telling your story (feelings, perceptions) to peers and teachers who are also working through this trauma is deeply therapeutic for your child and yourself.

Connecting with others allows us to express the shock, pain, and grief rather than repressing it. Children who do repress fear or grief initially may experience delayed stress symptoms later. A pattern of sleeplessness, anxiety, nightmares, or even depression may result if overwhelming feelings have no opportunity to be released. Encourage your child's physical, creative, and artistic avenues of expression at this time.

Signs of stress can include regressions to earlier behavioral patterns, such as clinging to your side, or the reverse, retreating from contact, depending on the child. Encourage your child to maintain a routine schedule, but remain connected and interested in talking about what is being discussed in the classroom. Encourage these discussions and stay in touch with your child's school experience.

Expect children to respond to this trauma according to their stage of development. Younger children will be more focused on safety alone. Older children in junior high and high school may come home debating interpretations of non-conformity and individualism. Adults will need to grapple with the absence of government programs that provide schools with the therapeutic, educational, and family support services required to address the violence happening in our schools. Our schools are, after all, a microcosm of our society.

Research on child development and prevention of criminal behavior points to a child's need for one caring adult to consistently believe in, and be committed to, their best interests. All children need a mentor. This adult can be a parent, an aunt, an uncle, a grandfather, or a teacher. There is no one family constellation that guarantees that a child will experience a quality, caring relationship with an adult. And single parents can and do provide such quality at the same rate as two parent families.

Children "fall through the cracks" because there is no one committed to their well-being, in a society that is getting increasingly difficult to navigate. The boys who perpetrated the tragedy at Columbine High were nearing the end of their high school careers. Was anyone helping them make plans for their future? Leaving high school for the adult world can be an overwhelming transition, when the future looks bleak and hopeless.

If "it takes a village to raise a child," the Columbine and other school tragedies tells us there is a gross miscarriage of caretaking by our society. Our government programs should provide our educational system with support necessary to children and families in trouble. And parents should feel there is somewhere to turn for help and resources when their own efforts to reach a disenfranchised teen are not enough.

Violence and boys

Dr. Gayle,

What can we do so that our boys do not turn to violence to express their pain?

"He's acting like a girl! Stop hiding him behind your apron strings," my father exclaimed in passionate disgust to my mother when she protested sending my ten-year-old brother out to play in a dress. At seven years of age, I did not know what, exactly, my brother had done to deserve such punishment, but I felt the pain and shame of my father's cruelty as I watched my older brother hide from neighborhood children who would taunt him. My father, a man who shielded his own sensitivity in military machismo, believed he was teaching his son to be a man.

William Pollack, in his book, *Real Boys*,[42] calls this kind of destructive behavior towards our sons a part of the "boy code" perpetuated by our society. His research validates what Olga Silverstein and femi-

---

42. W. Pollack, *Real Boys* (New York: Holt, 1999).

nist family therapists have warned us about previously.[43] Boys are shamed into early separation from their mothers and subsequently cut off from their own expression of sadness and vulnerability in favor of anger and detachment, in order to prove their manhood. Repression of feelings ("big boys don't cry") starts early for a male child in our society and mothers are warned from the beginning of the emasculating dangers of making their son a "Mama's boy."

Boys are diagnosed with significantly higher rates of learning disabilities, hyperactivity, and conduct disorder in our schools. In fact, Pollack tells us that boys are ten times more likely to be diagnosed with a serious emotional illness than girls. Is it any wonder that boys, ashamed to show emotional pain, reach out for help through aggressive conduct? After all, it is manly to punch, while it is "sissy" to cry. With suicide being the third biggest killer of young people ages fifteen to twenty-four, boys are four to six times more likely to succeed at committing suicide, than girls.

The push towards early separation and independence for a boy, usually by toddler age, can set the stage for depression when adjustment problems occur later. And conflicts of identity and sexuality that arise in adolescence are fertile ground for complications when boys are given a second "push" to be self-reliant and repress needs for ongoing nurturance.

But William Pollack warns us that a boy's pain may not stop there. Repression of vulnerable feelings can cause a boy to further "harden," and coupled with anger and rage as the only acceptable male emotions, can create a formula for violence. When this equation gestates over time, it becomes fertile ground for unexpressed inner grief to take the form of outward rage.

When disconnection has reached crisis proportions inside and out, violence can become the distorted cry for relationship. Anger and rage are emotions of "strength" and even power, while sadness, fear and loneliness are "weak." When a boy believes this, he acts accordingly. Cutting off from his own emotions, he becomes disconnected from himself. Perhaps it is when this disconnection becomes complete that the choice to kill ensures that others will know the pain he feels inside.

---

43. O. Silverstein, B. Carter, M. Walters, & P. Papp, *The Family Web: Gender Patterns in Family Relationships* (New York: Guilford Press, 1988), p. 166.

In the absence of any one committed adult who cares and is in touch with this child, things can worsen, with destruction expressed towards oneself, others, or as in the Columbine tragedy, both. Certainly there are many contributing factors in the formula for violence of this kind, notwithstanding the availability of illegal weapons and the potential for desensitization to caused by the violent imagery commonly found in the movies our children watch and the video games they play.

Still, the line between reality and fantasy is crossed because of serious emotional illness which has not been adequately addressed by people and the institutions we create as a society to raise and nurture our children. Our society's formula for "manhood" is a part of the equation for depression, which may help set a boy on a course towards "crying bullets" to express his sadness and break his isolation.

What can we do to help our sons?

1. Establish a safe environment to talk about the "boy code" as it comes up. Let your son know that all of his feelings are natural and that you do not expect him to "tough it out." If he is looking sad, say so. Ask him if he is feeling depressed and let him know you are available. But do not stop there!

2. Stay connected. Actively work to set the stage for contact that can lead to discussions. He may not choose to immediately open up to you, but he may open up when you are doing an activity together. Make weekly dates with your son to have lunch together, see a movie, attend a sports activity or some other event of his interest. I found that my teenage son loved to be tucked-in each night, although it took the form of massaging his back after football practice (and injuries.) It was during this time that he gradually opened up and talked to me about his day, his fears, and things that were not going well for him.

3. Go below the surface. Try to anticipate periods of transition or events that could be stressful to your son, even though he says "I'm fine, no big deal." Being rejected by a girl he asks out, failing to make the baseball team, being ridiculed for his sensitivity, or drifting apart from a friend should bring some "down" feelings. Let him know you expect him to have failures as well as triumphs, and share your experiences of disappointments as well as successes. This will help him feel less alone with defeat and less likely to harbor feelings of shame because of it.

4. Reward him for showing empathy to others as well as being able to express his vulnerable feelings when they arise. "I am proud of your ability to be a good friend," or "I am glad you can cry about that, it shows you care."

5. Affirm the kind of boy that your son is, outside of gender stereotypes. Let him know that sensitivity, creativity and avenues of pursuit, such as cooking or playing house, are as valuable self-expressions as the normal "rough-housing" or "action play" that boys do. In fact, it is worth pointing out that such homemaking skills are essential to a boy's eventual independence when he does leave home to live on his own.

6. Do not confuse "action" with "violence." A word of warning about seeing your son's natural aggressiveness through a distorted lens of fear, particularly in light of recent school violence. Help your son establish healthy limits and avoid self-destructive risk-taking, but assist him in finding healthy and constructive avenues for letting off steam, physically, too. Karate, sports, and punching bags can help him release pent-up energy while respecting and caring for others.

Testosterone does not equal violence, but it may contribute to differences in a boy's tendencies of self-expression. Do not shame your son for his aggression or label him because of it. Help him channel aggressive energy constructively and teach him to reach out for help, without humiliation.

Keep in mind that the major protection your child has against drugs, unhealthy risk-taking behavior, or crime is the ongoing relationship of one, caring adult who is committed to his well-being. More is better, but one is enough! This is you. It is up to you to know where your child is, which sometimes may take extra effort in these days of travel in cyberspace. Do you know, for example, what sites your child has been visiting on the internet? Time magazine (May 10, 1999) offers parents a list of software and tips to help you keep track of the sites your child has recently visited online.

Do not fall into despair or helplessness about violence in videos, music, or movies. Instead, stay connected with your child in talking about them. If necessary, consider limitations, but do not stop there! Talk about drugs, alcohol, violence, and crime. Take your children to movies that show the values you want to teach them. Watch shows with them you believe are violent and be willing to discuss what you see. Your input is your child's greatest ally against unhealthy influences. Know who your child's friends are and what they spend their time doing. Now, more than ever, the answer is to connect and communicate!

A word of support to single mothers: Single mothers are often encouraged to find male role models, leaving a mother to believe she cannot raise her son on her own. This is not true! Feminist therapists have voiced the belief that a boy's relationship to his mother forms the basis for being able to be intimate. Emotional intimacy between mother and son is a foundation for a boy's growth, not his demise!

Certainly, including more adults, male and female in your son's life is desirable, as any one single caretaker has limited energy. But searching out male role models to make up for a deficit in your own ability to effectively parent leads to false solutions.

Healthy parenting does require adequate self-esteem and in a single mother household, as with a two parent household, an attitude of respect for men (and women) is critical to a son's (and daughter's!) development. Mothers have long been held responsible for their children's development on the one hand, and ridiculed for their closeness to their sons on the other. The "boy code" binds both men and women. William Pollack encourages mothers and fathers to be close to their sons and acknowledges, rather than criticizes, mothers for their efforts. He writes:

"[I]t is not mothers who are crippling our boys masculinity. It is society's myths about manhood that are preventing boys from being seen and trained as whole human beings, men who can work effectively and live in close relationship to other people."[44]

Nurture your sons as much as your daughters. See their strengths and their vulnerabilities. The "boy code" does not by itself cause violence, but it can establish an environment where it can grow.

Raising teenagers can be as rewarding as it is stressful. When we are able to remain connected to our growing teenagers, we naturally evolve, as do our marriage relationships.

In our earlier example of Bill and Mary, the entry into the stage of raising adolescents was the breaking threshold in the marriage, as the accumulated stress of previous stages added to the challenge of the cur-

---

44. W. Pollack, *Real Boys* (New York: Holt, 1999), p. 98.

rent one. If couples have not maintained and strengthened their marriage over the years, the need to do so intensifies at this time. And the room to do so, as an adolescent's independence increases, can leave time free to address the intimacy issues in the couple's relationship. But without realignment, an already weakened marriage can be strained to the breaking point by the additional stress of adolescence.

NINE

Divorce

Choices in Growth and Pain

Over half of marriages end in divorce. But the dissolution of the marriage does not end the family. Relationships must adapt to tremendous change amid sadness and often bitterness. As we understand the changes inherent in divorce, we are left with many questions.

Although we are still attempting to understand the best approaches for helping parents and children through this transition, what is clear is that it should be treated as a normal, rather than an abnormal transition. The questions and answers in this chapter address common concerns and challenges of this very important transitional crisis in the family and offer guidelines for healthy adjustment. Parents need to consider how the divorce is handled, not just the divorce itself, so that their children come through this change with a greater sense of resiliency than may have been the case if the parents had remained in a marriage of high conflict. The following question and answer illustrates how and why children can fare worse in high conflict, intact families, than their peers in less conflicted, divorced situations.

Is divorce always damaging to children?

Dr. Gayle,

A friend of mine is miserable in his marriage. He and his wife hate each other and have tried to work through it. They are afraid of the damage a divorce would do to their child. I have tried to express that their constant unhappiness and conflict may do more

*damage than the divorce. What advice would you have that I can
pass along to them?*

Linda

Dear Linda,

Divorce and its effects on children are often misunderstood by parents. And in the last two decades public opinion has undergone dramatic pendulum swings. The media loves drama and proliferates the false belief that all divorce ravages children. As if it were the divorce itself, and not the way the family handles it, or what improvements are being sought in the family, that impacts a child in the long term.

There have been very few studies that document the long term effects of divorce on children before 1980 when J. S. Wallerstein presented her research project on children and divorce.[45] The positive influence of the project was to make parents think deeply about the process of divorce, and how it can be handled by the divorcing parents in the best interests of the child. This was, and still is, an important message. Prior to this time, divorce was seen more in light of a solution that was better for children if their parents had conflict. Clearly, as a society we were underestimating the potential negative impact that children can suffer in divorce. However, Wallerstein's work came under heavy criticism by her colleagues for skewed population and interpretation. But though her work came under fire, it spurred others to delve more deeply into the truly subtle and complex issues in divorce and spawned other studies of great merit. In the meantime, however, divorce began to be seen as the culprit, pure and simple, whether or not this was Wallerstein's intention. Newspaper headlines glared the newfound "truth" that divorce harms children! No wonder your friends, or others may feel the way they do.

When necessary, divorce can be in the best interests of the child. In 1982, E. M. Hetherington and her research team studied the effects of divorce on the family.[46] Her work has been heralded as one of the best designed research studies and clearly states that a conflict-ridden intact home is more detrimental to all family members than a stable home in which parents are divorced. Naturally, this is because the continued

45. J. S. Wallerstein, *Surviving the Breakup: How Children and Parents Cope with Divorce* (New York: Basic Books, 1980).

46. E. M. Hetherington, M. Cox, & R. Cox, "Effects of Divorce on Parents and Children." In M.Lamb (Ed.), *Non-traditional Families: Parenting and Child Development* (Hillsdale, NJ: Erlbaum Associates, 1982).

conflict drains the energy needed for a child's development, causing difficulties in learning, socializing, or other areas of growth; not to mention the role model of the marital relationship being played out and the effects on the child of living in a war zone. This kind of unresolvable conflict creates emotional insecurity for all family members. The experience of divorce and its long term impact will be unique to the child. We could imagine both negative and positive results, depending on the child and on their lives post divorce. There are situations where children fare better after the divorce. Divorce is a tool. Norma Walsh, a noted family researcher, is not alone in her field when she states that the family processes and quality of family relationships remain the most significant predictor for health in families, divorced or not.[47]

Tell your friend that divorce does not create dysfunction! Families experiencing divorce have the same range of functionality as intact families. Family researchers have found that it is not divorce that creates long term disturbance in children, but three other significant factors related to post separation changes. These are:

1. The quality of post-separation life on the children—for example, whether they are propelled into poverty or cannot pursue classes or education they enjoyed previously.

2. Change in quality of the relationship with a parent following divorce.

3. The number and degree of other stressors induced by the separation for the child.

Minimizing the above factors in a child's life increases stability and the child's ability to benefit from the divorce. Divorce does not change the fact that parents have a responsibility to continue to raise their child together and to keep in the forefront of their minds what is in the best interests of the child throughout the process. Marriage ends with divorce, but parenting does not!

We should not embrace divorce as an answer to all our problems, because it does cause more problems that need thorough consideration. Neither should we be afraid to divorce if it is in the best interest of the family.

---

47. N. Walsh, "Conceptualizations of Normal Family Processes." In F. Walsh (Ed.), *Normal Family Processes*, 2nd edition (New York: Guilford Press, 1993).

A family is a system. We cannot underestimate the pain inherited by our children for marriages that are unworkable. Children of divorce suffer. And so do children who are steeped in conflict and pain unchanged over years in their parents' marriage. These adult children may never marry, because of the pain they perceive as marriage. They do not expect happiness in marriage because it has not been their experience of their parents' relationship.

Some children will suffer more if the marital discord is covert instead of out in the open. Sometimes parents feel they can protect their child from pain by shielding them from the conflict. Children definitely should be shielded from the marital battle. However, after a point, if resolution cannot be achieved, the marital battle spills inevitably onto the unconscious of the child, and the atmosphere of the family. Communication is shortened. Depth of feeling is absent. Left unidentified and ignored, such unconscious conflict can be more destructive to our children's future than if it is brought out in the open and addressed in divorce. Fears of intimacy and commitment, thought to be results of divorce, are in fact phenomena often experienced by children who grew up in disturbed intact families. Parents that remain married "for the sake of the children" may for all intents and purposes be emotionally divorced. When this emotional alienation occurs, children may develop an aversion to intimacy or an inability to commit to a partner.

In addition we should keep in mind that when spouses divorce, they are not guaranteed of marital happiness with anyone else. However, they are eligible for future happiness! And this future happiness, if it becomes a reality, can be a real improvement in the family system. Children can definitely benefit when this is the case. However it is important to balance the pros and cons and take responsibility for providing the stability and guidelines for caring for your child through the trauma of divorce as the first order of business, if this is the avenue of choice. A book which can help parents with this process is *The Good Divorce* by C. R. Ahrons.[48]

But before proceeding towards divorce, it is important to turn over every stone to ensure you are not jumping out of the frying pan and into the fire. To not repeat our mistakes, we must understand our own contributions to them. And without effectively working

---

48. C. Ahrons, *The Good Divorce* (New York: Harper Collins, 1994).

through why the marriage is failing, we are vulnerable to regrets down the road. Have your friends tried to work through their marital difficulties? Do they know why things are not working? What are their individual contributions are to marital discord? Have they studied their families of origin for projections of past childhood ghosts onto their relationship? In short, have they tried to save the marriage through intensive marriage counseling? There may be reasons why they are not divorcing other than their child. It is important that if they do remain married, they continue to work on improving their relationship. This could lead to deeper and rewarding change at best, and provides the child with parental role models who are taking responsibility to search for solutions instead of creating an atmosphere of despair and victimization.

Whether or not it is divorce that is the best answer for your friends' marriage, it does seem apparent that some reflection and work on the relationship is in order. To not work on the partnership in some capacity, as long as they are remaining together, is to create an atmosphere of despair, leaving the child with unconscious responsibility for the parents' happiness. It is the parents' responsibility for staying in or getting out of the marriage. No child benefits from being an albatross.

The ongoing quality of the relationship and contact with your children following divorce is key to assuring them they are still loved and cared for by you, despite the breakup of the marital relationship. Studies have found that continued access and the quality of your ongoing connection is more important than the type of custody arrangements made. How you handle divorce makes the difference for your children's healthy adjustment.

Helping kids cope with divorce

Dr. Gayle,

My husband and I just told our children that we are getting a divorce. My eleven-year-old son is doing a lot of talking, which I perceive as a healthy way to understand the situation. My fourteen-year-old daughter is totally clamming up. I don't know what to do.

Heather

Dear Heather:

Arrange for the children to visit what will be their father's new residence as soon as possible to establish their ongoing connection and relationship with him. Also, he should let his son and daughter know how and where he can be reached and what arrangements he will make to spend time with them. If these details have not been decided, ease the pain by slowing this process down, if at all possible.

Whether or not one or both the children should be present when their father moves depends on their readiness to help him, as well as his readiness to have their help. Discuss what is in their best interests, before asking what their preferences are. It is likely, however, that it is you who will not want to be present.

Although things have not worked out in the marriage, the two of you still have two children to raise together. Speak with your husband about keeping the children out of your conflict as much as possible. Also, reassure them that they will continue to be loved and cared for by the two of you. Let your children know that your love for one another has changed, but that your love for them remains strong and constant.

Divorce is painful and it is traumatic for children and spouses. Still, how parents handle divorce makes the difference in their children's healthy adjustment or potential maladjustment. Here are guidelines that family researchers have identified to help ease this transition.

What you can do:

1. Make decisions whenever possible to reduce other changes your children will experience during this transition. Avoid a change in your residence, or change in the schools your children attend, if at all possible. Children need a support system of friends, teachers, and other adults to help them through this change.

2. Reduce immediate financial stress by taking a loan from relatives, if necessary. Use credit for temporary relief, until you can stabilize. Consider refinancing your home on a low adjustable mortgage and consolidating other debts, until you can get back on your feet, both emotionally and economically. This will also free up money for support services as you travel through this family crisis. Studies have found[49] that poverty resulting from a divorce—not father's absence—was associated with the greatest disturbance in kids. This is not to say that fathers are not important: They are!

---

49. E. Hetherington,T. Law and T. O'Connor, "Divorce: Challenges, Changes and New Chances." In F. Walsh (ed), *Normal Family Processes*, 2nd ed. (New York: Guilford Press, 1993).

But even in cases where fathers disappeared, financial support was also withdrawn, resulting in a lifestyle change and decreased resources for many children of single working mothers.

3. Make an agreement with your spouse to refrain from talking about the details of the divorce. Do not talk badly about the other spouse to the children. Refrain from arguing in front of the children and do your best to keep them out of your conflict!

4. Do not give children more responsibility than they are ready for during this period.

5. Do not make a child a confidant for the pain the divorce is causing you. Seek a support group to help you through this period. Share your feelings with friends and professionals, who can help you grieve and reclaim yourself from the marriage.

6. Support connections with extended family. Help your children avoid choosing sides or being caught in a conflict of loyalty between the two parents they both need and love.

Family experts also advise that parents establishing co-parenting after a divorce reduce conflict by staying clear of any discussion about their relationship. Focus instead on what is in the best interests of your children, and what you can reasonably do to support your child's positive and strong relationship with both parents. Establish clear, agreed upon boundaries to reduce pain and protect the children from any unresolved marital conflict.

Let your children know you are sad and be available for their feelings, too. Cry together and grieve together, but stop short of blaming. Look into programs in your area that connect children with others their ages who are going through a similar experience. Let them know they are not alone. Work to accept their anger, but do not fail to continue to set limits as appropriate to their age.

Your son is talking about his feelings, while your daughter seems to be keeping her feelings inside at the moment. Let your daughter know you are available to her when she is ready to talk about it, and acknowledge that you know it is very hard for her, too. Keep in mind that your daughter is further into adolescence, which is a time of pulling away and separating. Paradoxically, the divorce creates instability. This may make her movement toward independence more difficult for a while. Encourage her to spend time with her father. Both children should experience some reassurance and initial relief as they experience continued and consistent contact with their father, even though he is moving out of the family home.

Children fare best when parents are able to keep them out of the middle and work toward reducing their conflict post-divorce. *Quality* contact with both parents and low conflict are the two best predictors for adjustment in children.

High conflict, which continues to trap children in the middle, even after divorce, is the greatest predictor of poor adaptation in children. This held true for a variety of custody arrangements.[50]

Take care of your children, but do not forget yourself! Seek support through this period of mourning for your marriage. One year following divorce, over half of women report their lives are improved, and sixty-five percent credit positive emotional and psychological growth to their divorce.

Be assured, that while you are in the midst of crisis, you have the opportunity to work your way through grief and toward recovery. Take to heart the well-worn phrase so many family therapists use to describe this journey: a process of "crisis and transformation."

Establishing a stable schedule for contact with both parents is important in the early phase of separation. It is at this time that children need their questions answered and to know that they will still see both parents and on what terms. In fact it is best to slow things down so that separation does not take place until children are told what is happening and how and when they will continue to see both parents.

How to tell four-year-old that mommy and daddy are getting a divorce

Dear Dr. Gayle,

I would like some information on how to explain to a four-year-old about mommy and daddy not living together anymore. She has been through a lot, but has a hard time understanding that her daddy and mommy don't live together anymore. Also her father lives about nine hours from us. She used to see him all the time, now she's lucky if he comes to visit her once every four months.

---

50. F. Walsh, *Strengthening Family Resilience* (New York: Guilford Press, 1998).

What can I do to help her understand that her daddy still loves her
but we as a family can't live together anymore?

Connie

Dear Connie,

Four is a very tender age and your concern for your daughter
shows you are taking her needs seriously. A divorce is a dissolution of
a marriage, but it is not a dissolution of family. Family relationships
change, but you and your daughter's father are still her parents.

About fifty percent of couples following divorce are able to work out
an amicable relationship that promotes the job of co-parenting even
though the marriage relationship is over. It is not necessary, however,
to be friends with your ex-spouse in order to sustain and support relationships with both parents that are in the best interests of the child.

The initial period of separation is the most difficult because you
are reeling from the transition from a nuclear family to some form
of a "binuclear" family. But the equilibrium has not yet been established. It is important for a child to know that though mommy and
daddy's feelings have changed for one another, they both continue to
love her and remain committed to taking care of her. She will need
to hear this many times. And she will need to hear it from both of
you. She will need to be able to repeat the story of the divorce to
others. So it is important that you and her father together agree on
an explanation that is non-blaming of the other and simple enough
for a four-year-old to understand and repeat to others. Telling the
story about the change is one way children work through the grief
and adjustment to this separation.

Talk with your "ex" about your daughter's needs. Let him know
that she needs him. If he has trouble listening to you about this,
arrange for mediation to work out parenting in the best interests of
your child. He may be unaware of his importance to her, particularly
if he did not develop a separate relationship with her when he lived
in the home. Communicate this in a non-blaming manner. He is
divorcing you, not his daughter. It is necessary for him to initiate
extra effort at this time to create a separate relationship with his
child. It may be that when you lived together, he depended on you to
feel connected to his daughter. Now he must do this for himself. If
this is the case, doing so may make him a better father to his daughter living separately, than he was when living in the home.

Arrange a meeting with your daughter's father to talk with him about how often he will visit, how he will be available to his daughter, and how you can support their ongoing relationship even if he is not living with her any longer. Do your best to put aside your own hurt feelings or anger in your relationship with your "ex" in order to negotiate your continuing parental responsibilities. Ask for his best efforts to do the same. Your child deserves this effort for full cooperation. Raising your child continues to be both of your responsibilities and is one of the most important processes to be worked out in divorce.

Once you set up a schedule, let your daughter know when she will be seeing her dad. Give her a calendar with the dates circled. Also support phone and letter contact, e-mail, and sending him pictures or stories about her day if at all possible. Find out which of her friends have parents who have divorced or separated and talk about their adjustments to mommy and daddy living separately. It would be good for her hear about other children going through this process. It would also be helpful if she has a place or room for her things at daddy's house. Getting this place together for her visits can help her feel more secure with the changes. It would be helpful for dad to buy her a special gift to help her through his absence. Pictures or other objects that remind her of their connection and that he loves her will also be soothing to her during this transition.

Accept her tears, sadness, rage, and anger at this change, as it is one of the most significant changes in her life and one she has not asked for! She has no control over a major life event that is happening to her. Give her as much say in things as is possible and appropriate in the situation, such as being able to contact daddy at particular times of the day when he will be available to her. Keep other schedules and relationships in her life as stable as possible as she adapts to this transition. Do not change daycare, schools, or her primary residence unless it is absolutely unavoidable. Wait until she has adjusted to the separation to make any needed changes in these areas.

Establish new rituals for yourselves. Going out for pizza every Friday, or with friends to the movies once a week may help normalize your routine together. Check for local groups for children going through this transition and for single mother support groups for yourself. Taking care of your needs right now will benefit her, too.

Children do adjust and they are truly resilient. However they do need special attention to feel secure through such a major life transition. Increase the art supplies in your home. Be sure she has opportunity to express her feelings through play as this is a child's avenue for adaptation. Your daughter is mourning the loss of the family unit as she has known it since birth. Be patient with any tantrums or anger at this time. And offer her ways to draw, to paint, and to hear and tell stories about the changes she is experiencing.

Absorbing her anger and pain will also require that you have someone to talk to as well! Mourning is a process of letting go before you can take things in again. Be sure you are caring for yourself through this period of family transformation. Spending time with friends, eating well, socializing and getting exercise are some activities that can become fragmented.

The dissolution of a relationship is also an opportunity for personal transformation and healing if we can understand the meaning of the divorce to our personal histories and take responsibility for what we may have contributed to the failure in the marriage. Education, counseling, or psychotherapy can be powerful tools for uncovering what happened and help us heal through understanding our own needs and being better able to successfully address them the next time around. This kind of parental self reflection (for both mothers and fathers!) is the best insurance for a child that history will not repeat itself, as about fifty percent of remarriages end in divorce.

Recovering yourself from the relationship and helping your daughter adjust and maintain relationships with her biological parents is the first order of business. Doing what you can to insure that she does not suffer further loss in family cohesion in the future, however, begins with deep reflection on the past by both parents individually. This perspective on the future in caring for children is often missed during this transition.

Whether divorce is used as a tool for learning or becomes a legacy of aborted attempts at creating family, will become a part of your child's history. Divorce can be an opportunity for growth and healing if we reflect deeply enough so that history is unlikely to repeat itself.

Parents sometimes resort to the courts for answers, which may or may not end up being in the best interests of your child. Sometimes it is a good idea to attempt mediation a second time, or talk with your ex-spouse again, before letting a judge decide your fate. This next question and answer deals with this dilemma.

Working through visitation problems

Dr. Gayle,

After a long battle with my ex-girlfriend, I've been given visitation rights to see my three-year-old daughter every other weekend. Her mother has fought every step of the way to keep me from my daughter; even when we were together she never let me care for her. My little girl becomes upset when it's time to leave her mother, which is expected. But my ex says that if my daughter cries, I can't take her. What can I do to make her mother cooperate? Can I do anything without incurring more legal bills to make my ex cooperate?

Tim

Dear Tim,

Your situation is a difficult one. Although you can force the issue of visitation legally, the intense conflict between you and her mother may traumatize your daughter. This could be harmful in many ways, and may strain your relationship with your daughter. It's possible that your best intentions could end up backfiring over time, and your relationship with your daughter could suffer.

Your child is still quite young, and you and your ex-girlfriend apparently cooperated in making her the primary nurturer when you were together. Although you may have regrets about allowing this to happen, it is now history. This was the situation, for whatever reasons, that the two of you enacted.

It would be prudent to talk with your daughter's mother about cooperating with you at this point, for your child's sake, instead of forcing you to resort to legal coercion. Perhaps mediation could help resolve this conflict with some equanimity by providing a safe place where you can express yourselves. It is in the best interest of your child that the two of you strive to develop a working relationship to keep your child from being caught in the middle of your tension.

If you are so inclined, ask your ex-girlfriend how much visitation she believes would help your daughter adjust to separation from her at this age. What is in the best interest of the child depends heavily on the relationship you've had with your daughter from birth until the present and how familiar you are with her needs and personality. If your child has not been separated from her mother for any length of time, and you have not been very present in your daughter's life up to this point, it is possible that your daughter would adapt to you better on a graduated schedule. If this is the case, it may be more appropriate to start with half days twice or three times per week, eventually working up to full days and a full weekend over a much greater length of time.

Work together or with a mediator to see if you can forge some compromise that offers your daughter a less-conflicted experience. If she has never been apart from her mother for a period of forty-eight hours, you may find that she is emotionally unavailable for developing a relationship with you when you are with her. Your best course of action would be to try to develop a more cooperative relationship with the mother of your child to support your relationship with your daughter.

Though this approach may not feel "fair" to you, it is important to put your daughter's experience and needs ahead of your own. Attachment to a primary nurturing figure is a delicate phenomenon that should be treated with respect, whether it is fair to you or not. You have a right to have a relationship with your daughter. Appeal to your child's mother to offer cooperative suggestions instead of mere resistance. Let her know you would prefer very much to avoid the use of legal force on her for access to your child, and request that she offer a plan for beginning visitation with graduated increases as your daughter adjusts to the schedule. This will give you and your daughter time to adjust to one another in shorter periods, which are likely to be more satisfying and successful connections from the start. Building on these successes will more likely ensure continued strengthening of your relationship in the years ahead.

If you find that you have truly done your best in offering to hear her best suggestions for helping you develop a relationship with your daughter, and tried to reach her with the help of a mediator without obtaining any results, you will be left to make your decision unilaterally. Invite the mother of your child to be a part of the solution rather than an obstacle to your relationship with your daughter. It is in your daughter's best interests that she develop a safe and trusting relationship with you. Let your ex-girlfriend know that this issue will not disappear and that you need her help in setting up a cooperative parenting approach that will benefit your daughter rather than cause her further distress in separating from her.

Slow this down and see if the two of you can come to some mutually acceptable agreement that is in the best interests of your daughter. You once cared for each other and were able to conceive this child together. Is there some way to make peace with one another in order to truly offer your child the best of both of you, instead of the worst of a miscarried relationship?

Another example of court-ordered decisions shows why it is best to develop a cooperative parenting arrangement with your ex-spouse if at all possible, rather than depending upon the courts to determine your children's welfare. Many parents find they can put old marital conflict aside and discuss the activities and needs of their children, if they give it extra thought and effort.

Parental rights and children's welfare

Dr. Gayle,

It seems the case, rather than the exception that the needs of the parent or parents outweigh the needs of the children in a custody battle. In our case the court has ordered that my children must spend eight weeks every summer, and half the school vacations, and every other weekend at their father's. Their father lives three hours (one way) from where my children and I reside. The court has also ordered that we share driving, or mileage.

All and all my ex-husband got everything he asked for. The children got nothing they asked for. My son, who is twelve, wants to run cross country and all the other sports. His father has already told him, "Tough, guess you'll miss every other weekend!" All the meets are on weekends. I have tried to get a lawyer to look into talking to his father, but it is just out of my money range.

As for my daughter, she doesn't look at her father as her dad, as she was very young when he filed for divorce. She thinks of my husband as her dad, and doesn't even want to be forced to have to go to see her biological father.

I am put in the middle, as the court order says I must make them go, or be held in contempt. I really encourage them to have a rela-

tionship with their father, but he no longer upholds the values that our family believes in—God, family, hard work, and lots of love. Rather when the children are there they are exposed to drinking, and smoking, and told that both are okay.

Do you have any ideas for me? I really would like to be able to protect my children. The courts seem to think that it is not my job, but theirs. Yet, they don't have the best interests of my children at heart.

Lisa

Dear Lisa,

You have identified one of the most hypocritical situations occurring presently in our legal system. While it is very important that parental rights are protected, it is sometimes at the expense of what is truly in the best interests of the children. And our children's lives are not static! What works for them and for their separated parents at one point in time may change when outside interests naturally claim their focus. If we insist that children revolve around their parents' lives, separate locales can seriously inhibit their ability to develop independent interests and activities. An overattachment to "fairness" for each parent may become a distortion in which the child's time is divided like a piece of pie, with little respect for the child as a entity separate from the dissolving marriage.

Rigid maintenance of equal schedules that pull children away from involvement in important activities and interests only continues the marital conflict on the backs of the children. This kind of arrangement maintains the children in the middle of parental conflict instead of removing them from it. It is sometimes the case that children become "prisoners" to parental "rights" in the court's attempt to dole out justice.

Equality is not "sameness"! But somehow the courts have not found a way to understand that there is a difference between the "ethics of justice" that our legal system is based upon, and the "ethics of care," which is at the heart of female development. Carol Gilligan's book, *In a Different Voice*, marked the discovery of the very different nature of female development, unrecognized and devalued in our society.[51] Gilligan elucidates the point that our society values male development based on concepts of individual

51. C. Gilligan, *In a Different Voice* (Cambridge, MA: Harvard University Press, 1982).

"rights" to define "justice," rather than considering the value of nurturing relationships, which is at the heart of female development in the evaluation of "fairness."

Please understand that when I am using "male" and "female" I do not mean it to be interpreted as all women have their child's best interests at heart automatically and men do not. This is not the case. There are mothers who exploit their attachment to their children and men who sacrifice their immediate gratification for their children's needs. However, it is true that our justice system sometimes miscarries our children's needs in favor of parental rights, which are based on competition between parents instead of nurturance. And women's and men's development, although coming closer together, remain culturally laden with divergent perspectives on what constitutes morality.

Perhaps the truth lies in the fact that custody issues are far more complex than our judicial system can handle well. It is a system set up to protect us from criminality, where issues of right and wrong are more clear-cut. Divorce is not criminal, and children require better support than is currently available in this venue. Our justice system is set up to focus on fairness as a matter of "rights" of two conflicting adult parties, rather than ensuring a child's emotional and economic welfare. The bias of our legal system often results in miscarriages of justice for children. But it is also possible to continue to voice your objections and be heard!

As children mature, they develop their own lives. Their ability to pursue interests and activities should be taken into consideration. It is a current failure of the legal system to not require that parents inconvenience themselves rather than demanding that their children give up significant aspects of their lives in order to share and develop a parent-child relationship.

Children are susceptible to exploitation because they have no independent legal rights. However, in some states (such as California) it is possible to obtain help from the court at no charge through family court services. In this situation, you are entitled to request a mediation appointment to bring up the points about your son's truncated athletic development and the negative effects on him of the current implementation of the visitation schedule.

Do not give up on getting help! Oftentimes these situations require that you attempt an agreement that has been set by the court in order to see if it will work out. This possibility of "working out" of course includes the probability that your husband would adapt to his children's needs appropriately over time, without legal intervention. When this is not the case, it is necessary to return to mediation to establish this fact.

Continue to identify what prevents your husband and yourself from making adjustment that ensure your son's participation in programs that are critical to his happiness. Refrain from attempting to control your ex-spouse's environment or parenting relationship with his children, except as it interferes significantly with their pursuit of happiness or health. Respect his relationship with his son and daughter and his rights to teach his values to the children as you do in your home. But do not throw in the towel on your children's needs that are seriously curtailed by deference to locale over appropriate development of independent activities and interests.

Persistence is your best ally!

Single parent families are healthy and viable

When a situation clearly presents danger to a child, a parent must remove the child from danger. A parent who does not remove a child from a violent partner is also culpable of child abuse. When the situation is extreme, children need to be protected from abusive or insane partners.

One third of divorced families remain single parent families. Still, we have not empowered single parents to nurture and lead their families. Instead our society experiences and conveys a bias that single parent families are deficit. We often unwittingly encourage single parent families to feel inferior, and single moms are often left with guilt for having no father for their children.

Research clearly shows[52] that single parent families are as healthy and run the full range of dysfunctional to functional spectrum at the same rate as two parent households. Additionally, almost all of the violence recently occurring in schools has been perpetrated by children from two parent families, despite the initial assumptions that such children must have come from "broken homes." Single parent households are warm and loving families, not "broken" in any way! Yet, this myth is perpetuated by many, often undermining rather than empowering single mothers who commonly head single parent households.

---

52. F. Walsh (ed), *Normal Family Processes*, 2nd ed. (New York: Guilford Press, 1993), p.16.

Single parents must be competent on their own in the areas of discipline and nurturing, rather than looking to others to fill these roles. They must retain authority, while seeking and accepting support. But too often, teachers, clergy or other well meaning people try to help in ways that sabotage a mother's belief in her capacity to raise her child competently on her own. The following question and answer illustrates one mother's struggle with a father's withdrawal.

Father refuses child visitation

Dear Dr. Gayle,

My divorce was final just a couple of days ago. I left my husband because he was violent. We have a ten-month-old son also. Since I left him he did start going to counseling and anger management courses. But he only did this because he thought he would get me back. He did this once before and I did give him another chance after he started counseling, but he ended up beating me up even worse in front of our son (who was six months old at the time). That ruined all the trust I would ever have for him.

Now that he got the final divorce papers he refuses to see his son. I don't think this is right. My son deserves a father and for my ex-husband to desert our son is not right because I will not take him back. This has got me very depressed and I am also very confused. I'm starting to think sometimes that he has changed but he continues to yell and scream and put me down one minute and the next minute he is crying and begging for me back. It has been a very emotional roller coaster. I know going back to him would definitely be the wrong thing to do, especially because of our son. I don't want my son raised in that environment but I don't understand what I can do to make things better and make myself feel better about what I have done. How do I explain to my son when he is older why his father doesn't wish to see him? I am so confused and hurt but relieved all at the same time!

Monique

Dear Monique,

Your conclusion that your ex-husband "ruined all the trust you had ever had for him" is an accurate assessment. Your decision to end the marriage may be the best action you could have taken not only for yourself, but for your son as well.

Your sense of responsibility to provide a father for your son, while understandable, is misguided. Parenting (fathering) is a nurturing activity that requires skill and some level of self-sacrifice. Minimally, parenting includes care of a child that does not put that child in harm's way. You are in no way depriving your son of his "father" if you mean to include parenting in the definition of fatherhood. And it is your son's biological father who is making the decision to completely cut-off from his son, not you!

Your ex-husband continues to be himself, which includes threatening you in any way he might succeed at causing you guilt. You are best protected from this kind manipulation if you seek counseling and a support group for battered women to further understand the roots of your mistaken loyalties. This will not only curtail the potential for further harm to you and your son from this relationship, but will help ensure that you have your priorities clearly established before entering another relationship.

Something is haywire in your past experience of family. Seek to identify the roles that men and women played in your childhood and the nature of the marital contract between your parents. These are the blueprints for your recent choice of a mate. Without exploring your past, you are likely to repeat similar patterns. Taking care of yourself through self-exploration and emotional support is your son's best insurance against future relationship loss or harm.

Do not second-guess yourself regarding your decision to divorce. And do not make choices out of guilt or a false promise of "fatherhood" for your son. Clinical studies have shown that single parent families are quite capable of producing loving and well-adjusted children. And there is a plethora of two parent families that fail to provide the needed balance of affection and authoritative limit-setting that their children need!

You are not deficient. You are enough for your son's healthy development. Maintaining a belief in your independent capacity to parent your son will be communicated to him, as will any belief that he is deprived of parenting because his biological father cannot parent!

Do not create unrealistic fantasies for your son, and he will not be obligated to fulfill them. Children can cope with the reality of life when they are lovingly supported in doing so. Sensitivity is spawned from life's troubles. Do not avoid discussing questions and feelings he will have about his biological father, but do not confuse him with expectations that his father fulfill his needs for parenting in any way. This would be a set-up for unnecessary disappointment.

Research shows that when a single parent is capable of loving authority, children flourish. Become the best parent you can be. Do not ignore appropriate discipline (or love) as your son grows. Your capacity to set appropriate limits when needed in your child's future development will be best assured if you resolve misplaced guilt now. Unresolved guilt is often the culprit for disabling parents of their authority, resulting in misconduct and other difficulties of childhood.

Seek help to recover from the abuse in your marriage. Withdraw your energies from your ex-spouse. You are not in control or responsible for his life choices. Continued ruminations that revolve around him and his activities or threats only serve to distract you from your own life's path. Enjoy your son. He is fortunate to have a mother who not only loves him, but has the courage to remove him from an unhealthy and dangerous situation!

Recovering from divorce occurs for different people at varying rates. Sometimes it is necessary to take stock of whether you are moving forward or standing still after the dust has settled. The following question and answer addresses the depression that can linger if anger and resentment continue to determine the direction of your life, long after your spouse has left the marriage.

Recovering from divorce

Dr. Gayle,

I am angry and depressed after my divorce. I have not lived with my ex for two years, but see him almost every day as we work in the same profession. The only good thing is that he pays more attention to our twelve-year-old son now. I have someone in my life who says he loves me, but I just want my old comfortable life back. How do I get past this?

Lura

Dear Lura,

Divorce is the death of a relationship so it is natural to feel a great loss of self when a marriage ends. Reclaiming yourself from the marriage involves deep grieving, as well as discovering the personal meaning of this event in your life. (Seeing your ex-spouse on a daily basis does not give you much emotional distance for doing this inner work!)

Consider the possibility that you are living out a pattern of attachment to an absent lover. You imply that your ex is a more attentive father outside the home than he was in the marriage. This points to an emotional withdrawal from family relationships when you were married. Try to identify why you would have been attracted to a man who did not have much emotional energy for family relationships.

We commonly choose our partners to fulfill unmet development. The marriage holds unconscious promise for healing past wounds, or for repeating them. An early childhood bond with a remote father or mother could be at the root of "wanting your old life back" despite the fact that you are better off out of the marriage.

Your craving may be older than your marriage or divorce. It may be the craving for someone who was not there for you as a child that has caused you to remain stuck in longing, rather than moving toward love.

Divorce presents an opportunity to recover lost parts of yourself, if you are not afraid to look further back. Individual counseling aimed at understanding your choices and the meaning of the divorce in your life will help you let go of the past and move toward the future.

Your seeming disinterest in available men may also be a result of fear that you could lose in love again. Failure in remarriage is more likely if you do not explore childhood relationships and their impact on your past partnership patterns.

Do not let fear or nostalgia stand in the way of doing the emotional work necessary for your full recovery. You may not be happy now, but you are certainly eligible for future happiness!

Children continue to make sense of divorce when they are adults. Talking about their experience as children and helping them understand what the qualities are that make a committed partnership work helps them address their own lives and future relationships. When these issues do not come to light, the effects may serve to avoid relationships and intimacy altogether. The following example illustrates this situation.

Effects of divorce on adult commitment

Dr. Gayle,

I have a real problem, I can't keep a relationship for more than six months. For the past six years of my dating life the most serious relationships have ended by my choice. I feel as if I suddenly don't care about the other person in the same way. Someone asked me if I thought that it was because of my parents. My father left us (my mother, sister and I) three times before they finally got divorced.

I don't know what to do but I am now in the process of looking for a therapist to try to help me. I would really appreciate it if you could tell me whether their divorce has caused this problem or does it go deeper?

Kathryn

Dear Kathryn,

Your sudden change of heart is becoming a pattern of abandonment in your relationships. It is certainly possible that you are repeating the conflicts of attachment that you experienced with your father. It is also likely that you learned ineffective patterns of relating that abort, instead of sustain, relationship.

Therapy focused on what happens to your feelings six months into a relationship could prove enlightening. There are developmental challenges in any relationship that have to do with accepting your partner as a real person and not a perfect romantic figure. But seeing a lover's imperfections and weaknesses should not obstruct your view of the true nature of his worth and value. Nor should disappointment completely and irreversibly turn your good feelings off! Six months is about the period of time that is required in a relationship before considering more serious commitment. Your "turn-off" at this time may indeed be a defense against hurt.

It may be the case that when you get to the phase in a relationship that requires that you depend on your partner, you shut down. It is possible that you become overly critical in order to protect yourself from needing him. Opening up to let someone in deep enough to care for you could be frightening, as you may have experienced your parents unresponsive to your needs, due to their involvement in their own turmoil and instability. It is likely that all of the marital discord did siphon off energy that would have been available to answer the needs of developing children in the family.

You may have learned to distrust those you depended upon and even to disavow some of your own needs to depend upon others. You may find yourself "quitting" relationships when you feel dependent to avoid potential loss or disappointment projected from your past experience.

You may also find yourself ready to leave when differences arise because you do not believe they can be successfully resolved in a relationship. Working through differences and maintaining a positive connection to a partner through disappointment are phases all relationships must evolve through to be sustained long-term. But believing in stability and happiness may be difficult for you. Sudden cynicism or an abrupt desire to flee relationships is understandable given your vulnerability to the ongoing disruption and fall-out in your parents' prolonged and unresolved marital conflict.

The good news is that you seem to very much want to be in relationship. You are not shunning potential lovers or withdrawing from relationship due to disappointments in the past. Despite disappointment, you continue to reach out and are open to seeking help. Your capacity to turn inwards to find answers to your own behavior at this time is a sign of health.

The bad news is not so terrible. You may have learned patterns of hot/cold relating from your parents' on-again/off-again relationship. And you may have been afraid of commitment and getting trapped in a painful marriage, like the one you saw your parents experience. At least you are clear that you can cut things off. Perhaps "calling it quits" was what you wished your own parents had been better at doing.

Use your therapy to identify your needs and develop realistic expectations for what a good relationship can offer you. Develop insight into the past and skills to evolve and sustain a good relationship. Now that you know you can walk away, it is likely you can learn what you need in order to stay!

Children's lives develop and what is in the best interests of your child at any given moment in time is unique to your child and your situation. Consider the following question and answer with regards to changes that may arise over the years.

Re-evaluating and adjusting visitation

Dr. Gayle,

I am a full-time access father and although my ex has custody, I have statements in our agreement that give me joint custodial rights. This is one of the many issues that helped me stop my ex from relocating herself and my daughter many miles away.

My daughter is almost eight, and we have lived apart since she was two and a half. We see each other all the time. Our schedule is every other weekend Friday to Sunday night and every Wednesday evening 4:30 to 7:00 during school. I also take her out for lunch ever other Monday and see her at all of her school and extra curricular activities.

In my home (I am remarried) I have two stepchildren, a five-year-old girl and nine-year-old boy. Emily fits in wonderfully and the children who have known each other for four and a half years and are truly a brother and sister to her.

Emily has expressed an interest in sleeping over on Wednesday nights through out the school year. I know I can accommodate this and will drive her to school for the morning with homework done, bathed, fed, lunch packed (I guess what I am saying is that I am capable as I do this for my step children as well).

My ex is concerned about how this may affect her schooling and she wants Emily in a non-disruptive pattern during school months. I do understand that with swimming lessons and Brownie, our visit is yet another thing that Emily has on weeknights and this alone is disruptive enough.

To make a long story short, can overnight stays at my home affect her schooling or any other aspect of her life? I ask her teachers all the time if they notice any difference in Emily's performance after spending a weekend with me, and the answer from all four teachers is "no."

Please send me in the right direction, I do want to do what is best for Emily.

Mike

Dear Mike,

You should congratulate yourself on your obvious success in parenting your daughter after your separation and divorce. Though it may have been difficult in the beginning, the fact that you maintain your focus on what is best for your child reflects the quality of parenting she is receiving from you. It is likely that your daughter is doing well in school and other areas of her life not in spite of her overnight stays with you, but because, in addition to other positive influences in her life, you remain emotionally committed to Emily and she feels it! Maintaining a strong relationship with your daughter based on accommodating her schedule and needs has not proved disruptive, but stabilizing!

You are right to consider your daughter's needs with respect to other activities in her life, including her academics. However, if you are willing to ensure her ability to complete school assignments and step in to assist her to remain organized, there is no reason why an overnight should not be considered, if your daughter is asking for it. Be sure, if it is decided to do so, that your daughter understands what is involved. She may need to give up an activity for the extra overnight. But it may be the case that being in the household overnight is more important to her and her development than another extracurricular activity at this time. By the time she is a teenager she will be more likely to be spending increased time with her peers and outside activities and may want to decrease time with you. So enjoy it while it is here! This is the time to solidify your connection with her. Be clear about your expectations. If you and her mother agree to try it out, you can set a time to evaluate Emily's adaptation to her new schedule.

Your daughter's interest in spending more time with you and her stepfamily now may be an outgrowth of her budding independence and a sign that she feels secure enough to express her desire for a change. Her desire to remain overnight during the school year is a natural extension of what she has already experienced in the summertime. So there is little being introduced that is new. With your readiness to provide for her needs and her familiarity and comfort with her stepbrother and sister, I see little reason why this change would be disruptive to her. Her readiness and your willingness in addition to the stability of your situation suggests that this could be a positive change for your daughter. And responding to your daughter's naturally evolving independence by allowing her to make her own choices is beneficial to her development.

Your daughter's healthy adjustment is likely a result of her parents' careful negotiations for her stability and consistency. However, as Emily matures, she will be having ideas of her own about how she wants to spend her time. Support her ideas whenever they originate from a point of healthy independence, for this is usually a sign of her readiness for new challenge. Thwarting these impulses (repeatedly) at this age can lead to dulling her spirit and decreasing her assertiveness in the world. In her book, *Reviving Ophelia*, Mary Pipher writes about the potential for our culture to kill a young girl's independent spirit at this age by not supporting her emerging initiative.[53] Part of your daughter's development is to begin to have a say in the decisions made about her life.

Emily is fortunate in that you and her mother have the same goal, which is understanding what is in her best interests. With her mother's care and caution and her father's sense of responsibility and interest in her, Emily has a chance many children of divorced parents do not have——growth resulting from balancing stability with change.

True growth requires new challenges that upset the balance a little, but not too much. This allows Emily to master new situations. Determining the correct balance is the nature of a child's growth and the challenge of parenthood. The tension between stability and change is a dance that must be encouraged so that stability does not become stagnation and change does not produce chaos. Emily is trying her hand at choreographing a part of her life. Why not try out her dance?

---

53. M. Pipher, *Reviving Ophelia* (New York: Grossett-Putnam, 1994).

TEN

Making Healthy Stepfamilies

So complex is the process whereby the remarried family system stabilizes and regains its forward developmental thrust, that we have come to think of it as adding another whole phase to the family life cycle for those involved.[54]

Experts estimate that by the year 2000 there will be more stepfamilies in the U. S. than any other kind. Half of Americans have been or will be in a stepfamily constellation at some point in their lifetime.[55] About half of remarried spouses procreate a mutual child in addition to children from one or both former marriages, while the remaining fifty percent of stepfamilies fall into the categories of stepfather families, stepmother families, or complex families in which both spouses bring children from another marriage into their new union.

If the joining of two individuals in marriage is comparable to blending two different cultures, as many a family therapist has suggested, then the joining of two individuals with histories of past marriages, divorce and children must be the joining of two different galaxies!

Previous loyalties and relationship loss that predates the new marriage can wreak major havoc on well meant intentions in stepfamilies, along with other stressors. It is illuminating for couples at the helm of these fam-

---

54. M. McGoldrick & B. Carter, "Forming a Remarried Family." In M. McGoldrick & B. Carter (Eds.), *The Changing Family Life Cycle*, 2nd edition (New York: Gardner Press, 1988).

55. Paul Glick reported this finding from the 1987 National Survey of Families and Households in his address to the Annual Conference, Stepfamily Associates of America, Lincoln, Nebraska, October, 1991.

ilies to learn that family researchers have identified the best predictor of stepfamily happiness to be the quality of the relationship that develops between the *stepparent and children*.[56] Like any transition, timing can be one of the most important factors in favor of healthy adjustment. The next most important factor in stepfamily adjustment, as in any family, is the strength and quality of the couple's bond. These two important variables are obviously related, as all natural parents will attest to, if they have ever been placed in a situation where they felt torn between their children and spouse. And any stepparent can understand the awkwardness of finding his or her place as a family member and as a parent in a maze of relationships and shared history established prior to his or her arrival.

So, the task itself is fraught with paradoxes. It is often painful and difficult for the stepparent to find a place in an already established system that grieves the loss of a person you may have never met, including being the person who children "test" to see if you are "good" enough to earn membership. It is also important to remember that one of the developmental tasks of a family is to raise and nurture its young to adulthood in the best way possible. It is important to remember that as a stepparent, you had a choice in the situation while the children did not. As the adult your responsibility must encompass an understanding that you will be expected to be concerned and involved in caring for these children and ensuring their sense of security in traveling through this transition of adding you to their family! If the job is too big, don't sign up for it!! Remember you are the adult and you made the choice to marry a spouse who came with children. Very often stepparents suffer from unrealistic expectations regarding the transition of blending families, resulting in feelings of helplessness and victimization.

And very often natural parents share fantasies of the perfect family union, pressuring spouses to love children they do not even really know yet, or expecting a stepparent to discipline a child before an appropriate affection has grown between the two. Natural parents can play an important role in supporting the stepparent appropriately, including being understanding of the frustration this role can hold, particularly in the first two years of the new marriage. Pacing the role that a stepparent takes on in the family to match realistically with the development of the relationship between stepparent and child will go along way towards developing a positive relationship.

---

56. E. B. Visher & J. S. Visher, "Remarriage Families and Stepparenting." In F. Walsh (Ed.), *Normal Family Processes*, 2nd edition (New York: Guilford Press, 1993).

Helping husband become a supportive stepparent

Dear Dr. Gayle,

I am remarried, with two children from my first marriage, and feel torn between my husband and children. I have a seven-year-old and a five-year-old. My husband has no kids. My seven-year-old has a learning disability and cannot read or write. My husband thinks he is just lazy. How do I get my husband to understand that encouragement can do so much for a child?

Teri

Dear Teri,

Your husband is new to fatherhood and you are right to take the lead in expressing your beliefs about your son, as well as your overall views on child rearing. It is possible that your spouse is reflecting his own upbringing, which may have been long on criticism and short on emotional support or individual differences.

Not having had children, your spouse may not have given much thought to parenthood. It is likely that he has not experienced two critical insights that are common to the process of becoming a parent. The decision to have a child provides opportunity to 1) reflect on our own childhood and 2) discover the ways your own child is different from yourself. It is necessary to turn a discerning eye toward your own childhood in order to identify the kind of parent you want to be. It is also natural to try to understand others by identifying with them, before realizing that a child may indeed be uniquely equipped with strengths, weaknesses, and sensitivities that are unlike our own.

Now that he has taken on the responsibilities of becoming a stepparent, it is your partner's job to identify how the ways he was raised affect is way of responding to his own stepchildren. Give your husband the benefit of time and discussions about your own process of becoming a parent.

Given that you have already developed your own child-rearing philosophy and sensitivities to your individual children's needs, you are definitely several steps ahead. Engage in discussions about your beliefs and how you came to them. Share your perspective on what you believe contributes to a child's self-esteem, and on the particular unique needs of each of your own children.

Ask your husband to reflect on his own relationship with his parents and their child-rearing philosophy. Did they encourage him?

When he had difficulties did they make efforts to build his self-esteem and confidence, or make judgments about his "laziness"? It is also natural for your husband to experience some stirrings of jealousy if he sees you giving your child what his parents did not give him. This could result in his feeling critical towards your son, instead of encouraging.

I remember my own husband's journey as a stepparent. He initially repeated patterns of parent-child interactions that he had experienced growing up. Remember that the concept of "self-esteem" was not even a part of many of our parents' awareness in raising us. We had long (seemingly endless!) discussions of how to support a child's self-esteem, and what the job of parenting entailed.

Over a period of eight years, my husband grew to agree and implement many of these concepts, but not without initial disbelief and resistance. After all, if it was good enough for him, why did he have to change anything for this child? More significantly, these discussions caused him to look more critically at his own upbringing and make active choices about the kind of stepparent he wanted to be.

Invite your husband to become a part of the solution, instead of the problem. Your spouse's belief that your son is lazy contributes only negative energy to the situation. Be willing to listen to your husband's feelings, but insist that he consider a change in his own attitude, if he expects to facilitate a change in his stepson. If he wishes to motivate your child, encourage him to do so in a positive manner, and to understand any special needs a child with a learning disability may have.

Creating strategies for success or creative ways to pique your son's curiosity could result in greater effort to understand concepts that might otherwise be difficult for your son to grasp. Ask that your husband strive to accept your son's difficulties (and differences from himself) and find ways to help him cope, rather than criticize. You might discover that he can help your son develop much needed determination, if he pushes just hard enough, and in the right direction!

Characteristics of healthy remarriage

Because more than fifty percent of remarriages end in divorce, we can assume that information about the very complex process of blending families is not well known. Being able to identify common pitfalls, predictable feelings, and characteristics of successful remarried families will elucidate a more viable and realistic vision. In order to better understand this transition, let's take a look at what the characteristics of successful remarriage are according to family researchers.[57]

No instant bonding

Love takes time to develop. Relationships take time to adjust and to mourn the past family unit. Realistic expectations between stepparents and children must include a gradual period of getting to know one another. There is no such thing as *instant* intimacy. One of the most common pitfalls that stepfamilies can fall into is the expectation that "we are one big happy family." This kind of idealization is often the result of unresolved past loss and a set up for failure and disappointment.

Respect one another and take the time to become acquainted. Let the relationship build security and caring on its own merit, without pressure to fill the fantasy of loving one another before a solid "like" has been established. On the average, two to three years is the time period for developing these bonds and stabilizing the new family. The following question and answer illustrates the danger of believing in the allure of instant love and adjustment, when we as adults want to change our lives and leave the "pain" behind.

The pitfall of "instant love"

Dear Dr. Gayle,

I have been divorced for a year and am planning on getting remarried within the next eight months. My children love their new father very much, but our problem is that we will have to move to another state with this marriage. The children want to move, but their natural father has said that he is going to fight this action. I am prepared to battle that out if necessary.

How can I best handle this situation with my son and daughter (twelve and nine years old) so that they survive this in the best possible manner? What can I tell them and how do I help them deal with their emotions? They love their real father and I would never take that away from them, but this move can't be helped and the children would, at least for now, be better off in a family unit. I realize that my son will be ready to move back with his natural father

---

57. Ibid.

*in the coming years. I feel like I am stuck here. I know this is best
for the children but this is a really hard move for all of us! How can
I make this easier on them?*

Sherry

Dear Sherry,

Whoa!! Slow down. On what grounds do you believe that this
move is best for your children? Or that it "can't be helped"?
Choosing motherhood commits you to looking at this situation
more honestly. You cannot instantly give your children another
father. This is your fantasy, but not a reality! Did you know that
more than half of all remarriages end in divorce because of insuffi-
cient understanding of the significant conflicts involved in stepfamily formation?

There is no such thing as "instant family." Although your children may get along well with your new boyfriend now, it is only a
honeymoon phase. You are suggesting catapulting them into (at
least) three major life transitions at once. You may be deluding
yourself to believe that this kind of move following a divorce is in
the best interests of your children.

If you and you ex have joint custody it is not likely that the court
will see it your way. Barring significant abuse that would disqualify
your children's father of his parental rights, it is usually the case
that removing your children from a parent's locale and taking them
away from their community is not perceived as being in their best
interests. If you consider the changes involved, you will no doubt see
the reason for this perspective.

Your children have just come through a major upheaval and
loss of their family unit. Adjustment to this change and stabiliza-
tion of a new family unit usually requires about two years.
Mourning the loss of the intact family and adjusting to separate
relationships with each parent is a plateful! Requiring that they
make a geographic move that will not only reduce contact with
their father at a vulnerable and unstable time, but also cutting
them off from the supportive relationships of friends and familiar
surroundings while simultaneously plunging them into a "new
family" situation, is courtship with disaster.

You are not looking at this situation realistically or from your
children's perspective. You are clearly putting your own wishes first

and creating a fantasy picture to match your desires. This is not only being blind to your own children's needs but to your long term happiness as well.

There is no instant love between stepchildren and stepparents. Over half of remarriages fail, in part because of highly idealized visions of becoming "one big happy family." Television shows like "The Brady Bunch" only helped proliferate these destructive myths. The lack of education about stepfamily development is largely responsible for unresolved tensions and failures in remarriages.

The other reason remarriage can fail is because unsuccessful ways of coping with conflict continue in the new marriage. Inability to resolve conflict results in fractured relationships. Your willingness to believe that your children "love" this new husband-to-be as a "father" and they would be better off in a "family unit" suggests that you are not dealing with the mourning and readjustment necessary after divorce, but attempting to solve the problem by running away from it.

As a parent, you are a leader in the family. It is your job to consider the future impact of your decision to remarry and move to another state on your children.

Reconsider your move! Slow things down a bit. You can maintain your relationship with your boyfriend without rushing marriage. Let him know that you are a "package deal," which means that he may have to bide time, consider relocation, or relate from a distance until things have settled and your future with him is clear. As a future stepparent it is his job to consider your children's needs as well as his own. This is a part of the real picture!

Losses and mourning

By the time of a second marriage, it is often a child's third family unit, the first being the biological parents' marriage, the second being a separate or single family unit, and the third being the new relationship involving a stepparent. Children need parental permission and understanding to grieve these losses, before embracing the new family system. Failure to accept mourning as a natural feeling may result in angry outbursts and potential alienation. One way to build relationships at this transitional time, is to allow stepparent-child relationships to be initially more distant. Eventually, if given the space to express themselves and resolve past loss, children do show genuine interest or liking for this new person who has been brought into their home. Children will eventually respond to the health and love present in the couple's relationship over time, as they do want their parents to be happy.

Parents also suffer loss, particularly if their own biological children are not living with them. Loyalty to previous members who used to live under one roof can make it a difficult process to bond to new members, but given time and respect for each others' feelings and boundaries, these bonds do grow. Relationships become what they are meant to be. A small child will tend towards accepting the stepparent in a parental role differently than a teenager. Coming into a teenager's life may involve more of a friendship, depending on the individuals and needs involved, while coming into a family with a one-year-old will usually require parental nurturance and attachment similar to that of a primary parent.

Strengthening your marital relationship

Even though taking on certain responsibilities, particularly discipline, may take some time for a stepparent, the key to any healthy family system is the mutual love, caring and respect that the spouses share. Working through the predictable stresses of becoming a stepfamily secures your relationship. Taking time to be together is also important, as in this situation the honeymoon phase of the relationship has no doubt been curtailed. Take time to be alone and develop your bond independent of the children and parenting roles in the family. This is not a step that can be skipped! The couple relationship needs some breathing space of its own to grow. Getting away for a weekend may be difficult with all that is going on, but it is essential to the health of your marriage.

Resolving difficult parenting issues through honest sharing and understanding will build intimacy. Just remember to be patient with the desire for change. And do not hesitate to seek the help of a counselor to help you resolve and understand the very tumultuous feelings you may experience in building your new family.

The following question and answer addresses the mourning and adjustments that face the couple leading a stepfamily.

My wife treats my children differently than hers

Dr. Gayle,

I don't know how to deal with my wife's treatment of my natural children. She treats her son, who is the youngest, like a little angel.

My children are considered trouble by her and her family. The kids are five, six, and seven years old. I work long hours, so I'm not home a lot. She doesn't see the difference, except to say that her son is good, why aren't yours?

Ron

Dear Ron,

You and your wife are experiencing the challenges of becoming a stepfamily. Your particular circumstances define you as a "complex stepfamily," meaning that you both bring children to the marriage. This is the most complicated stepfamily formation. All children have suffered loss of their original intact family situation and these losses need to be mourned. All too often unresolved sadness and loyalties do not get a place for safe expression in the family and a second family dissolution is the result.

It is natural for both of you to experience feelings of belonging to your own biological children. But you are rapidly taking on traditional roles and expectations, which increase the pressure to be one big happy family! Which only increases the likelihood of an explosion.

There is no "instant love" between stepchildren and stepparents and in situations where a stepparent, particularly a stepmother is taking on primary responsibility for stepchildren you can expect trouble. In addition, your wife has gone from caring for one child whom she has known for years, to primary caretaking for your three children, with whom she did not experience a primary bond. Perhaps both of you are falling prey to highly unrealistic expectations for one another, which leads to alienation and blaming.

Take a step back and put yourself in your wife's shoes. Certainly her negative expression of feelings towards your children needs to stop. But her feelings that your children are a burden are quite real. If you were the primary caretaker for three new children that came with your spouse, in addition to the work of caring for your own, you too might feel overwhelmed. But instead of resolving these feelings, your wife may be contributing to greater polarization and disharmony by villainizing her stepchildren and sanctifying her own biological child.

Acknowledge your wife's feelings, but request that she change her behavior. Ask her what would be helpful to her in taking a step back herself and accepting the complexity of the situation. Does she need hired help or your help in some way? Because you are the biological parent, it is you who should be disciplining and setting limits. It is a set-up for failure for your wife to be the one who doles out consequences. Your children will act out their anger on her, as she is not their "real mother." And there is no affectionate foundation yet established on which your wife can effectively gain your children's respect. The result is a self-perpetuating pattern of splitting the positive and negative feelings natural to family life, into biological war camps.

It is your job and your wife's job to sort through these difficult issues and get back on track as a couple so that you can more effectively lead the family together. Research shows that the most significant predictor of successful stepfamily formation is the quality of the relationship between stepparent and stepchildren. The second most important predictor is a strong couple's bond. You and your wife need to work on both.

Take responsibility for educating yourself to the task at hand. Remember that each of you chose to be married to the other. Choice includes responsibility. You each made the choice to become a stepparent to one another's child(ren). No one promised you that it would be easy. Your children did not have this choice. It is your responsibility to create an environment that works for everyone. You owe it to your children and to your marital commitment to one another.

Satisfactory step relations develop gradually

Too often a stepparent expects, or is expected, to fill in as a full-blown parent, including administering discipline. This may happen after children and stepparent have developed a bond of trust and caring. It also might not ever happen, *particularly if the children are teenagers when the stepparent arrives on the scene.* Adjust to the situation according to its natural evolution. It is unrealistic to assume your authority will develop the same with a teenager as a young child. Respect boundaries and what has come before as well as being open to a different form of relating than your idealized interpretation of what family "should" be.

How to avoid becoming the "wicked stepmother"

Dear Dr. Gayle,

I need advice on disciplining my five-year-old stepdaughter. I am basically required to do all of the correcting when she is in our home because her father is reluctant to do so. I have discussed this

*with him on several occasions and he says he is going to take an
active role but usually does not! How can I get him to take an active
role and not let this five-year-old corrupt the household with her
behavior?*

Denise

Dear Denise,

You are on the road to becoming the "wicked stepmother"! This is
a common pitfall for stepmoms. The terrain of the stepfamily needs
to be carefully navigated if you are not to make this fairytale character come true. Should you continue to be the disciplinarian in your
family your relationship with your stepdaughter will suffer. This
should be her father's role, as you suggest and not yours.

One of the strongest predictors for success in stepfamily development is the relationship between stepparent and stepchild. The second strongest predictor is a good couple's bond. Since the biological
bond between parent and child predates the couple's relationship,
the need to honor and respect the boundaries of this previous bond
is essential prior to fully incorporating a stepparent as a major
authority figure. Any shortcuts precipitate problems later.

Oftentimes, because of cultural expectations that mothers act as
the primary caregivers, stepmothers are susceptible to being placed in
this role precipitously. Men more than women, following divorce, tend
towards looking for a "replacement mother" to continue the work the
biological mother did in the biologically intact family unit. This is a
set-up for failure and frustration! Do not take this role on. Step back
and require that your husband play the "heavy" or you are likely to
end up the scapegoat for everyone's negative feelings in the family.

Love includes discipline. Your husband is failing to cope with parenthood. Perhaps the dynamic in his last marriage was to leave this
part of the job to mom and he is attempting to do the same here.
This could have also played a part in the failure of the first marriage,
if responsibility for parenting was left to one parent! But you are not
the parent. Your stepdaughter has a mother and a father. It is not
your job to take over.

Tell your husband you do not want to discipline his child, as it
gets in the way of your forging a friendship with her. It takes time
for a stepfamily to bond. Let him know that his lack of limit setting
as a parent is jeopardizing the future of your family—and simultane-

ously undermines whatever authority you do muster in the situation! By putting you in charge of discipline, he is setting up a situation in which he is the "good guy" and you are the "bad guy." This void in parenting by him runs the risk of communicating to his daughter that he does not love her enough to do the hard part of the job! And leaving it to you ensures that your relationship to your stepdaughter will become wrought with conflict, before you have ever have the opportunity to secure your bond.

This kind of situation is not fair to any of you! Refuse to take this on, even if it means leaving him alone in the room with his daughter and her out-of-bounds behavior. Continue to develop a positive relationship to your stepdaughter. Take her on special outings the two of you can enjoy together if possible. But keep it simple and the interaction positive. Try to develop a good friendship with her. However, do not get drafted into the middle between your husband and his daughter. If your husband experiences difficulty developing this aspect of his parental responsibilities, ask him to seek out the advice of other fathers. Perhaps a fathers' support group could serve to help him reflect on his own relationship with his father, and why this part of parenting is so hard for him. It is his job to do whatever it takes to develop his ability to cope with parenting. Developing his parenting skills is his obligation as a parent. He owes this to his daughter, as well as himself.

Try instead to forge a special friendship. Over time, as your bond grows, you may gradually and quite naturally acquire the status of an authority figure who can also discipline. But you will not be filling in for your husband's lacks. With time and patience on your side, you may have the opportunity to grow into a workable stepfamily. Otherwise you may find yourself seeking a divorce as refuge from the "wicked stepmother" you could become!

Establishing family rituals

Every family develops its own culture. This gives members a sense of belonging to an intimate group. Holiday rituals can be developed that are unique to the present constellation. For example, a mother of two children marries a Jewish man. Chanukah celebrations might be added to Christmas, and the children learn new rituals and philosophies for living. Other elements, like specific kinds of jokes or well-intentioned humor can also go a long way in weaving a family together. Be open to the unique characteristics and pleasures that develop naturally and spontaneously between family members. Humor is a powerfully bonding experience. Finding ways to laugh *together* will go along way towards establishing a sense of belonging. Humor can be a form of intimacy, as sharing fun builds relationships in which people tend to seek each other out.

Keeping children out of the middle of conflict

Supporting children's relationship to biological parents who do not live in the stepfamily is important to healthy development. Keeping these situations separate will decrease chances for conflict, with children being caught in the crossfire. The following question and answer gives guidelines for helping parents keep children out of the middle of their conflict when a spouse remarries. Remarriage presents predictable stress in the post-divorce stage of readjustment. The spouse must relinquish any subliminal wishes for reconciliation. The ending of the marriage is once again made fresh, as spouses adjust to the remarriage of their ex-partners.

Remarriage and keeping children out of the middle of conflicts

Dr. Gayle,

What do you say to an ex-husband to get him to understand that his refusing to speak to me unless absolutely necessary since I have remarried hurts no one but the children? He signs my child support checks with my first name only. He says in front of the children that we're living off his sweat. When I was still single he gave me more child support than he had to when I asked.

He no longer does anything else for the kids unless I throw a fit. My husband and I try not to say anything negative in front of them, but they can see it too. There has got to be magic words to let him know he isn't hurting me like he thinks he is.

Sandy

Dear Sandy,

The remarriage of an ex-spouse is a predictable stressor in the aftermath of divorce. It is a clear and undeniable marker to your ex-husband that you have moved on. Any fantasy of reconciliation is quashed. This event often resurfaces old grief about the loss of the family unit and ushers in a renewed period of mourning, but this is no excuse for putting children in the middle of your conflict.

You have enjoyed a relatively smooth adjustment to initial separation and divorce, judged by your ex-husband's willingness to exceed the granted amount of child support. Clearly he is feeling hurt and possibly left out as he imagines his family going on without him. Perhaps he fears that he will be replaced by a new father figure or in some way lose the relationship he now has with his children. Though these thoughts and imaginings can be quite painful to him, his inability to contain his feelings can result in actions that can be harmful to his children.

Do not expect your husband to do or give more than is required right now. Encourage his contact with his children and support their relationship to their biological father as inviolate. In other words, make it clear through your words and actions that your children's father is not being replaced in any way by their stepfather. You may be adding to the tension in your interactions by overreacting to your ex-spouse's withdrawal from doing "extra." Refrain from throwing fits to get your way. Instead, examine your own expectations, and adjust them accordingly.

Since you have enjoyed a more cooperative relationship in the past, it is likely that your ex-spouse will adjust to your remarriage and equanimity will return to your relationship. In the meantime, consider writing your ex-husband a letter about the changes you have noticed and your concern for the effects his behavior might be having on the children. But be cautious in your tone. Express appreciation for his past generosity and sadness that this has changed. Do not blame him or express anger that he is not as forthcoming in his generosity as in the past. Instead, focus on keeping your children out of the path of his anger and resentment. Ask him to refrain from commenting on child support to the children. Express that you know it must be difficult for him but that it is critical to act in the best interests of the children in keeping them safe from feeling to blame for their emotional or financial needs.

Acknowledge to your ex-spouse that the children will be experiencing a lot of adjustments to your remarriage and that you want to assure him that you see his relationship to his children as important and unchanged. Let him know that you want to do everything you can to stabilize their lives during this transition. Recognize that your remarriage will necessitate adjustments for the children and you need his help to remain as emotionally consistent as possible in their lives. Recognize his importance to them. In this context, bring up your concern that they could get caught up in negative emotional reactions that could arise between the two of you, since you have remarried.

Reinforce your intent to maintain the quality of your parenting relationship with your ex-spouse. If you feel comfortable doing so, invite him to discuss (with you and/or a mediator), concerns he might have about this transition. Maintain your boundaries around your life and your remarriage, but respect his feelings and reach beyond your resentment to show your good will and intent related to parenting issues.

Research repeatedly concludes that your best insurance in assisting your children through divorce is to keep them out of the middle of your conflicts.[58] Likewise, the greatest predictor of maladjustment in children following divorce occurs when they are frequent victims of a parent's anger toward his or her ex-spouse.

Your remarriage is a new phase that precipitates change in family relationships and a resurgence of the past. You have every right to move on in your life. But be careful that you do not fuel the problem by responding to your ex's anger in kind. Do not get involved in finding "magic words to not let him know he is hurting you like he thinks he is." Instead, refrain from getting embroiled in these anger games.

Take the high ground. Work to separate your emotional response to your ex's reaction to your remarriage from your children's welfare. Seek solutions, not retaliations. Accept the challenge to be the voice of reason rather than reaction in getting your parenting relationship back on track. If you succeed your children will benefit!

There are situations that are not ideal but can be carefully managed to bring out cooperation. Still, there are situations in which experts recommend against making co-custody arrangements. In more extreme cases of mental imbalance, parental dysfunction, or severe childrearing conflict, family researchers recommend decreased contact and sole custody, with visitation rights for the non-custodial parent. However, with

---

58. E. Hetherington,T. Law and T. O'Connor, "Divorce: Challenges, Changes and New Chances." In F. Walsh (Ed.), *Normal Family Processes*, 2nd ed. (New York,: Guilford Press, 1993).

professional help, parents are often able to get over past hurts and work in the best interest of the children.

Advice from stepparents

Perhaps the best advice comes from the parents and stepparents who have made it work! In a study by Dahl, Cowgill, and Asmundsson,[59] families that have succeeded in creating a healthy remarriage and developing strong bonds with children gave the following advice to people embarking on this journey of family-making:

1. Go slow. Take time. Settle your old marriage (divorce) before you start a new one. Accept the need for continual involvement of parts of the old family with the new. Help children maintain relationships with biological parents.

2. Stepparents should try for mutual courtesy, but not expect a child's love. Respect the special bond between biological parent and child.

3. Communicate, negotiate, compromise, and accept what cannot be changed.

In the end fathering and mothering are a result of the time and effort we put into it. It is true that anyone can be a biological "parent." But we all know of far too many cases where there are natural parents but no true parenting. Stepparenting is always a conscious choice, whereby biological parenthood may be accidental. Wherever there is a choice to bring forth life, or be involved in intimate relationship to developing children, we must remember that it is not the children who have asked to be born or to "become married."

Our children deserve our superior effort at understanding what is in their best interest, especially when feelings and struggles are intense, as they often are in the transition to a remarried family constellation. And it is a parent's job to be able to consider the needs of the child and expect to put them first when appropriate. This is the nature of parenthood. Whether you come by it biologically or through marriage, parenthood requires maturity.

As with anything in life that involves soulful effort and an amount of personal sacrifice, the rewards are reaped by those who sow. One seven-

---

59. A. S. Dahl, K. M. Cowgill, and R. Asmundsson, "Life in Remarriage Families." *Social Work*, 32 (1), pp, 40–44.

teen-year-old who had lived in a remarried family since she was thirteen summed up her feelings for her stepfather this way, "He's my dad. Anyone can be a father, but he's been there for me. I have a father, too. But he's my dad!"

Remember, too, that children fare better the more adults they have who are *committed* to their growth and well-being. There can be room for two dads or two moms, if each relationship is respected for what it is and supported in its' uniqueness. Perhaps the newly constellated stepfamily network at its best holds promise for a return to a kind of extended family system. In any case, with support and knowledge for the natural feelings and challenges of this kind of system, perhaps we will be able to recognize the unique opportunity for conscious love, caring, and commitment that a stepfamily holds. Learning the value of nurturing is, after all, the core of healthy relationships of all kinds.

ELEVEN

Trouble-shooting and Preventing Predictable Pitfalls

Many family therapists use the family life cycle as a map for assessing trouble in a family, and for making the appropriate intervention. For example, a common glitch that can occur in single parent families is increased difficulty launching a child, due to worry about how the parent will fare alone. Talking through these emotional issues of separation can increase the likelihood that children will be able to do well in their new independent endeavors (college, or leaving home to work and live on their own), especially when they are assured by the parent that he or she can manage without them at home. Likewise marriages that have been held together "for the sake of the children" may result in the youngest child's continual return home due to failure in the world outside the family. Talking about these situations may help a family move through the launching stage and get "unstuck."

Parents may also find themselves under increased stress when they travel through a part of the family life cycle in which unresolved feelings from childhood are buried. The following exercise will help you to trouble-shoot potential stages that may put you under increased stress. Getting help, professional or otherwise, to talk through these stages in your past will help you adjust to the present family's tasks when it passes through the same stage.

For example, if you lost a parent at the age of three, you will experience feelings related to this loss as you travel through the stage of raising young children. Research carried out by Paul and Paul[60] in the early 1980s, demonstrated that when grief goes untreated, families in counseling felt threatened by the possibility of marital dissolution. Looking at a family's history, this loss can be revealed. The Paul's research showed that the trajectory towards divorce is halted, and present family issues are resolved when the parent suffering the early loss experiences a full release of his or her previously suppressed emotional pain. Resolving past loss allows families to remain intact at a statistically significant rate.

Exercise: Predicting your sensitive stages

Draw an "X" on each stage in the life cycle that represents a period of increased stress in your childhood due to losses such as parents' divorce, death of a significant relative, stressful move, or parental job change. Mark also if a particular stage was difficult in other ways, such as abuse in adolescence, unresolved strife and conflict at any given period, or a period when physical or mental disability in a family member first appeared.

Unattached adult	Coupling	Pregnancy and birth	Raising young children	Raising adolescents	Launching children	Later Life

If you are doing this exercise with a spouse, interview one another about these stages, prompting the partner if he or she forgets to name something you know about in the family history that you feel is significant. Plot one another's significant childhood stressors in the appropriate stage when each initially occurred, below:

SELF:

Unattached adult	Coupling	Pregnancy and birth	Raising young children	Raising adolescents	Launching children	Later Life

SPOUSE:

Unattached adult	Coupling	Pregnancy and birth	Raising young children	Raising adolescents	Launching children	Later Life

60. N. Paul & B. Paul, "Death and Changes in Sexual Behavior." In F. Walsh (Ed.), *Normal Family Processes*, 1st edition (New York: Guilford Press, 1982).

Finally, if you are doing this exercise as a couple, you can combine all of the stressors that appear on both lines and plot your family life cycle stage stress composite below:

COUPLE'S FAMILY STAGE STRESS COMPOSITE:

Unattached adult	Coupling	Pregnancy and birth	Raising young children	Raising adolescents	Launching children	Later Life

This composite will give you a sense of which of the family life cycle stages may be the most stressful for your family. Knowing this can help you obtain a larger perspective and avoid the pitfalls of tunnel vision when a particular stage is harder than the previous one. You will be more likely to wonder about the impact of your own childhood on your present moods and determine whether you feel you are reacting appropriately to a given situation or charging it with unresolved tension from your past. It will be easier to get help if you need it and to talk through your feelings rather than overreacting to situations. Armed with this overview, you are more likely to help each other navigate the family life cycle through rough as well as smooth waters. The diagram below illustrates an example of one couple's family stage stress composite.

Bob and Susie: family stage stress composite

Unattached adult	Coupling	Pregnancy and birth	Raising young children	Raising adolescents	Launching children	Later Life
		X X		X		

Bob experienced the loss of his mother who died soon after he was born from complications of childbirth. His wife, Susie, experienced the loss of her mother's presence soon after her birth due to postpartum depression, which necessitated her mother's hospitalization for a period of three months. Susie was cared for by her grandmother and father during that time. Therefore, Susie and Bob may have increased stress above and beyond the usual adjustments to new parenthood. Such additional stress at this time could prove overwhelming if they were not aware of the fact that this stage of pregnancy, birth, and postpartum adjustment will be tinged with sadness from the past. Knowing this, however, Bob and Susie are likely to understand and forgive one another more easily and to seek help from one another or others sooner. As the adjustment takes hold, they will also have an opportunity to heal old wounds in a way that can strengthen their bond and bring them closer as a couple and as parents, rather than lapsing into withdrawal or depression, thus deadening their connection with each other at this important stage of their own family's life cycle.

Susie's parents divorced when she was thirteen, and her father moved away from the family home. She continued to see him several times a year in her teens. Therefore, Susie may experience increased stress when her children become teenagers and she is reminded of the age when this loss occurred for her in her own childhood. Being aware of this will help her express the grief of any renewed or previously unreleased sadness about that loss, allowing her greater clarity in her own relationship to her teenagers and husband during this stage. Without this insight, she may have struggled in her marriage, pushing her husband away to recapitulate loss of her father. When grief is expressed below the level of consciousness, it gets projected onto current life relationships. Many family therapists believe this happens because the younger part of ourselves has been traumatized by loss, becoming "frozen" or forgotten in the past. When travel through a particular familiar stage of the life cycle stimulates this trauma, the younger part of us "thaws" a bit and seeks expression of suppressed emotions. It is natural for us to project the reasons for our feelings onto our spouses or our children when we are unaware of the true origins of these emerging feelings.

By plotting these stressors out on the family life cycle composite, Susie and Bob will be more sensitive to their own needs and to the needs of their partner. Alienation and isolation can be circumvented when deep feelings from the past are not unwittingly projected onto our loved ones. It will be easier to travel through these stages with love and support instead of unintentional polarization.

Once you have finished your joint family composite and discussed it with one another, put it in a place for safe keeping. Take it out for review and updating as you travel through the family life cycle together. Once in a particular stage, you will find you may remember more about what these stages were like in the past. Discuss feelings that arise around the "X"s you have placed in particular stages and feel free to add events that you may have left out previously. Making a tradition of sharing feelings in the present will secure your bond with one another in the future. And being able to *predict* feelings that might otherwise surprise and confuse you can be a real benefit on your journey through the family life cycle!

Further family challenges in the life stages of the family life cycle will be the focus of volume two of *Making Healthy Families*. This second volume will address launching children, multicultural families, grandparenting, reproductive changes and the effects on family development, dual-career marriage, gay and lesbian families, and more on single-parent families and complex stepfamilies. Questions and answers on all of these subjects can be found on the author's family column.[61]

In our complex and rapidly changing society, marriage is stressed no less by gender shifts in expectation than any other one phenomenon. The following question and answer closes this part of our study of family development with the focus on the very critical issue of equality in marriage.

Can wife and husband have an "equal" relationship?

Dr. Gayle,

I work full time, as does my husband. He helps with laundry and dishes, even puts dinner on the table once in awhile and bathes our four-year-old daughter on weekends. He says he does more than any other husband he knows. But I feel he doesn't appreciate that I do a much greater share of the housework and am employed full time, just as he is. He thinks we have an "equal" relationship. He is a great father to our child, but I find myself angry at him for the smallest things, like leaving the cap off the toothpaste. Why can't I get past this?!

Lucille

Dear Lucille:

Traditional relationships, as portrayed on "Leave it to Beaver" and other early television programs, have left us with a legacy of expectations that is difficult to alter. Women specialized in home-making and caretaking children, while men were expected to secure the financial health of the family. In the perfect world of TV, specialization appeared to work. Husbands and wives respected and appreciated each other, and were fulfilled by their respective roles. But in the real world, the divorce rate climbed to fifty percent. Traditional marriages were far from ideal, with sociologists declaring the American family to be in a state of crisis.

Times have changed. Women's role in the workplace has evolved, but not a lot has changed on the home front. Most men still measure

---

61. www.AskDrGayle.com and www.parentsplace.com/expert/family.

their worth by the amount of money they provide, and women are prone to feel more responsible for their children's welfare and household appearances. The unpaid work of raising children and housework remains largely invisible in our families and society at large.

As women have moved into the work force, they have shared the financial burden, but still find themselves doing more of the housework and childcare coordination than their partners. When your partner does not acknowledge that you do more of the running of the household, salt is poured into the wound. Because he is doing more than his father did in the home, he feels he is surpassing expectations. No wonder you are upset!

If your husband gave you credit for the extra effort you extend in caring for your family, you might feel less frustrated. For it is really a matter of love that brought the two of you together. You feel unloved when he does not value your contribution. This exacerbates your feelings that the workload is unfair.

But what is your agreement in your marriage? Did you both agree to equal household and financial responsibilities? If so, you must return to the drawing board. It is up to both of you to decide what is really fair in your relationship. Discuss the household responsibilities and make a list of what each of you will do. Consider household help if what is to be divided is too much for the two of you to actually split up and achieve by yourselves. Work on this until you can both feel that your agreement is fair. But take a deeper look at what level of appreciation is expressed in your marriage, too.

We do things for the people we love because we know it is emotionally meaningful to them. This is the nature of love. And it is the quality of a good marriage. The question to ask ourselves is, "How can I have a positive influence on my relationship?" and "How can I make my partner feel special?" For if you succeed, the good feeling will come back to you in the form of increased affection and consideration in your marriage.

Research studies revealed that men who reported high satisfaction in their marriages did more housework! When asked about this correlation, individual men said that they simply had come to understand how much their doing such work meant to their wives. These men loved their wives and this extended to their understanding of what was important to them. Love was translated into action in the marriage. Housework by these men increased due to love, not equality! But clearly, there must be a connection between the two.

"Equality" does not necessarily mean partners do the same work in a relationship. Partners who agree on different, or even special-ized, areas of work in the family can also succeed at having a satisfy-ing marriage. An important key to a satisfying marriage is genuine appreciation and acknowledgment.

You are suffering because your husband does not acknowledge your efforts. Your efforts are also your way of expressing love to your family. Talk with your partner about a fair division of household and childcare responsibilities. But do not stop there! Let your husband know how his lack of appreciation is making you feel.

When our relationships are truly loving, we allow our partners greater leeway for mistakes, even inequities. If you feel loved in your marriage, leaving the cap off of the toothpaste will no longer sym-bolize the ways you feel taken for granted!

The exercise in this chapter allows us to look back on the past to better prepare us for our future. When society's values shift, we can be left with a legacy that is in collision with our present lives. The models of our parents' marriages may have worked within the culture of their times, better or worse than they would for us now. Explore gender expectations in your parents' respective marriages and your own. Consider placing an "X" on any point in the life cycle composite that you feel might be a stress point due to colliding expectations.

Keep this composite in mind as you create your future. Unpredictable twists and turns may throw you, but having each other can help steady your course. The family life cycle takes us on a journey through time. It is my hope that this book will help you in your travels. Happy family-making!

WEB WISDOM

On-line family seminars and articles by Dr. Gayle Peterson available on the world wide web

www.AskDrGayle.com from the "Making Healthy Families" series:
Making Healthy Stepfamilies.
Becoming Parents.
What is "Good Enough" Parenting?
Childbirth: The Ordinary Miracle.
When Women Become Mothers.
Traveling Through Time on the Family Life Cycle.
Communication and Problem Solving.
Making Healthy Families: Characteristics of Healthy Family Systems.
Making Healthy Families: Developing Your Family Style.

www.parentsplace.com/expert/family/ on the "Making Healthy Families series" from the author's family column
Developing Your Family Vision: An on-line family seminar.
Say What You Mean and Mean What You Say: an on-line family seminar.

List of Links to Questions/Answers on "Ask Dr. Gayle" for above seminars:
Marriage turning bad due to inability to discuss
http://www.parentsplace.com/expert/family/general/qa/0,3488,5910,00.html

How can I control my angry outbursts?
http://www.parentsplace.com/expert/family/familydyn/qa/0,3488,5814,00.html

Mothers are people, too!
http://www.parentsplace.com/expert/family/familydyn/qa/0,3488,5931,00.html

Communication or mind-reading?
http://www.parentsplace.com/expert/family/relationships/qa/0,3488,5982,00.html

Husband doesn't follow through on agreements
http://www.parentsplace.com/expert/family/relationships/qa/0,3488,5851,00.html

Taking responsibility for defining "love" in marriage
http://www.parentsplace.com/expert/family/relationships/qa/0,3488,5930,00.html

I want a date with my wife!
http://www.parentsplace.com/expert/family/relationships/qa/0,3488,5983,00.html

Cultural loading of "motherhood" and creating a parenting team
http://www.parentsplace.com/expert/family/familydyn/qa/0,3488,5932,00.html

Creating Romance: A shared vision
http://www.parentsplace.com/expert/family/general/qa/0,3488,6000,00.html

Resolving child-rearing differences with partner
http://www.parentsplace.com/expert/family/general/qa/0,3488,6001,00.html

Helping husband become a supportive stepparent
http://www.parentsplace.com/expert/family/general/qa/0,3488,6002,00.html

Nagging is not the same as talking
http://www.parentsplace.com/expert/family/relationships/qa/0,3488,5990,00.html

Arguing in front of the kids
http://www.parentsplace.com/expert/family/relationships/qa/0,3488,10464,00.html

Marriage and Money: Communication and control
http://www.parentsplace.com/expert/family/relationships/qa/0,3488,5790,00.html

Blowing up and making up damages marriage
http://www.parentsplace.com/expert/family/relationships/qa/0,3488,5978,00.html

How to choose a marriage counselor
http://www.parentsplace.com/expert/family/relationships/qa/0,3488,5967,00.html

My husband and I aren't communicating effectively
http://www.parentsplace.com/expert/family/relationships/qa/0,3488,5756,00.html

═══ BIBLIOGRAPHY AND RESOURCES ═══

Additional books and articles on aspects of marriage, parenting and family health

Ahrons, C.,*The Good Divorce* (New York: Harper Collins, 1994).

Clarke, J. & Dawson, C., *Growing Up Again: Parenting Ourselves, Parenting Our Children*, 2nd edition (Center City, MN: Hazeldon, 1998).

Clinton, H., *It Takes a Village* (New York: Touchstone, 1996).

Doherty, W.,*The Intentional Family* (New York: Addison-Wellsley, 1997).

Eyre, L. & Richard, B., *Teaching Your Child Values* (New York: Simon and Schuster, 1993).

Gilligan, C., *In a Different Voice* (Cambridge, MA.: Harvard University Press, 1982).

Gottman, J., *Seven Principles of Marriage* (New York: Crown Books, 1999).

Gottman, J.,*Why Marriages Succeed and Fail* (New York: Simon and Schuster, 1995).

Hendrix, H.,*Keeping the Love You Find* (New York: Pocket Books, 1990).

Hendrix, H., *Getting the Love You Want: A Guide for Couples* (New York: Harper and Row, 1988).

Huber, C. & Guyol, M., *Time Out for Parents: A Compassionate Approach to Parenting* (Mountain View, CA: Compassionworks, 1994).

Johnson, K., *Trusting Ourselves* (New York: Atlantic Monthly Press,1991).

Linton, B., *Finding Time for Fatherhood* (Berkeley, CA: Father's Forum Press, 1998).

Lynch, J., *Language of the Heart: The Human Body in Dialogue* (New York: Basic Books, 1985).

McGoldrick, M., *You Can Go Home Again: Reconnecting with Your Family* (New York: W. W. Norton, 1995).

McGoldrick, M. & Carter, B. (Eds.), *The Changing Family Life Cycle: A Framework for Family Therapy*, 2nd edition (New York: Gardner Press, 1988).

McGoldrick, M., Anderson, C., & Walsh, F. (Eds.), *Women in Families* (New York: W. W. Norton, 1991).

Peterson, G., *An Easier Childbirth: A Mother's Guide for Birthing Normally* (Berkeley, CA: Shadow and Light Publications, 1993).

Peterson, G., *Birthing Normally: A Personal Growth Approach to Childbirth* (Berkeley, CA: Shadow and Light Publications, 1984).

Peterson, G., *Body-Centered Hypnosis for Pregnancy, Bonding, and Childbirth: An Audiotape* (Berkeley, CA: Shadow and Light Publications, 1991).

Peterson, G., *Body Centered Hypnosis for Childbirth: A Training Videotape in the Technique of Gayle Peterson* (Berkeley, CA: Shadow and Light Publications, 1989).

Peterson, G., "Chains of Grief: The Impact of Perinatal Loss on Subsequent Pregnancy." *Pre- and Perinatal Psychology Journal* (Winter, 1994).

Peterson, G., *Hypnosis for Childbirth*. In B. Katz-Rothman (Ed.), *Childbearing: Critical Perspectives* (Phoenix, AZ: Oryx Press, 1993).

Peterson, G., "Unlocking the Door to Healing: Understanding the Effects of Sexual Abuse on Childbirth." *Midwifery Today,* No. 28 (Winter, 1993).

Peterson, G., "Body-Centered Hypnosis for Pregnancy and Childbirth." *Mothering* (Spring, 1992).

Peterson, G., "A Preventative Prenatal Counseling Model: A Method for Improving Childbirth Outcome Through Body-Centered Preparation." In R. Klimek, (Ed.), *Pre Perinatal Psycho-Medicine* (Cracow, Poland: DWN Dream Publishers, 1992).

Peterson, G., "Prenatal bonding, prenatal communication, and the prevention of prematurity." *Pre- and Peri-Natal Psychology,* volume 2, No. 2 (Winter, 1987).

Pipher, M., *Reviving Ophelia* (New York: Grossett/Putnam, 1994).

Pollock, W., *Real Boys* (New York: Holt, 1999).

Stein, M., *In Midlife* (Dallas, TX: Spring Publications, 1990).

Tannen, D., *You Just Don't Understand* (New York: Ballentine, 1994).

Viorst, J., *Necessary Losses* (New York: Simon & Schuster, 1986).

Visher, J. & Visher, E., *How To Win in a Stepfamily* (New York: Dembner Books, 1982).

Wallerstein, J. & Blakeslee, S.,*The Good Marriage* (New York: Warner Books, 1996).

Walsh, F. (Ed.), *Normal Family Processes,* 2nd edition (New York: Guilford Press, 1993).

Walsh, F., *Strengthening Family Resilience* (New York: Guilford Press, 1998).

Walters, M., Carter, B., Papp, P., & Silverstein, O., *The Invisible Web: Gender Patterns in Family Relationships* (New York: Guilford Press, 1988).

Winnicott, D.W., *The Family and Individual Development* (Routledge: London, 1989).